NEW STUDIES IN THE HISTORY OF EDUCATION

Providing a wide-ranging, critical and up-to-date introduction to the history of education, this book explores its true meaning and value for education studies. With no assumption of prior knowledge, it considers key themes, individuals and situations in depth, highlighting the specific ways in which current educational practice is historically conditioned or, conversely, has been very different in other times and places and, by implication, might be different in the future. Chapters cover a diverse range of key topics, such as:

- the history of 'big ideas', such as liberal education
- the impact of state intervention on education
- the effects of imperialism
- the education of orators in ancient Rome
- the impact of Covid policies on British education
- the history of individual subjects, such as Geography
- the development of educational sectors

Accessible and engaging chapters model a range of critical approaches to the past, while discussion questions challenge the reader to consider links with the present.

New Studies in the History of Education introduces the sub-discipline to students of Education Studies and will help students and tutors to develop a more in-depth and critical understanding of the history of education, supporting them to develop their own historical awareness.

Nicholas Joseph is Lecturer in Education at the University of Derby. His current interests include developing a historically informed Education curriculum at Level 7, designed to enable students to reflect on practice across a wide range of international settings.

The Routledge Education Studies Series

Series Editor: Stephen Ward, Bath Spa University, UK

The Routledge Education Studies Series aims to support advanced level study on Education Studies and related degrees by offering in-depth introductions from which students can begin to extend their research and writing in years 2 and 3 of their course. Titles in the series cover a range of classic and up-and-coming topics, developing understanding of key issues through detailed discussion and consideration of conflicting ideas and supporting evidence. With an emphasis on developing critical thinking, allowing students to think for themselves and beyond their own experiences, the titles in the series offer historical, global and comparative perspectives on core issues in education.

For more information about this series, please visit: www.routledge.com/The-Routledge-Education-Studies-Series/book-series/RESS

NEW STUDIES IN THE HISTORY OF EDUCATION

CONNECTING THE PAST TO THE PRESENT IN AN EVOLVING DISCIPLINE

Edited by Nicholas Joseph

Routledge
Taylor & Francis Group

LONDON AND NEW YORK

Designed cover image: Children being taught geography from Rev. J. Goldsmith [R. Phillips], *A Grammar of Geography for the Use of Schools*, improved and enlarged by G. N. Wright (c1840)

First published 2024
by Routledge
4 Park Square, Milton Park, Abingdon, Oxon, OX14 4RN

and by Routledge
605 Third Avenue, New York, NY 10158

Routledge is an imprint of the Taylor & Francis Group, an informa business

British Library Cataloguing-in-Publication Data
A catalogue record for this book is available from the British Library

Library of Congress Cataloging-in-Publication Data
Names: Joseph, Nicholas, 1982- editor.
Title: New studies in the history of education : connecting the past to the present in an evolving discipline / edited by Nicholas Joseph.
Description: Abingdon, Oxon ; New York, NY : Routledge, 2024. | Series: The Routledge education studies series | Includes bibliographical references and index. | Identifiers: LCCN 2023012445 (print) | LCCN 2023012446 (ebook) | ISBN 9780367483685 (hardback) | ISBN 9780367483692 (paperback) | ISBN 9781003039532 (ebook)
Subjects: LCSH: Education–History. | Education–Philosophy–History. | Educational change–History.
Classification: LCC LA126 .N48 2024 (print) | LCC LA126 (ebook) | DDC 370.9–dc23/eng/20230517
LC record available at https://lccn.loc.gov/2023012445
LC ebook record available at https://lccn.loc.gov/2023012446

ISBN: 978-0-367-48368-5 (hbk)
ISBN: 978-0-367-48369-2 (pbk)
ISBN: 978-1-003-03953-2 (ebk)

DOI: 10.4324/9781003039532

Typeset in News Gothic Std
by SPi Technologies India Pvt Ltd (Straive)

Contents

Contributors

W. Martin Bloomer is Professor of Classics at the University of Notre Dame. His research has focused on Latin literature and the history of education. His books include *Valerius Maximus and the Rhetoric of the New Nobility*, *Latinity and Literary Society at Rome*, *The School of Rome*, and *The Wiley Blackwell Companion to Ancient Education*.

Stephen Daniels is Emeritus Professor of Cultural Geography at the University of Nottingham. His research interests include eighteenth-century British landscape art and the history of geographical knowledge and imagination. His books include *The Iconography of Landscape* (1988), *Fields of Vision* (1992), *Joseph Wright* (1999) and *Humphrey Repton: Landscape Gardening and the Geography of Georgian England* (1999).

Christine Eden was Assistant Dean of the School of Education at Bath Spa University for many years and recently retired as Professor of Education. She has a background in Sociology and Education Studies and is particularly interested in understanding how the implementation of education policy reproduces or challenges inequalities. She has taught Educational Studies to undergraduate and postgraduate students with a focus on inequalities, with a particular interest in gender. She has published *Key Issues in Education Policy* with Stephen Ward and contributed to a number of student textbooks in Education Studies. She has undertaken considerable evaluation research into the interface between education and the needs of the labour market, and this book reflects the concerns and interests of the many students she has taught across the years.

Paul Elliott is Professor of Modern History at the University of Derby. His research interests include the social and cultural history of science and medicine, local, urban and regional history, historical geography, landscape and environmental history and the history of education.

Peter Harwood is Senior Lecturer in Special Educational Needs, Disability, and Inclusion at the University of Wolverhampton. He has nearly 40 years' experience in education inclusion and educational policy as a teacher, leader, senior manager and commissioner. Peter has worked as Head of Special Educational Needs with responsibility for statutory assessment and Higher Needs provision commissioning in two local authorities in the West Midlands. Prior to that he spent much of his career in the Further Education sector working in curriculum development, senior management and leadership roles. Peter currently teaches on master's in education, the NASENCo award and undergraduate programmes.

Nicholas Joseph is Lecturer in Education at the University of Derby, having completed his PhD and lectured in History at the University of Keele. Current interests include developing a historically informed Education curriculum at Level 7, designed to enable students to reflect on practice across a wide range of international settings.

Gavin Rhoades taught ICT and worked as an assistant headteacher in secondary schools in Staffordshire and Cumbria for ten years before moving into teacher training with the University of Wolverhampton. Over a 16-year period, he was course leader for PGCE Secondary ICT, then a course leader in the Education Studies team, before becoming a cross faculty Principal Lecturer with responsibility for teaching and learning and student experience. His current role is Associate Dean for Foundation Year at Global Banking School, a private higher education provider. His research interests include online dialogic learning and the impact of expectations on student perceptions of their university experiences.

Harley Richardson is the author of *The Liberating Power of Education* (Academy of Ideas, 2021) and writes about Learning Through the Ages at https://historyofeducation.net. He has worked in education publishing for over 20 years and organises public debates for the Academy of Ideas Education Forum.

Richard Riddell is an educationist who has worked for over 40 years in and with state schooling in England. Following teaching in comprehensive schools in Oxfordshire and Berkshire, including four years as a head of department, he was a senior local authority officer for over 20 years. He held appointments in Wiltshire, Nottinghamshire, the County of Avon and the City of Bristol, where he was Director of Education for seven years. After leaving Bristol, he worked first as a consultant advising local authorities and (the then) Learning and Skills Councils, and was then Head of Education for three years at the international NGO Amnesty International. From 2009 until 2020, he worked part time as a senior lecturer in Education Studies at Bath Spa University, combining this with research and being a school governor. He is now a Visiting Research Fellow at the University. His books include *Schools for Our Cities* (2003), *Aspiration, Identity and Self-Belief – Snapshots of Social Structure* (2010), *Equity, Trust and the Self-Improving Schools System* (2016) and *Schooling in a Democracy* (2023).

Deborah Robinson is Professor of SEND and Inclusion in the Institute of Education at the University of Derby. During her a career as a teacher and teacher educator, Deborah has focussed on how mainstream classes could become more inclusive for pupils with SEND. Her specialist research has explored inclusive teacher development in the context of school and university partnerships.

Claire Tupling is currently Research and Development Manager with AQA, an educational charity providing GCSEs, A-Levels and other qualifications. For many years she was a senior lecturer in Higher Education, contributing to Sociology and Education Studies programmes as well as supporting the development of postgraduate students' research skills.

Stephen Ward is Emeritus Professor of Education, Bath Spa University, formerly Dean of the School of Education and Subject Leader for Education Studies. A founder member of the British Education Studies Association, he has published on the primary curriculum, primary music teaching and education studies. His research interests are education policy and university knowledge.

Series editor's preface

Education Studies has become a popular and exciting undergraduate subject in some 50 universities in the UK. It developed in the early 2000s mainly in the post-1992 universities which had been centres of teacher training but, gaining academic credibility, the subject has been taken up by post-1992 and Russell Group institutions. In 2004 Routledge published one of the first texts for undergraduates, *Education Studies: A Student's Guide* (Ward, 2004), now in its fourth edition. It comprises a series of chapters introducing key topics in Education Studies and has contributed to the development of the subject.

Education Studies is concerned with understanding how people develop and learn throughout their lives, the nature of knowledge and critical engagement with ways of knowing. It demands an intellectually rigorous analysis of educational processes and their cultural, social, political and historical contexts. In a time of rapid change across the planet, education is about how we both make and manage such change. Education Studies includes perspectives on international education, economic relationships, globalisation, ecological issues and human rights. It also deals with beliefs, values and principles in education and the way that they change over time.

It is important to understand that Education Studies is not teacher training or teacher education. However, its theoretical framework in Psychology, Philosophy, Sociology, and History is derived from teacher education, and undergraduates in the subject may well go on to become teachers after a PGCE or school-based training. However, Education Studies should be regarded as a subject with a variety of career outcomes, or indeed, none: it can be taken as the academic and critical study of education in itself. At the same time, while the theoretical elements of teacher training are continually reduced in government-controlled PGCE courses and school-based training, undergraduate Education Studies provides a critical analysis for future teachers who, in a rapidly changing world, need so much more than training to deliver a state-defined curriculum.

Since its inception in the late 1990s there has been continuing discussion about the roles of the so-called 'contributory disciplines' in Education Studies. Some have argued that Psychology, Sociology, Philosophy, History and Economics should form its theoretical basis. Others urge that Education Studies should be seen as a 'discipline' in itself, that the other disciplines should be less prominent and make the study of education too difficult and complex. This book is based on the former assumption that, for a rigorous analysis of education, a grounding in the disciplines is essential: students should have an understanding of the nature of each of the disciplines, be aware of the theoretical issues in the subject and familiar with its publications in education. Intended for second- and third-year undergraduates and masters students, this book is the tenth in the Routledge Education Studies series which builds on the introductory guide and looks in depth at the history of education. It is the fifth in sequence of books on the disciplines five disciplines; books on Psychology, Sociology, Philosophy and Economics are in print.

As noted, the disciplines for Education Studies are drawn from the theoretical framework for teacher training drawn up in the 1960s. The Robbins Report (Committee on Higher Education, 1963) recommended that school teaching should become a graduate profession and the Bachelor of Education Degrees (BEd) was offered in the various teacher-training colleges. The colleges did not have degree-awarding powers, and so the degrees were to be validated by each college's local university. Not surprisingly, the universities were insistent on their awards having a rigorous theoretical basis, not to be simply practical teaching methods. Crook (2002) relates the story of how the education disciplines were selected. RS Peters, of the London Institute of Education, argued that philosophers should determine the subject balance, and he met with CJ Gill, HMI for teacher training, in a closed seminar at the DES to agree the subjects to be included in the new degrees. The first proposal was for Psychology, Sociology, Philosophy and Economics to be the theoretical basis. It was later decided that Economics would be too difficult, and the history of education was substituted. It is interesting that Peters and Gill should have first selected Economics, probably a somewhat obscure subject at the time, but it was prescient given the way that education in the UK has been dominated by neoliberal economic politics. Some knowledge of Economics is now essential to an understanding of education in the twenty-first century.

The history of education was then something of a second choice in the original thinking about educational theory, and it must be said that the subject has suffered some neglect, often being overshadowed by high-profile developments, particularly in Psychology and Sociology. It tends to appear merely as 'a little bit of background' to a given topic. This book is intended to give History its proper due as an academic discipline: a way of thinking with its methodologies which reveal a critical understanding of education today and in the past.

References

Committee on Higher Education (Robbins) (1963) *Report*. London: HMSO.
Crook, D. (2002) Education studies and teacher education. *British Journal of Education Studies*, **50**(1), pp. 55–75.
Ward, S. (2004) (Ed.) *Education Studies: A student's guide*. London: Routledge.

Books available to date in the series

Brendan Bartram (Ed.) (2017) *International and Comparative Education: Contemporary issues and debates*. Abingdon: Routledge.
Brendan Bartram (Ed.) (2020) *Understanding Contemporary Issues in Higher Education*. Abingdon: Routledge.
Zeta Brown (Ed.) (2016) *Inclusive Education: Perspectives on pedagogy, policy and practice*. Abingdon: Routledge.
Zeta Brown and Stephen Ward (Eds.) (2018) *Contemporary Issues in Childhood: A bio-ecological approach*. Abingdon: Routledge.
Christine Eden (2017) *Gender: Education and Work: Inequalities and intersectionality*. Abingdon: Routledge.
Tom Feldges (Ed.) (2019) *Philosophy and the Study of Education: New perspectives on a complex relationship*. Abingdon: Routledge.
Jessie Bustillos Morales and Sandra Abegglen (Eds.) *The Study of Education and Economics: Debates and critical theoretical perspectives*. Abingdon: Routledge.
Catherine A. Simon and Graham Downes (Eds.) (2020) *Sociology for Education Studies*. Abingdon: Routledge.

Catherine A. Simon and Stephen Ward (Eds.) (2020) *A Student's Guide to Education Studies*. Abingdon: Routledge.
Cathal Ó Siochrú (Ed.) (2018) *Psychology and the Study of Education: Critical perspectives on developing theories*. Abingdon: Routledge.

British Education Studies Association (BESA)

Many of the editors and contributors to the Education Studies book series are members of the British Education Studies Association. Formed in 2005, BESA is an academic association providing a network for tutors and students in Education Studies. It holds an annual conference with research papers from staff and students; there are bursaries for students on Education Studies programmes.

The website offers information and news about Education Studies and two journals: *Educationalfutures*; and *Transformations*, a journal for student publications. Both are available without charge on the website: https://educationstudies.org.uk/

Stephen Ward, Bath Spa University, Series Editor

Abbreviations

AD	Anno Domini
ALFIE	Alliance for Inclusive Education
ASD	Autistic Spectrum Disorders
BC	Before Christ
BCE	Before Common Era
BEd	Bachelor of Education (degree)
BTIC	Business in the Community
CE	Common Era
CSIE	Centre for Studies on Inclusive Education
CYP	children and young people
DfE	Department for Education
DoH	Department of Health
EHC	Education Health and Care
EHRC	Equality and Human Rights Commission
ESN	Educationally sub-normal
GIST	Girls into Science and Technology
HMI	His/Her Majesty's Inspectors
ITE	initial teacher education
LEA	local education authority
NLCS	The North London College School
NSS	National Student Survey
NUT	National Union of Teachers
OfS	Office for Students
ONS	Office for National Statistics
PMLD	profound and multiple learning difficulties
PPE	Politics Philosophy and Economics
QTS	qualified teacher status
SEND	Special Educational Needs and Disabilities
SLD	severe learning difficulties
SPCK	Society for Promoting Christian Knowledge
TEACCH	Treatment and Education of Autistic and Related Handicapped Children'
TEF	Teaching Excellence and Student Outcomes Framework

UCU	University and College Union
UPIAS	Union of the Physically Impaired Against Segregation
UUK	Universities UK
WEC	Women and Equalities Committee
WIST	Women into Science and Engineering

Introduction

Some dry bones for an evolving discipline

Nicholas Joseph

The field of history of education has long suffered a reputation as being boring for students, and practically if not also theoretically pointless within the broader discipline of Education.

> No Ezekiel's wind can make dry bones live in some valleys. Nothing seems more dead and gone today than the educational battles of the early seventies of the Victorian age.
>
> (Garvin, 1932: 102)

The preceding quotation has been used more than once to hint at the irremediably boring and futile nature of history of education, and I follow Briggs (1972) in using it as a foil for my argument. Of course, it relies for its effect upon a biblical allusion. As the Book of Ezekiel may not be intimately familiar to all readers, the relevant text is reproduced as follows:

> The hand of the LORD was upon me, and carried me out in the spirit of the LORD, and set me down in the midst of the valley which was full of bones, and, lo, they were very dry. And he said unto me, Son of man, can these bones live? And I answered, O Lord GOD, thou knowest. Again he said unto me, Prophesy upon these bones. So I prophesied as I was commanded: and as I prophesied, there was a noise, and behold a shaking, and the bones came together, bone to his bone. And when I beheld, lo, the sinews and the flesh came up upon them, and the skin covered them above: but there was no breath in them. Then said he unto me, Prophesy unto the wind. So I prophesied as he commanded me, and the breath came into them, and they lived.
>
> (Ezekiel 37, 1–10 [excerpts], Authorised Version)

In the last few years, many Education Studies programmes have been remodelled to include a significant component of history of education. That *can* be understood as a return to the roots of the discipline, but it is only half true. History of education was part of the discipline of Education designed by the Robbins Committee in the 1960s for the Bachelor of Education (BEd) degree. However, Education Studies broke away from BEd programmes, becoming established as a separate degree programme in its own right, only in the 1990s. By that time, history of education had already ceased to be taught in all but a few BEd programmes. History of education has therefore never previously been a major part of Education Studies. Bringing it in now is a new development.

Like Ezekiel in his vision, Education Studies is entering this valley of dry bones for the first time. Like him, we may wonder why we have come to this dead and barren place, and question whether any good can result from our visit. In addition, there are long-standing doubts about whether

DOI: 10.4324/9781003039532-1

students can find anything to interest or engage them in a subdiscipline of which they 'do not readily "see the point"' (Tibble, 1970: 21). This book is intended, in part, to help the reader answer these questions.

In Chapter 1, I deal with the question 'Why study history of education?' from the perspective of an Education Studies student. That perspective is crucial to the answer. Unlike the BEd, a degree in Education Studies is not a mode of Initial Teacher Education (ITE). Instead, Education Studies is a liberal academic discipline. This means that students are challenged to look beyond their own vocational considerations. The student voluntarily focuses on a field of study – a subject – and not (primarily) on herself or her own professional development. To do that, the student needs a defined field of study upon which to focus. It is argued that education can be constructed as such a field, but only if education itself is understood in historical terms. Turning to history of education is therefore part of the evolution of Education Studies away from its roots in ITE. In ITE, education is – ultimately – whatever government dictates. By contrast, Education Studies is the critical study of the whole field of education, with neither scope nor conclusions foreclosed by contemporary politics.

I argue that what defines education in all times and settings is the propagation of (elements of) the past. The history of education is therefore intimately connected with the meaning of education itself. However, though cultural reproduction is always part of any educational activity, it is not the only purpose that education has served. In Chapter 2, Harley Richardson explores the roots and development of 'liberal education'. This highly influential, but deeply contentious, model looks at first sight like a fossil from the classical world of ancient Greece and Rome. Indeed, Chapter 7, which highlights the impact of the first-century Roman educationist Quintilian, will deepen the reader's understanding of liberal education and its influence. Nevertheless, Richardson shows that liberal education is not simply a heritage of Antiquity, but was constantly reinvented and recast in different contexts and to meet different needs. Educational practices and content were translated between radically different cultures, and reinterpreted. More than once, the whole concept of liberal education has been 'appropriated' by a different ethnic, religious or cultural group. Initially, the 'liberal' in liberal education merely described the status of those who received it: free male citizens of high status. But what developed was a model of liberal education as actually liberating – a sense that it transformed those who received it in such a way as to set them free. Richardson leads us to question what is meant by 'a liberating education', and whether all children would benefit from learning in such a way.

Chapter 2 is the first of Richardson's two chapters concerned with English education before the era of state funding and control. Before his discussion of 'mass education' in Chapter 4, Christine Eden focuses on the crucial topic of the education of girls and women. In Chapter 3, she teases out the influence of 'concepts of femininity'. Across the nineteenth century and well into the twentieth, women were widely believed to be inferior both physically and intellectually to men. This configured ideas about the education appropriate to girls and women. At the same time, women were expected to fit into subordinate social roles, so in addition to differentiating education to the inferior capacities of women, it was also important that they should be prepared for adult life on that basis. Eden emphasises the role of women in campaigning for change and inclusion, and in actually making the change themselves by taking education into their own hands on their own terms. There are parallels to be drawn here with Chapter 11, in which Deborah Robinson and I emphasise the agency of people with disabilities in campaigning for educational inclusion. Eden highlights the growing role of the state as a positive force. She casts the state, not indeed as rescuer, but certainly as the appropriate object towards which campaigners direct their persuasive energies.

Richardson takes a somewhat darker view of the state. He understands the expansion of state funding and intervention as motivated by a desire to take control of education, with the aim of keeping working-class people in a subordinate position from which they might otherwise have freed themselves. In Chapter 4 on mass education, Richardson tracks the expansion of liberal education throughout society, including working-class people and women. This was not initially the result of any deliberate planning. The intentions behind eighteenth- and nineteenth-century charity schools, for example, were strictly limited to a wish that working-class people should be able to read the Bible and be sufficiently employable to keep out of trouble. Intellectual liberation was not the plan, but it was the result, because even limited education gave people the basic tools – such as literacy – to go on and educate themselves. The state involved itself in education, in Richardson's view, in order to head off the perceived threat to the social order posed by an educated working class. Needless to say, that raises uncomfortable questions about the nature and purposes of state education.

Ambivalence about the role of the state is paralleled in Paul Elliott and Stephen Daniels's Chapter 5: 'The transformation of scientific and geographical education in eighteenth-century England'. On the one hand, geographical education developed in the service of expanding empire. It equipped generations of young men, particularly those aiming at a career in the Royal Navy, not only to chart but to subjugate great expanses of the globe. In so doing, it cemented the power of established military and commercial elites at home. On the other hand, Geography was a rapidly advancing science, often taught in new and even progressive ways. Geographical knowledge also enabled some upward social mobility for those boys from poorer backgrounds lucky enough to be taught it. So geographical education was both a means to colonial conquest and a catalyst for intellectual liberation.

In Chapter 6, focus shifts to the teachers themselves, as the social ecosystem of state education developed in the nineteenth and early twentieth centuries. Claire Tupling reconstructs an account of 'The Lax family of Staindrop and the making of a teaching dynasty'. Questions are raised about the nature of state-school teaching as a profession, and about the social status of teachers, that are suggestive of troubling contemporary parallels. Nevertheless, this case study of one family shows that teachers, and the teaching profession, were not merely the playthings of government. Individual agency enabled teachers to define a role in their communities quite different from that envisaged for them by those in political power.

From Tupling's discussion of a family of teachers, we move in Chapter 7 to consider the influence of a single teacher. W. Martin Bloomer explores 'Quintilian's educational impact' which continues to be felt after almost two millennia. Unlike many philosophers of education, Quintilian was throughout his career a practising teacher. His work on *The education of an orator* was a practical guide to the craft of teaching. It was at the same time a powerful statement on the curriculum and purposes of education that remains relevant to the concept of liberal education (see Chapter 2). In fact, Quintilian produced a complete educational programme rooted in a remarkably developed pedagogical understanding. His name ought to be familiar to educationists, partly because his ideas explicitly influenced many of those whose names are more familiar, such as Rousseau. But nor should his influence on contemporary educational practice be neglected. The 'rounded curriculum', after all, was designed as the preparation of an orator – it would enable him to speak with some knowledge on a full range of subjects. Contemporary educators continue to put great emphasis on the importance of a rounded curriculum. Understanding what it was originally for may help us to consider whether that emphasis remains justified.

Quintilian's ideas, and their impact, were to some extent products of empire. In Chapter 8, Jody Crutchley shows that English education in the later nineteenth and early twentieth centuries was no less affected by empire, notwithstanding the differences between Roman and British imperialism. Education in England became 'for, about, and because of empire'. Education was developed and transformed as a tool for advancing a particular agenda. The political and commercial interests of an elite minority were defended, and given broad social legitimacy, by defining empire in terms of a national project and shared identity. In all phases and sectors, albeit in different ways, promotion of empire became a core purpose of education.

Implicitly, that poses uncomfortable questions for us today. We are likely to see education for, about, and because of empire as indoctrination, a perversion of the legitimate purposes of education. But there is an undeniable parallel between the use of education to promote empire in the past, and contemporary use of education to promote projects such as 'decolonisation' itself, or environmentalism. Today, English universities are committed to promoting the United Nations Sustainable Development Goals (SDGs). When updating or designing new modules, whatever their discipline area, lecturers are required to show how we are promoting the SDGs through the curriculum. It might be questioned whether this is really so different in principle from schools a century ago celebrating Empire Day. Just like environmentalism now, empire then was politically correct and promoted by those in positions of cultural and political authority. That should give us pause for thought; of course, it does not imply that killing whales or chopping down rainforests is necessarily a good idea after all.

If Crutchley has shown how the whole project of education was instrumentalised for a political agenda, and perhaps degraded thereby, Chapter 9 offers a powerful counterpoint. Claire Tupling takes documentary films as historical sources to explore 'Documentary visions of the secondary modern school'. Secondary moderns were the destination of those children who 'failed' the 11+ examination and did not gain access to a selective grammar school. For that reason they were widely associated with failure, and seen as inferior schools. Tupling shows that *some* secondary moderns, at least, were able to transcend their ascribed inferior status and to educate the children in their care innovatively and well. They developed broad, holistic curricula that enabled inclusion of a great diversity of learners. Secondary moderns pioneered some of what would come to be seen as excellent practice in the comprehensive sector. As in Chapter 6, Tupling emphasises the transformative agency of teachers.

From the educational sector with probably the lowest ascribed status of any in British history, we move to a consideration of elite education with Richard Riddell's chapter on 'Independent schools'. The independent sector remains an undeniably powerful anomaly, operating at the same time inside, outside and above the education system accessible to most children in England. Riddell explores the development of that complex and paradoxical relationship, before tackling some contentious but unavoidable questions:

- Have independent schools been the best schools, judged in educational terms?
- Given the material and social advantages of most of those who attend independent schools, what actually has been the contribution made by the school to the measurable success of their 'old boys' (and girls) later in life?

Riddell gives the reader food for thought and directions for further research, while suggesting the inadequacy of simplistic answers to these questions. Finally, he points to the highly partisan nature of debate and research in this area. Political commitment on all sides may be impeding efforts to understand what is a decisively influential part of the educational ecosystem.

In Chapter 11, Deborah Robinson and I consider 'The history of Special Education in England: Divisions, divergences and coalitions'. A key concept developed in the nineteenth century to divide young people was the distinction between the 'educable' and the 'ineducable'. While those identified as educable gained the right (and were required) to be educated, those labelled ineducable were excluded. Despite changes of terminology, that remained the case until 1970. Between 1970 and 1993 came a period of 'divergence', in which Special and Ordinary education developed in separate directions informed by different underlying philosophies. While all young people were now educated, it was questionable whether education really meant the same thing in both sectors. Finally, from 1994 we can see an era of 'coalition' – but this has been paradoxically characterised by conflict over the meaning of inclusion. I cannot in this short Introduction summarise that conflict. Instead, I can say something about why it matters. Quintilian in c.95 wrote this:

> For on the contrary you shall find most children both very imaginative and willing to learn. Indeed, that is natural to mankind. Just as birds come to flight, horses to running, and wild beasts to ferocity; just so, our property is mental activity and care for the mind. For that reason our thinking mind (*animus*) is believed to take its origin from heaven. There are stupid and unteachable (*indociles*) people who are formed not so much according to the nature of human beings as omens and monsters, but there are very few of these.
>
> (1.1.1–2)

Quintilian's idea seems to have been that the great majority of children were educable, but those who in his view were not educable were not really human either. Precisely this attitude was reproduced in the rhetoric of the educable and the ineducable. The debate over inclusion, therefore, reveals a further purpose of education: honouring the common humanity of all children and young people.

Chapter 12 by Gavin Rhoades and Peter Harwood, which concludes the book, focuses on the kind of institution in which students of Education Studies are likely to be situated. 'Adult to adult *in loco parentis*: The changing roles of the university from 1968 to 2018', explores the evolving relationship between universities and their students. From the late 1960s and into the 1970s, students fought against universities treating them like children (which is what those under 21 legally were, in the UK, until 1970). Their apparent victory paved the way for a transactional relationship in which adult students paid universities for a defined – educational – service. However, this relationship was unstable because 'the customer is always right'. The need to satisfy students as consumers created a dynamic in which it was safer for universities to pander to student demands than stand up to them, and this created a new kind of student-led infantilisation. Rhoades and Harwood explore the example of (some) students demanding that material they find upsetting or offensive be removed from the curriculum. When those demands are met, students appear to have been empowered, but at the cost of changing – perhaps diminishing – the quality of their own education. In considering the period of Covid, Rhoades and Harwood show how students became victims of the 'safety culture' they had previously used to assert power over universities. Now, students themselves were stigmatised as 'super spreaders', denied the education they had a right to expect, and in some cases treated in ways that were not humane. This fits with Rhoades and Harwood's underlying thesis, that students have been duped. They have been tricked, ultimately, by government into throwing away their own rights as adults and their own intellectual freedom.

It is necessary to acknowledge some flaws in this volume. Many readers will regret the lack of non-Western content. Though the case is made in these pages that all history of education is part of the field of Education Studies, the focus of this volume is largely parochial. Secondly, though issues of methodology are discussed, the book would be much the stronger for a chapter devoted to the various methods used in researching and creating history of education, and perhaps another exploring and critiquing the different kinds of history that are produced. Alas. Still, this book had ambitious goals, and I hope the reader judges that they have been met. I must give particular thanks to Stephen Ward, the series editor, both for his remarkable patience and forbearance, and for the very considerable work that he has put into this project. It is hoped that readers will find this book enjoyable, but also disconcerting. Several chapters present uncomfortable parallels with contemporary educational practice and rhetoric. We need to acknowledge and engage with those parallels for at least two reasons. Most obviously, doing so will force us to confront our own unspoken purposes and assumptions and take a more critical view of contemporary education. But no less important from our perspective in Education Studies, it will enable us to empathise and understand more deeply how education in the past actually was. Returning to Ezekiel's vision, this book will have succeeded if its readers feel that these dry bones belong to them.

References

Briggs, A. (1972; repr. 1989) The Study of the History of Education. In P. Gordon and S. Szreter (Eds.) *History of Education: The Making of a Discipline*. London: The Woburn Press.

Garvin, J. (1932) *The Life of Joseph Chamberlain. Volume I*. New York and London: Macmillan.

Tibble, J. (1970) The Development of the Study of Education. In J. Tibble (Ed.) *The Study of Education*. London: Routledge.

1 Why study the history of education?

Nicholas Joseph

Questions for discussion

The textbook quoted here was intended for children. It was primarily an aid to teaching reading and writing, but aimed at the same time to explain the fundamental nature and moral significance of language itself. The schoolmaster defines letters (as in *a, b, c*) very differently from the way in which a modern primary phase teacher would explain the concept of a letter.

> *PIPPINUS. What is a letter?*
> *ALBINUS. The guardian of history.*
> > (From the *Discussion between Pepin and his schoolmaster*, a ninth-century
> > textbook in catechetical form attributed to Alcuin)
> > (Bowen, 1975: 11)

- How might a twenty-first-century primary phase teacher explain to early readers what letters are?
- To what extent does it make sense to see the written word as Alcuin did, as a tool for preserving the past? Is that perspective outdated?

An answer

The question explored in this chapter is that of why you (presumed to be a student of Education Studies) should engage with history of education. That is a different question from that of why those of us who already study history of education keep on doing it. It is a different kind of question that demands a different kind of answer. The latter can quite legitimately have a multiplicity of complementary, or even contradictory answers. Indeed, it is in the nature of historical study itself that historians, unlike natural scientists, look to identify multiple motives and causes for what has actually happened and what people have already done (Elton, 2002). But our question is of a different order. The point is not to explore why those who already do it, do it. The point is rather to establish whether there is any compelling reason why those who do not, should. That kind of question demands not descriptive plurality but normative simplicity. In other words, we need to identify just one main reason, and it needs to be a good one.

DOI: 10.4324/9781003039532-2

There are many benefits to studying history of education, but none is sufficient to justify giving it time in an Education Studies programme. History of education deserves inclusion in Education Studies not because it is useful, but because it is essential. Without history of education, Education Studies makes no sense as a discipline.

History of education defines the field of Education itself as a subject capable of being studied. That assertion may be shocking to those used to the idea of Education Studies as a discipline focused on contemporary education. The premise it rests upon is that the only universally tenable definition of education itself is cultural reproduction: education is tradition (the act of passing something on). Other definitions and purposes are applicable in specific times, places and cultural settings. Examples of such avowed purposes of education include spiritual salvation, individual liberation and the economic well-being of society or the state. But none of those, however passionately they may be embraced, can serve as a universally applicable defining purpose of education. What defines education in all times and settings is not any agenda for the future, but unavoidably the propagation of (elements of) the past. The history of education is therefore intimately connected with the meaning of education itself.

Why ask the question?

In that light, it would be tempting to agree with Brian Simon (1988 [1966]: 55) that history of education is so obviously 'an essential aspect' of the discipline that 'there is no need to make a case' for its inclusion. Today, Education Studies programmes across the UK are putting renewed emphasis on the history of education. Programmes which until recently lacked any explicit reference to the history of education are introducing new modules entirely dedicated to that subdiscipline. This could be seen as a return to the roots of Education Studies. The metadiscipline of Education, as designed by the Robbins Commission in 1964 as the Bachelor of Education (BEd) degree, was made up of four contributory disciplines: Psychology of Education, Sociology of Education, Philosophy of Education and History of Education. Of these, history of education was probably the best established as a discrete field. Indeed, the history of education was already a core component in the non-graduate two-year teacher training courses that had been provided by teacher training colleges (TTCs) for more than a century. For most of the time that the academic study of education has existed, it has seemed obvious that history of education should form a part of it.

However, the long hiatus between the 1990s and the start of the 2020s, during which history of education was generally not given explicit prominence in Education Studies, is not inexplicable. In the early 1990s Depaepe noted, in a book entitled *Why Should We Teach History of Education* (Salimova and Johanningmeier, 1993), that there were already more than 600 published works related to that question. The large number of attempts to answer it suggested a lack of confidence among practitioners in the value of their discipline. It has to be recognised that their lack of confidence was not simply in the willingness of others – especially political decision-makers – to understand that value. History of education had been under political attack, at least in the UK, in the 1980s (Richardson, 1999), but that was not the root cause of the insecurity. There had also been constant discussion of this question in the context of American teacher education in the first decade of the twentieth century. At that time, history of education was the dominant content of teacher education: 'No other kind of course was offered by as many institutions, and no other kind of course enrolled as many students' (Chambliss, 1984: 34). Even when the discipline of history of education was at its greatest prominence, and its practitioners had every reason to be confident in their employment prospects, there was an acute felt need to justify its value.

There were two key areas of weakness that repeated attempts were made to address: usefulness and quality. Because history of education was taught as a part of initial teacher education (ITE), it was necessary to claim that it would be useful to teachers in their practice. But neither historical knowledge nor familiarity with the historical method could really be equated with practical tips for teachers. The case made for history of education as useful to beginning teachers was always weak and unspecific. Unfortunately, any attempt to answer that criticism through tailoring the curriculum of history of education tended to undermine its perceived quality as an academic discipline. The more the discipline of history of education was designed in content and method to demonstrate practical relevance and utility, the weaker was its claim to be a branch of 'proper' History. Mainstream historians traditionally defined History as a liberal discipline, fundamentally different in nature from vocational training (Evans, 2000). History was understood as the disinterested, rigorous application of the historical method (basically source criticism), in the pursuit of truth about the past. The historian's aim was to reveal, in the words of the pioneering nineteenth-century historian Leopold von Ranke, '*wie es eigentlich gewesen ist*' ('how it actually was'). Such History could be a form of education, but it could not be training for a job (except that of the professional historian). If the aim is training in preparation for a job, then the historical inquiry cannot be disinterested; it is motivated by an agenda different from and possibly in tension with the pursuit of truth. That in turn undermines the commitment to rigorous application of historical method, since the aim is to find teachable 'lessons from history', and not to engage with the sources in ways that could disrupt those lessons. So there was a widespread and corrosive belief that history of education was neither useful as teacher training, nor credible as 'History'.

That persistent belief lay behind the Robbins Commission's reluctance to include history of education within the BEd degree (Richardson, 1996). The history of education produced and taught in TTCs was held in contempt by mainstream historians who worked in universities. It was seen as superficial, derivative and uncritical. At the same time, disciplines that had a contemporary focus – Psychology, Sociology and even Economics – promised to be more obviously useful to the teacher in practice. The architecture of Education as a metadiscipline, with its two social sciences (Psychology and Sociology) balanced by two humanities (Philosophy and History), is itself an accident of history. History of education was included more because of the ready availability of staff to teach it, and the lack of staff able to teach Economics as an alternative, than because there was any great faith in its value.

Education Studies today is in a substantially different position, and the value of history of education within it must be judged differently. For a quarter of a century Education Studies has developed independently of the BEd. A degree in Education Studies does not award Qualified Teacher Status (QTS), and is therefore not a mode of ITE. Education Studies is a liberal academic discipline, not a vocational training course. Students have the opportunity to break away from the predicament identified by Muir (2019: 172) as 'the presupposition that academic Educational Studies is a teacher training service of government, and consequently tasked less with the study of education than with training teachers in conformity to the requirements of state schooling'. As a student of Education Studies, your business is the free critical study of education itself, as an end in itself. The field is not defined, nor is debate foreclosed, by any political requirements. For that reason, the question of whether history of education equips a practising teacher with usable pedagogical tips is irrelevant.

What becomes relevant instead, however, is the question of what does define the field of education. In the context of ITE the question hardly matters, because, as Muir points out, the requirements of government provide a kind of cohesion. If you are studying a course of ITE, it may be of little importance to consider what defines education as such. It is unlikely to worry you to discover cogent arguments that education does not even exist in such a way that it can be an object of study (Scruton, 2001). Teaching does exist as a paid occupation, and it is reasonable to hope that completing a course of ITE will enable the student to get a job. That is what matters. But for a student of Education Studies, the question of what education actually is, is fundamental. It is argued in this chapter that history of education is the subdiscipline that gives the only universally tenable answer to that question.

Questions for discussion

- What is the point of reading for a degree in Education Studies?
- Is it not obviously preferable to enrol on a QTS-bearing programme?

Consider Scruton's critique of 'Education' as a field of study. This is most succinctly expressed in the section entitled 'The Artificial Degree' in *The Meaning of Conservatism* (Scruton, 2001: 136–139), excerpts of which follow.

- Does he have a point? Does it matter?

A subject is therefore invented, called 'Football Studies'. It contains a variety of papers (or 'modules', as they are now called). For example, there is the sociology of football (involving the study of the structure of crowds and the 'charisma' of players); the philosophy of football (beginning from Aristotle on catharsis and centring on the role of alienated labour in spectator sports); the psychology of football (containing dry reflections on how the motion of the ball is perceived by the human eye, together with much wetter reflections on 'football and the unconscious'); the ethics of football . . . the history of football and its relation to class structures; and so on . . . What is wrong with the subject [Education as a metadiscipline] is simply that it involves no critical reflection on an identifiable field of study, and, for that reason, embodies no educational value.

(Scruton, 2001)

History of education cannot be defended in the same terms as History

If Education Studies is, like History itself, a liberal academic discipline, that has implications for the approach taken to history of education. In principle, there is no reason why Education students cannot do history on the same basis that History students do history. In fact, it has long been argued that history of education is of a piece with the broader field of cultural history (Simon, 1977). That being the case, it might seem reasonable – even necessary – to collapse the question *Why study history of education?* into the broader question: *Why study history?* The discipline of History has a strong theoretical self-awareness. There is a huge literature debating the value, meaning and purpose of History as a discipline. Once freed from the need to make dubious claims about the practical utility of history of education to teachers, there would seem to be no reason not to lean upon that existing work to give a ready-made answer. However, that would be a mistake, because the position of Education Studies students is different from that of History students. Bluntly, History students signed up to study History; Education students signed up to study Education.

To summarise the debate, answers to the question *Why study history?* boil down ultimately to the personal choice and enjoyment of the student. A long list of collateral benefits to the study of history can be enumerated. History teaches logical and methodical argument. It promotes attention to detail. It may inoculate the student against the techniques of propaganda. It may, more controversially, inspire the student to transform the world in ways welcome to her teacher – which is allegedly not indoctrination or propaganda if good people do it for good reasons, in a spirit of 'sincerity' (Southgate, 2005: 137). Through practice and exposure, it hones some of the persuasive techniques that were in the ancient world taught to the aspiring orator. For a period in the twentieth century, History was seen as a replacement for Classics as the most suitable preparation for the aspiring political leader, for these and similar reasons (Kenyon, 1983). History also broadens the sense of what human beings are or can be, through what is sometimes called 'temporal anthropology' – see Paul Elliott and Stephen Daniels's contribution in this volume (Chapter 5). It enables the student to see that people could believe and act in very different ways from those seen at present, and thus to maintain consciousness of the possibility of change or even progress.

However, every one of these collateral benefits could be delivered as well by some other academic discipline. Temporal anthropology is not obviously superior to contemporary anthropology; it would seem rather to be inferior given the impossibility of direct observation. In Education Studies, the subdiscipline of Comparative Education provides those benefits of diversity. Literary fiction is surely no less effective than the study of history in raising consciousness of alternative possibilities. Programmes such as Politics Philosophy and Economics (PPE) – like Education itself, a metadiscipline – took over as the degree of choice for the politically ambitious. Most if not all academic disciplines aspire to instil analytical and critical habits of thought. What remains is that History is understood as a consumer good. It is validated by the willingness of students to spend their money as well as their time on it, thus keeping professional historians employed (Lowenthal, 1985). Yes, all the identifiable benefits of History could be attained through the study of other disciplines; but as those benefits can be gained through the study of History, and as History is such fun that students are willing to pay for it, historians often respond to the question *Why study History?* with a *Why not?*

That is not an adequate response when students of Education Studies are considered. They enrol in a programme expecting to study Education, perhaps with contemporary education explicitly in mind. They are entitled to ask why so much of their degree is taken up with history of education, and they are unlikely to be satisfied with the answer: *Because it's fun.* Some students may have different ideas about fun. Very few will enjoy what they believe to be irrelevant content being forced upon them at their own expense. For students of Education, there needs to be a stronger and more positive answer.

Many inadequate answers

The many hundreds of books and articles that have been written to defend the value of history of education present no shortage of answers. The problem is that most of the many reasons offered for studying history of education are not conclusive. Often the claims that are made are instrumentalist in nature. That is to say, it is argued that history of education should be studied as a means to an end, rather than an end in itself. Unfortunately, it turns out on inspection that most of the ends proposed either cannot be met through the study of history of education, or can be met with less effort in other ways.

The noted historian of education Richard Aldrich (1996) was well aware, in the context of the school History curriculum, of the danger inherent in presenting too many different – even contradictory – rationales. The result is confusion of purpose, even the suspicion that there might after all be no credible purpose to the activity. Nevertheless, in attempting to defend his own discipline, Aldrich gave a number of different purposes at different times, and often several together at the same time. He finally condensed them down to four key 'lessons from history' (Aldrich, 2006). All are interesting, but none is satisfactory as a justification for the discipline. They are worth exploring in some depth, not only because Aldrich himself was such a significant historian of education, but because they are representative of the kinds of argument generally made.

Aldrich's first

> lesson . . . is a response to the general question of what can be learned from history overall: My personal answer would be couched in terms of: an acquaintance with a much greater range of human experience than would be possible simply by reference to the contemporary world; an enlarged understanding of that experience which may promote an enlarged understanding of one's own potential and possibilities.
>
> (Aldrich, 2006: 2)

The obvious problem, as touched on previously, is that literary fiction is at least as effective as the study of history in promoting 'an enlarged understanding of one's own potential and possibilities'. If the aim is to enable a 'much greater range of human experience', the method suggested by Aldous Huxley in *The Doors of Perception*, published in 1954, may be more promising and more likely to result in high satisfaction ratings in the National Student Survey (NSS). It is, of course, possible that the Office for Students (OfS) would disapprove of the provision of mescalin in educative doses to students.

To express the same point in more general terms, the benefits outlined here need not be gained through the laborious pursuit of historical truth; they can be delivered more easily by telling lies. That sounds like an extreme statement. But consider the following historical claim made in a Level 7 Education module I myself taught on:

> In England, the rise of education started in earnest with the 1944 Education Act, which gave every child the right to a basic education.

This statement, whatever it was intended to mean (which is not obvious), is false. Education in England, regardless of its altitude, has a history that goes back long before 1944. Elementary Schools had provided every child with a basic education for decades before the 1944 Education Act. (It is true that those who were demonstrably being educated otherwise, at home or in the private sector, did not attend Elementary Schools. Nor did those professionally deemed 'ineducable' – see Robinson and Joseph, Chapter 11 in this volume. But the latter continued to be excluded from education until 1970, and in any case such exceptions were not indicated in these course resources). But this is the kind of statement that is widely made in teaching resources and, one can only presume, widely accepted by students. Some lecturers at least do confabulate in teaching, quite often, regarding matters of secondary importance. And if contemporary education is of primary importance, then telling the truth about past education can only be of secondary importance. Fiction, or gross oversimplification, or naïve unchecked assumption about what must have been the case, will do as well. The point here is that the study of history is hard. It is time-consuming. If there are easier ways to attain the same benefits as can be gained by the study of history, then it will always make sense to use those easier methods.

Aldrich's (2006: 2) second rationale for the study of history of education is that it 'includes a concept of value or merit . . . A study of history of education therefore has the potential to demonstrate not only how people have lived their lives in the past, but also how we may live better in the present and future'. That sounds plausible. A common-sense reason often given for studying history is the hope that it will enable us to avoid repeating past errors. However, with respect to history of education, that 'concept of value' is fatal. It creates a self-defeating circular logic, such as to destroy the whole value of the discipline. Our criteria of 'value' can be drawn only from present norms. The only judgement we are able to make, therefore, is that education in the past was more or less worse than at present. History of education becomes at best an index of errors to be avoided. Ultimately, for the vast majority of students, it would be more effective and more parsimonious to present them with the summary checklist of errors than to ask them to engage directly in the activity of history. Even that, however, would be of doubtful value, because what is an error in one time and place may be correct and successful in another time and place. Whether a particular method or approach is appropriate depends very much on specific context. Therefore, the list of errors, resulting from that 'concept of value or merit', would actually be misleading.

Leaving Aldrich's third lesson to one side for a moment, the final rationale for study of history of education offered (2006: 3) is that 'historical study shows the complexity of human events, including the co-existence of continuities and changes'. The discipline of History is indeed often focused on issues of continuity and change. But no argument is made for the educational significance of continuity and change, or for their worth as objects of study by students of Education. Aldrich gives a narrative account of how the Institute of Education has occupied a variety of buildings through the course of its existence, followed up by a descriptive example of a history book that uses continuity and change as a unifying conceptual framework. The impression is given that history really is just one thing after another and, worse, that some of those things do not even have the decency to end. As discussed in the next section, the concept of continuity is important in providing a rationale for history of education, but it is not self-evidently so.

By contrast, Aldrich's third 'lesson' appears persuasive: 'our journeys in the present and the future may be enhanced by having as accurate a map of the past as possible. Informed decision-making depends upon locating ourselves and our society accurately in time' (p. 3). This goes much further than the weak plea that history of education provides students with 'context' (Aldrich, 2006 [2003]: 20). Context *per se* is of little value. When Education students write essays, they often start with a narrative section supplying historical context ('Piaget was born in . . . His early research dealt with . . . Later on . . . Piaget died in . . .'). That section is padding. It adds no value to the essay whatsoever. If history of education is taught within Education Studies merely to provide context, then it is likely that Education students will relate to the entire subdiscipline much as their lecturers relate to the context sections of their essays. But here Aldrich makes a far more attractive claim. His 'map of the past' is a similar concept to the 'charts' by which Selleck (1983: 13) argued that educators could navigate the present and future. Selleck took the view that historians of education should be at least as willing as researchers in other fields to predict the future and make recommendations on that basis.

This is no less an instrumentalist rationale for history of education than some of those discussed earlier in the chapter. But scouring the past for pedagogical hints and tips, or alternatively for a list of errors to avoid, might be understood as a simplistic 'thin' instrumentalism. Selleck and later Aldrich were arguing for a more sophisticated instrumentalism, broader in scope and more ambitious: what might be called a 'thick' instrumentalism. History of education was still conceived as a means to an end. But the end was more exciting. Crucially, it was also an end that could not be attained through the study of any other discipline. If a significant benefit had been identified that could be delivered only by the study of history of education, that would indeed provide a strong rationale for its inclusion.

Selleck (1983: 3) saw historical continuity as a decisive force: 'history cannot be left in the past, because it is part of the present'. Because knowledge of the past makes the present intelligible, it should put the competent historian of education in a position of power: a prophet whose foreknowledge makes her advice indispensable. However, the unwillingness to engage in prediction which Selleck recognised in his colleagues may, after all, have been well advised. Even conservative historians who understood the force of historical continuity in terms similar to Selleck's have condemned historical prophecy as charlatanism (Elton, 2002). The actual record of the predictive power of historians is risibly bad (Kenyon, 1983). So even this 'thick' instrumentalist rationale fails.

Questions for discussion

- Does historical material have any place in an essay on the psychology, sociology or philosophy of education?
- What is it for?
- Is there a better way to incorporate it than with a descriptive, uncritical 'context section'?

Can we understand anything without putting it into its historical context? Consider the following examples:

- A play by Shakespeare. Do you need to be aware of Tudor beliefs about Jewish male menstruation in order to appreciate *The Merchant of Venice*?
- Genetic theory. Do you need to know the life story of Gregor Mendel to understand the expression of dominant and recessive alleles?

Continuity and relevance

Probably the major question underpinning mainstream History is that of continuity and change. The most obvious way to relate to any historical place or period is to ask what was changing, and what was staying the same. But as we have just seen, the idea of continuity has a further significance. It allows the claim to be made that the past is integral to the present and is therefore relevant. However, neither continuity nor relevance itself are simple ideas. The fundamental question is

Relevant to what or *whom?* In considering Education Studies, the focus of relevance is necessarily the field of education itself.

Traditionally, it seemed obvious that educational continuities exist over long periods of time, and that this constitutes a rationale for the study of history of education. Marrou (1956: xi) made this claim:

> The history of education in antiquity is not without relevance to our modern culture, for in it we can trace the direct ancestry of our own educational tradition. We are the heirs of the Graeco-Latins, and everything of importance in our own civilization derives from theirs. Most of all this is true of our system of education.

Understanding the interplay of social and political forces, philosophical commitments and lived experience that drove the evolution of that 'system of education' was indispensable. Without that knowledge, Western education even two and half millennia later would be inexplicable. We would be limited to *post hoc* rationalisations, essentially guesswork. However, Bloomer (2011: 2) takes a somewhat different view: 'The identity of culture is not a historical reality but a fiction, an imaginative act that takes the student beyond his place, present abilities and even background'. Discontinuity and difference were the reality of educational practice even within the ancient world itself. The myth of continuity was paradoxically one of the few enduring aspects; but the myth endured (or was continuously reproduced) only because it was of present use for engaging learners. Learners found the myth motivating because the idea of continuity happened to have a positive cultural value, not because the continuity itself was real.

This scepticism about continuity is paralleled in the wider discipline of History. Geary (2003), in *The Myth of Nations*, attacked the ahistorical 'myths' on which contemporary Western European national identities are founded. But he actually went further than that, ridiculing the idea that knowledge about a country's medieval past could reveal anything of importance about its present. Continuities across long stretches of time are seen as either fictional or facile and unimportant. Hobsbawm's (1995: 3) judgement of young people, that they are unaware of history and therefore live in an 'eternal present' likened to amnesia, might have been applied with equal justice to many of his own colleagues: professional historians for whom the idea of connection between the past and the present had become unfashionable.

Like Hobsbawm, Lowenthal (1985) lamented the lack of historical awareness among the young, which among other consequences rendered them unable to interpret even the significance of their own built environment. It also divorced them from much of the written heritage of their own culture, which they did not have the reference points to interpret. This, for Lowenthal, was the result of deliberate failure on the part of Western educators.

In other words, cultural continuity is an artefact of education; but if educators do not deliberately and explicitly maintain it, then it will cease to exist. Marrou implicitly accepted the same view. He deemed that which was not explicitly remembered and deliberately maintained to be unworthy of study by the historian of education. In fixing the starting point for his history of ancient education, he explained: 'By its "origins" I mean the end of the sixth century – there is no point in going back any further, for all we are concerned about are the immediate origins that were consciously remembered and so had an effect on tradition' (Marrou, 1956: 230). Though Lowenthal and Hobsbawm might regret it, the implication would seem to be that educators can, through curricular omission, cut the young off from the past of their own society, such that continuity stops. It is beyond the scope of this chapter to discuss whether and why educators have actually sought to bring that about.

What is within the scope of this chapter is to question whether such an alienation is actually possible. The ideas of Richard Dawkins and Daniel Dennett regarding memetics, by analogy with genetics, have relevance here. Richard Dawkins is famous in the UK for his opposition to all religions, and also for his reductionist theory about genetics. He coined the term 'selfish gene' (Dawkins, 1976). His position is that while human beings may think of themselves as conscious, moral, reasonable people who make decisions – and in one sense, we are – in biological terms we are just carriers for our genes. It is genes, not people, that are important in evolutionary terms. More pertinent to this chapter is Dawkins's parallel theory about memes. A meme is an idea. Dawkins's memetic theory is much like his genetic theory: just as our bodies are merely vectors for our genes, our minds are carriers of memes, of ideas. While we may originate a few ideas ourselves, and some spread invasively like viruses, the memes that are most important for us – and have the best chance of transmission from one mind to the next – form part of a mutually supporting system. We might call that system a memetic complex, we might describe it almost as a unified intellectual organism – or we might call it a culture. In this view, a culture is a network of ideas that has evolved over time to maximise the chances of its own propagation. So, we humans are merely carriers of the memetic system, the culture, that has colonised our minds and is using us as a means to colonise other minds. Dennett (2001: 310) explains how memes can use their human hosts to propagate themselves, even when those hosts consciously recognise them and 'are positively dead set against' allowing them to go any further. Even if educators attempt to break continuities with the past, some at least are likely to be reproduced in spite of those efforts.

Memetic theory brings historical continuity back as a source of relevance. The past cannot be escaped. Ignorance of the past does not liberate us from it. If that is true in general, it is especially so for education:

> One characteristic of education is outstanding: perhaps more than any other cultural process it carries almost all of its past with it into the present, even if this past rests rather in covert assumptions, practices, attitudes and beliefs.
>
> (Bowen, 1972: xv)

Even the most radical and deliberate attempt to break with the past is unlikely to achieve its end, if children have succeeded in learning anything at all. The task of the historian, especially the historian of education, is 'making the present intelligible' (Bowen, 1972: xvi) by explaining how the past has formed it.

A huge field of educational history is thus opened up as potentially relevant. From a British perspective, all Western educational history from its earliest traces could be defended as more or less relevant in these terms. That certainly takes us well beyond the limited scope of the discipline as it was generally taught in the decade before its disappearance from undergraduate Education programmes by around 1990. The need to demonstrate relevance to contemporary practice had led to a narrowly focused curriculum, dealing with nothing earlier than Victorian educational reforms and tending to favour the most recent developments as the most relevant. Richardson (1999) presents an account of how the pursuit of narrow relevance made the discipline increasingly limited and, in all likelihood, boring for students.

However, even that expanded sense of relevance is flawed in the context of Education Studies. The unstated assumption behind it is that relevance is to the students themselves, or to the contemporary educational context in which they might later work as teachers. A demand for relevance on those terms would exclude any history of education for which influence on contemporary Western practice could not be demonstrated. Much non-Western history of education could easily be neglected on that basis, or those who wish to study it forced to justify their choice by reference to strained or spurious connections. In Education Studies, relevance centres neither on the student, nor on contemporary Western educational practice. Instead, relevance is defined by the broad field of education itself. That scope distinguishes Education Studies from ITE. In ITE, the focus is on the beginning teacher herself. Everything that is taught and learnt has the ultimate rationale of contributing to her practice as a teacher. Education Studies, by contrast, challenges the student to look out beyond his own vocational considerations.

With that in mind, it is vital to define the field of education. There have been many attempts to define education in terms of specific agenda, such that whatever apparently educational activity does not conform to that agenda is not 'real' education. Instead it is something less than education, such as training or indoctrination. The discourse around 'liberal education' provides a good example of this pattern – see Harley Richardson's contribution in this volume (Chapter 2). Brian Simon (1993: 13) made what is a standard Western liberal claim: 'Education is about the empowerment of individuals'. The problem is that such a definition excludes too much activity that is obviously educational, both in the present and in the past. Indeed, the idea that education is defined in terms of individual liberation, or should even aim to achieve it, is parochially Western and quite recent in origin. To consider one example, the first scheme of universal compulsory education in the English-speaking world was established in colonial New England (Tocqueville, 2004). It had nothing to do with individual empowerment in Simon's sense. Rather, the agenda was to save the souls of the children by enabling them to read the Bible. In twenty-first-century terms, it might be called indoctrination. Nevertheless, it would be perverse to exclude these schools from the field of history of education.

A more fruitful definition of the field is provided by Lowe (2002: 502), who saw '"education" as dealing with "acculturation" in a fairly wide sense'. If education is defined in terms of acculturation, then the field is not limited to institutional settings such as schools but can encompass education in the home and informal education in the community. Nor is acculturation seen as irrelevant, simply because the specific culture in question is non-Western, or because it lacks demonstrable links to contemporary education.

Acculturation may be very deliberate, as in the educational approach celebrated by Scruton (2018: 29):

> True teachers do not provide knowledge as a benefit to their pupils; they treat their pupils as a benefit to knowledge. Of course they love their pupils, but they love knowledge more. And their overriding concern is to pass on that knowledge by lodging it in brains that will last longer than their own.

The parallel between Scruton's understanding of education and Dennett's memetic theory is obvious. For Scruton, the educator puts herself consciously in the service of a memetic complex, and sets out deliberately to replicate it. But as Dennett points out, that replication of memes – acculturation – need not be consciously intended. It could be the opposite of what is intended. Or it may have no connection with the conscious agenda of the educator, whether that be salvation, empowerment or anything else. Regardless of what the educator intends, the essence of education is tradition.

For that reason, education is inherently historical in nature. It is always about the perpetuation of the past. Education therefore cannot be fully understood, either as an activity or as a field of study, without the capacity to explain it in historical terms. If Education Studies is to exist as a discipline focused upon the field of education, broadly but coherently defined, then history of education is vital.

Questions for discussion

Consider a traditionalist classroom, such as what Scruton would approve.

- What, if anything, does the learner contribute?
- Is the learner just a blank slate for the teacher to project memes upon?

Consider a progressive classroom, in which the teacher is a facilitator and teaching is learner-centred.

- Can the teacher avoid transmitting his own ideas to the learners?
- What kinds of memes might be transmitted without the teacher's conscious intention?

Conclusion

In the context of Education Studies, the question *Why study history of education?* cannot be collapsed into the question *Why study history?*; instead, it collapses into the question: *Why study education?* Unlike ITE, Education Studies is a liberal academic discipline, and it therefore requires precisely what Scruton believed education could not be: 'an identifiable field of study.' It has been argued here that the only universally tenable definition of education is tradition. That definition of education, as the activity of cultural reproduction through time, is obviously historical in nature. It is history of education therefore that makes the field of study 'identifiable'. History of education is also indispensable in making that field of study intelligible.

This is not an instrumentalist argument. The position is not that the subdiscipline of history of education is useful or even necessary to the study of education. Instead, it is that history of education is in itself (part of) the study of education. To return to the question raised at the start of this chapter:

Q: Why should you engage with history of education?
A: Because you want to study education.

Summary points

- History of education is being given a new prominence in Education Studies programmes, but the rationale for that is not self-evident.
- Inclusion of history of education cannot be justified in terms of instrumental utility. Nor can it be justified to Education students in the same terms that the study of history is defended for History students.
- The only universally tenable definition of education is tradition. It is inescapably, perhaps among other things, the activity of perpetuating (elements of) the past.

- Students of Education Studies are committed to studying the field of education 'for its own sake', and not as a form of professional training. History of education both defines that field of study and makes it intelligible.
- History of education therefore enables Education Studies to develop as a liberal academic discipline, and empowers students to engage with it as such.

Recommended reading

Gordon, P. and Szreter, S. (1989) *History of Education: The Making of a Discipline.* London: The Woburn Press.
Lowe, R. (2002) Do We Still Need History of Education? Is it Central or Peripheral? *History of Education,* **31**(6), pp. 491–504.

References

Aldrich, R. (1996) History in Education. *Paedagogica Historica,* **32**(1), pp. 47–64.
Aldrich, R. (2006) *Lessons from History of Education.* Abingdon: Routledge.
Bloomer, M. (2011) *The School of Rome.* Berkeley and Los Angeles: University of California Press.
Bowen, J. (1972) *A History of Western Education, Volume I, the Ancient World.* London: Methuen.
Bowen, J. (1975) *A History of Western Education, Volume II, Civilization of Europe.* London: Methuen.
Chambliss, J. (1984) The Study of History of Education in the United States: Its Nature and Purpose, 1900–1913. *Paedagogica Historica,* **25**(1), pp. 27–47.
Dawkins, R. (1976) *The Selfish Gene.* Oxford: Oxford University Press.
Dennett, D. (2001) The Evolution of Culture. *The Monist,* **84**(3), pp. 305–324.
Depaepe, M. (1993) Some Statements about the Nature of the History of Education. In K. Salimova and E. Johanningmeier (Eds.) *Why Should We Teach History of Education?* Moscow: Rusanov. 31–36.
Elton, G. (2002) *Return to Essentials.* Cambridge: Cambridge University Press.
Evans, R. (2000) *In Defence of History.* London: Granta Books.
Geary, P. (2003) *The Myth of Nations.* Princeton: Princeton University Press.
Hobsbawm, E. (1995) *The Age of Extremes: The Short Twentieth Century 1914–1991.* London: Abacus.
Kenyon, J. (1983) *The History Men.* London: Weidenfeld and Nicholson.
Lowe, R. (2002) Do We Still Need History of Education? Is It Central or Peripheral? *History of Education,* **31**(6), pp. 491–504.
Lowenthal, D. (1985) *The Past Is a Foreign Country.* Cambridge: Cambridge University Press.
Marrou, H. (tr. G. Lamb) (1956) *A History of Education in Antiquity.* London: Sheed and Ward.
Muir, J. (2019) *The Legacy of Isocrates and a Platonic Alternative.* New York and London: Routledge.
Richardson, R. (1996) Historians and Educationists: The History of Education as a Field of Study in post-war England Part I: 1945–1972. *History of Education,* **28**(1), pp. 1–30.
Richardson, W. (1999) Historians and Educationists: The History of Education as a Field of Study in Post-war England Part II: 1972–1996. *History of Education,* **28**(2), pp. 109–141.
Salimova, K. and Johanningmeier, E. (Eds.) (1993) *Why Should We Teach History of Education?* Moscow: Rusanov.
Scruton, R. (2001) *The Meaning of Conservatism.* Basingstoke: Palgrave.
Scruton, R. (2018) *Culture Counts.* New York and London: Encounter Books.
Selleck, R. (1983) 'Is He to Be a Little Lord God Almighty?' – A Reflection on the Study of the History of Education. *History of Education Review,* **12**(1), pp. 1–14.
Simon, B. (1966, repr. 1989) The History of Education. In P. Gordon and S. Szreter (Eds.) *History of Education: The Making of a Discipline.* London: The Woburn Press. 55–71.
Simon, B. (1993) The History of Education: Its Importance for Understanding. In K. Salimova and E. Johanningmeier (Eds.) *Why Should We Teach History of Education?* Moscow: Rusanov.
Simon, J. (1977) The History of Education in Past and Present. *Oxford Review of Education,* **3**(1), pp. 71–86.
Southgate, B. (2005) *What Is History For?* Abingdon: Routledge.
Tocqueville, A. (tr. H. Reeve) (2004 [1835]) *Democracy in America.* New York: Bantam Dell.

2 Liberal education

Harley Richardson

Note: This is the first of two chapters exploring the development of English education before the era of modern state funding and control. For a full treatment of the subject, read in conjunction with chapter 4 on mass education.

Introduction

It's tempting to believe that the history of education in England began with the creation of the national system in 1870, or perhaps with Rab Butler's 1944 Education Act which put many elements of our modern system in place, but more than 2,000 years of educational, social and philosophical development occurred before the state got involved. The roots of modern debates between academic and vocational education, to give one important example, can be traced back to antiquity and the distinction between 'liberal arts' and the 'mechanical arts' of Ancient Greece. Knowing what these ancient and modern concepts have in common, and what has changed in the intervening centuries, can help us appreciate the historical human achievement that modern-day State education represents, and provide insights into the work still to be done.

The liberal arts were particularly noteworthy because they went beyond what was immediately practical or necessary, at a time when life for most still involved a struggle for survival. From around the fourth century BC, the liberal arts were taught to male Athenian citizens who had free time on their hands and choices about what to do with it. The word 'school' contains a distant echo of this fact, as it derives from the Greek *skhole*, meaning 'leisure' (Bykes, 1976).

The purpose of an education in the liberal arts was to foster moral and intellectual excellence and an appreciation of beauty and the finer things in life. The great philosopher Aristotle said that the liberal arts liberate man by enlarging and expanding his choices (Gutek, 1972). They enabled citizens to lead full and interesting lives and participate as active members of society. Underlying the liberal arts was the ability to read as the means of engaging with the great classics of literature and philosophy, most importantly the epic poems of Homer – the *Iliad* and the *Odyssey* – which were rich with examples of heroic, moral conduct to emulate and learn from.

The freedom to study the liberal arts was a product of Greek civilisation, but it was not equally distributed. Free male citizens made up perhaps a tenth of the population of Athens. The slaves whose work society depended upon to function were neither citizens nor free. Instead of the liberal arts, they were taught the mechanical arts which included activities such as making clothes and weapons, agriculture, hunting, baking, butchery, cooking, navigation, medicine and, perhaps surprisingly to a modern mind, the theatrical arts. The mechanical arts were considered to be

DOI: 10.4324/9781003039532-3

repetitive and narrow in scope, each having a specific aim: to become skilled at that activity and no more.

Although the mechanical and liberal arts both fulfilled important roles in society, the latter were believed to be inherently superior. So were there aspirations to extend their study to the whole of the population? In his *Politics*, Aristotle considers this question. Freedom for the few was made possible by the slaves who did the work and operated the tools. If only tools could operate themselves, he reasoned, there would be no need for slaves; all could be free and all could have a liberal education. But for Aristotle, that was just a thought experiment, a fantasy. If most people were slaves, that must have been the natural way of things. And the same applied to the role of women whose role in life was thought to be domestic. This was an early form of 'know your place', with that place allotted by nature and unchangeable (Aristotle, 1995).

For most of human history, education has indeed been the privilege of a lucky few. Nevertheless, within that narrow confine, it did evolve in profound ways that would eventually contribute to the spread of human freedom and thus help bring about universal access to education. The ideal of a liberal education, which has been expressed in different forms at different times, has been at the heart of this remarkable transformation.

This chapter describes the beginnings of that process, showing how the pagan classical education of the Greeks and Romans was transformed under Christianity, leading to a quest for knowledge that would culminate in the Enlightenment. Its companion, Chapter 4, will explore what happened in the wake of the Industrial Revolution, when the tools did begin to operate themselves and education for the masses became possible.

From *romanitas* to religion

Christian education in a classical world

The classical educational model of antiquity was brought to Britain in AD 78 by the Roman general Agricola. The Romans had inherited the liberal arts from the Greeks and took them to all the lands they conquered, because education was central to promoting '*romanitas*', the collection of political, religious and cultural values and practices that formed the Roman identity. Vanquished peoples were expected to *become* Roman, a process that began with the education of the sons of nobles, although the extent to which this approach cascaded *romanitas* to the rest of society is debatable (Lawson and Silver, 1973).

The Greek system originally involved one-to-one tutoring, but had given way by this stage to private schools for collective instruction. These usually consisted of loose communities of teachers and students who would set up shop wherever space could be found, rather than in the fixed institutions and buildings we think of today. Something akin to the modern phasing of education was also in place. Children stayed at home till they were seven, then attended primary school where they were taught the alphabet, syllables and numbers, along with simple moral concepts. In secondary school they would study grammar, using works of literature and history as their source material, drawn from both the classical Greek canon as well as newer Roman works by authors such as Virgil and Cicero. Those who made it to higher education would learn the liberal arts of rhetoric and oratory: the end of a Roman education was to be what the educator Quintilian (see Chapter 7) described as *vir bonus, dicendi peritus* ('the good man skilled at speaking'), a person who could participate effectively in civic life. Over time, specialist schools were created to teach the new Roman sciences of law and medicine.

This was the world the early Christians inhabited. Christianity required its adherents not only to have knowledge of the Bible but to achieve a level of personal and intellectual maturity in order that they could perform meaningful acts of faith. The classical education model provided a ready-made system for teaching reading and for civilising young children; so Christians sent their children to Roman schools where they were expected to do their best to ignore and rise above the pagan content they encountered. Their religious education was provided separately by the Church and the family (Marrou, 1956).

This situation put Church leaders in a quandary. From their point of view, all worthwhile moral lessons were to be found in Scripture, which at that time was most widely available in Latin. But if young Christians learned to read Latin, that also gave them access to a world of illicit pagan material which might lead them astray. Even Saint Jerome, who had translated the Bible from Greek into Latin, was not above reproach. He was famously said to have been admonished by God in a dream for putting his love of secular literature above religious devotion: 'You are not a Christian, but a Ciceronian' (Ferguson, 1990).

This ambivalent attitude to knowledge – recognising its necessity, whilst being wary of where it might lead people – will be a theme throughout the history of education right up to the modern day.

Education for salvation

When the Western Roman Empire collapsed in the fifth century AD, the classical education system went with it. The only education that survived was provided by and for the Church. Christians appropriated aspects of the old system and redirected them to a radical new end. The purpose of education was no longer the preparation of an effective citizen for this world, but the creation of a citizen of the city of God, with the skills and knowledge required to enable the salvation of others and to prepare them for what came after life in this world.

Over the following centuries, as classical culture faded away and 'barbarians' spread across the West, education acquired a heightened importance and urgency for Christians. This took Christian schools to Britain, thanks to the missionary work of Pope Gregory I (590–604). In Bede's *Ecclesiastical History of the English People* (c. 731) we are told that Gregory, some years prior to becoming pope, encountered several Anglo-Saxon children at an Italian slave market. Impressed by their pale skin and blond hair, he enquired as to their origins. 'They are called Angles', he was told. 'That is right', he is said to have replied, 'for they have angelic faces, and it is right that they should become joint-heirs with the angels in heaven' (Bede, 1955). This story is illustrated in a nineteenth-century mosaic which can be seen on display today in Westminster Cathedral. Its legend adds an important detail: '*Non Angli Sed Angeli Si Christiani*' (They would be angels . . . *if only they were Christian*). Gregory was informed that the pagan inhabitants of Britain were ready to embrace the Christian faith in great numbers, if only a suitable preacher could be found to instruct them.

On becoming pope, Gregory chose the Benedictine monk Augustine for this role and, in 597, sent him to Kent. Augustine swiftly converted the king of Kent, Æthelbert, to Catholicism and was allowed to establish a Christian see, becoming the first Archbishop of Canterbury. One of his first acts was to establish a school to teach young monks. Today it is known as King's School, Canterbury, the King in question being Henry VIII who re-founded the school in the sixteenth century (Curtis, 1963).

As Christianity spread across England during the seventh century, the school at Canterbury provided the model for other monastic schools, such as Dorchester, Winchester, Hexham, Malmesbury, Lichfield, Hereford and Worcester, along with a handful of nunneries (Gillard, 2018). Schools were also attached to the 'chantries' established by wealthy benefactors in return for annual services in which their souls would be sung on their way through purgatory to heaven. The founder of a chantry knew that children not yet born would owe their education to him and would owe him their prayers for that service. Chantry schools stood for something that has always been true about education: they drew together generations, including those too widely spaced in time ever to meet in the flesh.

By the end of the Middle Ages there were around 300 Christian schools, each consisting of anything from a handful of scholars to as many as 100 (Ogilvie, 1957). Over time these would come to be known as 'grammar schools', in honour of the subject they devoted most attention to. Studies in 'grammar' by this stage had expanded beyond learning the formal structure of a language. They also involved comprehension and commentary on the content and were effectively vocational, with students learning to read and understand the Gospels in order to become members of the clergy. Grammar school lessons were mostly oral, since manuscripts were rare, and the master made use of hand-copied textbooks such as the *Ars Minor* of the fourth-century grammarian Donatus. In addition, some 'vernacular' schools taught basic reading and writing in English to children under the age of seven, acting as a form of preparatory school for the grammars (Curtis, 1963).

The more liberal understanding of 'grammar' would eventually herald the full-blown return of the liberal arts. As far back as the fourth century AD, Saint Augustine of Hippo (354–430, not to be confused with the Augustine of Canterbury mentioned earlier) had convinced sceptical church leaders that these pagan arts could provide a useful intellectual basis for understanding Scripture (West, 1912). But it took another four centuries for Christian education to embrace the liberal arts wholeheartedly. The person responsible was Alcuin (c. 740–804), a master of York school who was famed for his love of knowledge. In an echo of Aristotle's views, Alcuin believed that education should look beyond what was simply required to understand the Gospels and embrace wider aspects of knowledge, such as the ideas found in the classics of Latin literature which could still be found in a few libraries by those who cared to look.

In an era still referred to by some as the 'dark ages', Alcuin put in place features of education we now take for granted. Indeed, a case could be made for him as a very early pioneer of what would become known in the twentieth century as 'progressive', child-centred education. He developed innovative teaching methods which went beyond learning by memorisation, challenging his pupils to think by setting them tricky mathematical and logical puzzles. He also radically changed the way knowledge was recorded by promoting the use of the Carolingian minuscule script with its then-novel features such as punctuation, spaces between words and capital letters, all of which made manuscripts easier to read and understand (Reitz, 2004). Carolingian minuscule is described today as a 'humanist' script, and we can see that Alcuin was thinking not only about what knowledge to transmit but also how to transmit it most effectively. As we shall find out, consideration of this 'human' element of education would become increasingly important from here on.

The liberal arts provided Alcuin with a powerful medium through which to develop his ideas about teaching. By this stage there were considered to be only seven liberal arts, perhaps because that number was associated in Scripture with anything that was entire and complete (West, 1912). The Seven Liberal Arts (as they were known) had also acquired a structure and were subdivided into two groups. The 'trivium' of Grammar, Rhetoric and Dialectic (or logic) was taught to younger children. The scope of Grammar had expanded well beyond the mechanics of language and now encompassed the most important knowledge of the time (meaning that found in classical literature and the Bible). In Rhetoric, children learned to put that knowledge into their own words; and in Dialectic, their understanding was tested and developed in discussion with others. Here knowledge provided the basis for expression, discussion and understanding, although still within a relatively narrow religious framework. Building upon this foundation, the 'quadrivium' of Arithmetic, Geometry, Astronomy and Music – the different aspects of mathematics, as it was then – was taught to older children and eventually university students (Curtis, 1963).

Thanks to Alcuin, the Seven Liberal Arts were not only studied in York. Such was his renown that he attracted students from the continent to the school, and in turn was tempted away to Frankia (the territory roughly equivalent to modern France and Germany), where he became an advisor on education to King Charlemagne, a ruler who believed strongly in the value of learning. In 800 the latter was crowned emperor of a revitalised Roman Empire (and so effectively ruler of the West). Alcuin made the Seven Liberal Arts the basis of Charlemagne's education programme during the Carolingian renaissance that followed. In England, the Seven Liberal Arts would be taught in grammar schools for hundreds of years.

Question for discussion

The liberal education described so far was given only to a small elite, mostly boys entering a career in the Church. Imagining the resources existed to provide it, would such an education have been beneficial for other social groups?

The cumulative impact of education

Education imperilled

The achievements of Alcuin and other medieval educators were significant but could still be trumped by the struggle for survival. During the ninth century, education went into a decades-long decline while the inhabitants of Britain reckoned with successive Viking invasions. Monasticism and the schools associated with it all but disappeared. Alfred the Great, who united the kingdoms of England against the Vikings, believed the invasions were God's punishment for neglecting the learning required to both live in accordance with God's will and make wise and just decisions. As one historian put it, to repel the invaders, 'the revival of learning was as badly needed as the building of forts' (Wormald, 2004).

Alfred had a liberal educator's love of knowledge and is alleged to have said 'I know nothing worse of a man . . . than that he should not know'. In emulation of Charlemagne, he learned Latin as an adult and invited famous scholars to his court. His concern that few could understand Mass led him to establish a school for the children of the nobility as well as more able children of lesser birth. He forced his officials to learn to read under threat of losing their positions and ordered vernacular translations of the books he thought 'most necessary for all men to know', including works by Gregory I and Bede. In his preface for Gregory's *Pastoral Rule*, which outlined the responsibilities of clergy, Alfred considered how its principles could be applied to statecraft, in an early example of religious knowledge being put to broader secular use.

The intellectual atmosphere propagated by Alfred would generate knowledge as well as celebrate it, giving rise to the *Anglo-Saxon Chronicle*, which was written in Old English and provides much of our knowledge of the times. Wormald argues that the boost Alfred gave to the vernacular turned English into a viable language of prose literature which helped secure its survival after the Norman conquest, when Latin and French became the official languages. Alfred's contribution to education would be acknowledged several centuries later by Oxford University, when it retrospectively claimed him for its founder.

Alfred's success in containing the Viking threat seemed to vindicate his intellectual project, and the revival of education would continue under his grandson Æthelstan (924–939) and through the Benedictine reforms of the tenth century which put monks back in monasteries and revived ecclesiastical standards.

The glamour of grammar

As the structures and practices of the newly united English society became more complex during the tenth and eleventh centuries, increasingly sophisticated administrative processes were required, and a liberal education began to create career opportunities. Educated monks, since they could write as well as read and had been taught arithmetic for purposes such as calculating the date of Easter, found themselves with an effective monopoly on any work involving letters and numbers – the equivalent of modern office jobs. These religious 'clerics' would eventually evolve into secular 'clerks'.

Knowing Latin became the mark of an educated person, a status with considerable significance at the time. If you could read Latin, then you were deemed to be in clerical orders and could claim 'benefits of clergy'. Clerics were free men and agents of God who were above secular laws. Unsurprisingly, there was resistance to poor children going to school to 'learn clergie', and parents could be fined for sending children to school without permission. Some were driven, in desperation, to pretend that they were educated. A person accused of a crime could attempt to prove their membership of the clergy in court by learning and reciting in Latin the 51st Psalm, known as the 'neck verse' – so called because it could save their neck from the noose (Lawson and Silver, 1973).

In the rigidly hierarchical society of feudal England, it is hardly surprising that ordinary people came to view education as a gateway to a better life. A grammar school offered a passport to a form of liberation that must have seemed almost magical. Perhaps this is the reason why the word 'grammar' would eventually produce an offshoot, the word 'glamour' (as in 'enchantment' or 'spell') (Cresswell, 2010).

At the same time, the mechanical arts did undergo a revival of sorts thanks to the medieval craft guilds that were imported from the continent in the wake of the Norman invasion. A young person could now be apprenticed to a master craftsman to learn a trade, although the permission of the local lord was required, and this permission was not often given. The 1406 Statute of Artificers overturned this rule, allowing anyone to send their children to schools, but in practice a stipulation that the parent had to own land worth 20 shillings made it an unachievable goal for most (Curtis, 1963).

Young girls had even fewer options than boys. Some were admitted to elementary schools, but were barred from grammar schools. Apprenticeships were available in trades such as metalworking and silk manufacturing, but most girls were taught practical skills in the home, such as cooking, spinning and sewing, by their mothers and grandmothers. Girls from more privileged families were taught to read and write by their parents or tutors, and daughters of nobles might be sent to nunneries to receive a spiritual education. The end aim in each case, however, was the same: preparation for domestic life as a wife and mother (Kersey, 1980).

Specialisation and higher education

Notwithstanding these considerable restrictions on access to education, collective knowledge was accumulating across Europe. Medieval libraries grew and scholars distilled the knowledge they had acquired about different aspects of life into books known as *summae*, such as the *Decretum* (c. 1150) of the monk Gratian, which dealt with canon law, and the *Sentences* (c. 1150) of Peter Lombard which covered theology (Lawson and Silver, 1973). Some schools began to specialise, too, and from the ninth century what we now think of as higher education started to take shape with the foundation of a dedicated medical school at Salerno. This was followed in 1088 by the law school at Bologna, where we find the earliest use of the term *universitas magistrorum et scholarium* ('community of teachers and scholars'). Others evolved out of the prestigious schools associated with cathedrals. These had begun to attract more students than they could manage, and their masters and students responded by organising themselves into scholastic guilds in emulation of the craft trades (Gutek, 1972). The most notable example was the *universitas* formed (c. 1150) around the cathedral school of Notre Dame in Paris where we find the first 'doctorate' (from the Latin *docēre* – 'to teach') which granted the recipient a license to teach. These scholarly communities would eventually obtain the recognition of secular and religious authorities and evolve over time into the institutions we know today as universities (Curtis, 1963).

Universities first arrived in England after 1167, when Henry II's ongoing quarrel with his archbishop Thomas Becket (who had been educated at Paris) prompted him to issue a ban on studying in Paris. Students went instead to Oxford, where they formed a new scholarly community which grew rapidly. Oxford in turn went on to experience its own student mutinies. In 1209 the killing of a local woman and the execution of several students who were held responsible provoked an exodus to Cambridge, where the second great English university was founded (Lawson and Silver, 1973). The famous colleges we now associate with 'Oxbridge' were originally communities of around a dozen scholars each, with student halls appearing only in the late sixteenth century.

The advent of universities was perceived to be both a boon and a potential threat by Europe's rulers. They welcomed the prestige and economic prosperity that universities brought, but were concerned by the intellectual activity that was part of the package, and the risk of its leading to heresy and subversion. On the continent, political and religious divisions meant that centralised control was difficult, but in England the Crown came to a subtle mutual understanding with Oxford and Cambridge. In return for a privileged existence, they would contain theological debate along relatively uncontroversial lines. If necessary, the monarch could play them off against each other to keep them both in check. The founding of a third university at Northampton was blocked by Henry III in 1265, and the last exodus from Oxford, to Stamford in 1334, came to nothing when Edward III ordered the migrants to return. From this point on, graduates had to take Edward's 'Stamford Oath' and swear that they would not teach anywhere else, which effectively gave Oxford and Cambridge a duopoly on higher education in England.

Universities continued to proliferate elsewhere, however, and several were founded in Scotland during this time – St Andrews (1413), Glasgow (1451), Aberdeen (1495) and Edinburgh (1583) – along with Trinity College Dublin in Ireland (1592). The situation in England would persist until the relationship between the Anglican Church and the state broke down during the 1820s as a result of disputes over Catholic emancipation, opening the way for the founding of the Universities of London and Durham (Whyte, 2018).

Question for discussion

Compare the role of universities in England and elsewhere. Has the Oxbridge duopoly had any positive results?

Synthesising the old and the new

The universities used the 'scholastic method', a grown-up cousin of dialectic, which had been developed in the schools of the Carolingian renaissance. This, along with the Quadrivium, formed the basis of university studies which culminated in Theology, the 'queen of the sciences'. In scholasticism, texts were pored over line by line and discussed in intense detail by a master and his students with the aim of resolving the apparent contradictions and ambiguities found in Scripture in order to get closer to God's meaning. The combative and dynamic nature of scholasticism made traditional monastic studies seem limited, and intellectual life soon passed to the universities.

The rediscovery of books and manuscripts from Ancient Greece during the Renaissance gave university masters a wealth of new material to draw upon in their scholastic debates. Perhaps most significant were Aristotle's writings on logic, which had been lost in Europe for hundreds of years but were reintroduced to the West by Arab scholars around 1120 AD. Initially, the high medieval Church thought his ideas would encourage heresy among Christian readers. By implying that knowledge could be acquired through rational investigation of the world, without the need for divine revelation, they represented a challenge both to Scripture and the authority of God, and in 1210 study of Aristotle's work was banned. Nonetheless his writings were too compelling and persuasive to be suppressed for long, and 50 years later the ban was overturned (Curtis, 1963).

One of those who was fascinated by Aristotle's ideas was the Italian theologian Thomas Aquinas (1226–1274), a Dominican friar who would spend years attempting to resolve the tension between Aristotelian logic and Christian thought. What Augustine of Hippo and Alcuin of York had done centuries before for the Latin classical heritage, Aquinas did for the Greek. Aristotle had believed that rationality was humanity's defining feature, but Aquinas added faith as its necessary underpinning (Gutek, 1972). In doing so, he carved out a space for a thinking, intelligent Man to coexist alongside God. Aquinas provided intellectual support for the idea that people have free will and the moral responsibility to direct that will to good purpose, a responsibility which rests upon having knowledge. His philosophy, Thomism, with the license it granted to rational enquiry, became the dominant strain of Catholic thought and education, inadvertently helping lay the ground for the flowering, over the coming centuries, of humanism.

Humanising knowledge

The concept of 'Renaissance Man'

By the fifteenth century, the highly formalised structure of scholastic debates had become an end in itself, with scholasticism gaining a reputation for pointless attempts to answer conundrums such as 'How many angels can dance on the head of a pin?' It took the development of humanism in Renaissance Italy to reinvigorate intellectual enquiry, by placing the individual at its core. Humanism involved a belief in the ability of people to understand the world through rational enquiry and, by understanding it, to open up the possibility that we could change it to our advantage.

As we have seen, the aim of medieval education had been to prepare students for death and what came after it. The historian Arthur Leach claimed that, following the Renaissance, the purpose of education became to prepare students for life (Curtis, 1963). In theory at least, this took educa-tion full circle back to the classical ideal. In order to engage successfully in the world, humanists believed that learning was the best way to develop oneself as a whole person – *L'uomo universale*, more familiar to us as 'Renaissance Man'. For the Italian diplomat Baldassare Castiglione, this meant cultivating the characteristics of an educated member of the Renaissance court – courtier, scholar, soldier – as described in his widely read *The Book of the Courtier* (1528). For Vittorino da Feltre (1378–1446), it extended to physical fitness, so he set up a school in Mantua with gymnas-tics and physical exercises on the timetable, a novelty in the post-Ancient world (Burckhardt, 1990). Although God and religion were still central to life, secular ideas about what an educated individual looked like were beginning to take shape.

By 1480, Renaissance humanism had reached the English universities, and from that foothold would go on to influence the values of Tudor society and higher education. Classical studies pros-pered once again and, with the encouragement of Henry VIII, Oxford introduced the study of Ancient Greek. Interest in Latin literature thrived, and Latin was now taught for its beauty rather than its utility. The English diplomat and scholar Thomas Elyot (a distant ancestor of the twentieth-century poet T.S. Eliot) wrote the popular treatise *The Boke Named The Governour* (1531), in which he recommended reading the best authors in Latin and stressed the importance of clarity and refine-ment of speech, as well as the literary value of poetry over prose. Elyot's 'boke' was primarily intended for the training of the statesman, echoing the purposes of Roman education 1,500 years earlier, although, as a humanist with a more open view of people's place in society than any Roman would have had, Elyot believed his methods could in principle benefit everyone.

The English vernacular also got a humanist boost, from Richard Mulcaster, the head of Merchant Taylor's school, whose *Elementarie* (1582) did much to win public support for its formal use. He argued that it could be as beautiful and useful as Latin if taught well, and he advocated standardised spellings for ease of reading (Ogilvie, 1957). Over time the wider use of vernacular English in edu-cation would encourage the creation of literature written with the general public as its intended audience, and facilitate public interest in the new sciences of the Enlightenment. Mulcaster arguably deserves to be recognised alongside Alfred the Great for his role in promoting its use.

Not all his ideas were so well received, however. His claim that physical education and organised games would be beneficial for children's health proved to be too far ahead of its time: the idea would not properly catch on until the nineteenth century. In fact, humanism's short-term impact on English schools was limited, and may even have been counter-productive. Ironically the ideal of the *L'uomo universale* seems to have encouraged middle-class parents to send their children to private tutors for a broader education than they would receive in a school, and in doing so contributed to the decline in demand for grammar school education that was to come (Curtis, 1963).

Enter the individual

Nevertheless, the humanist spirit found a more direct route to the populace, thanks to the introduction of printing to England in 1476 by William Caxton and the publication of the first mass-produced English-language Bible in 1539. The latter was derived in part from translations of the New Testament by scholar William Tyndale, who intended it to be understandable by everyone, even the illiterate 'boy that driveth the plough'. Tyndale was not an educator, but, like Alcuin hundreds of years before him, gave great thought to how the knowledge he was concerned with could best be transmitted. The language he used was designed to be read aloud and easily remembered, and was replete with simple but striking phrases, which have become part of our everyday language, with 'signs of the times', 'let there be light', 'my brother's keeper', 'fall flat on his face', 'the land of the living', and 'the parting of the ways' being just a few examples (Bragg, 2017).

The clergy were directed to place a copy of the new English Bible in every parish church. But, once again, the prospect of wider access to knowledge was not universally welcomed, with some expressing concern about the unpredictable conclusions people might reach if they read Scripture without the mediating influence of a priest. In 1543, the Act for the Advancement of True Religion banned artisans, husbandmen, labourers, servants and almost all women from reading or discussing the Bible (Lawson and Silver, 1973). The prohibition proved impossible to enforce. The brief availability of the book had already encouraged many to learn to read and had made them think about the nature of society and the church. This inadvertently opened the door to an early form of self-education, which would flourish in the coming centuries, as we shall find out in Chapter 6.

Tyndale's influence can be seen all over the plays of William Shakespeare, whose grammar school education arguably showed the potential of the trivium at its greatest (Baynes, 1894). His writing certainly provides abundant evidence of the breadth of knowledge and ideas that sixteenth-century grammar school children were exposed to, and his characters were emblematic of the humanist outlook; they were fully formed individuals with personalities and consciences, who grappled with universal human dilemmas.

Enlightenment – but not in schools

Paradoxically, humanism would go on to drive a nail in the coffin of the trivium and the Seven Liberal Arts. Its emphasis on Latin literature was to the detriment of dialectic, which was largely dropped from the trivium after Shakespeare's time. To rub salt into the wound, the enthusiasm for teaching literature would be short-lived, and the study of grammar soon reverted to a mechanical ritual. Without a humanist spirit to breathe life into it, liberal education became an empty shell (Curtis, 1963).

As humanist enquiry began to bear fruit in the scientific and philosophical Enlightenment of the seventeenth and eighteenth centuries, there was a proliferation of new knowledge and ideas. Francis Bacon (1561–1626), one of the leading figures in the scientific revolution, argued that the era demanded a new form of education that accommodated science, in order to 'extend more widely the powers and greatness of man's estate, to secure the sovereignty of man over nature' (Ogilvie, 1957).

Bacon's challenge was taken up, in a limited way, by Dissenters from the Anglican Church. Ironically, this was a consequence of attempts to restrict their education. Dissenters were barred from attending universities by the 1662 Act of Uniformity, but responded by setting up at least 20 illegal academies for older children. As these were unregulated, they were free to offer a wider, more modern curriculum, with subjects such as Hebrew, English, modern languages, history, geography, mathematics and natural science alongside Latin and Greek. The 1689 Act of Toleration legalised their academies, which provided an important alternative to Oxbridge until the liberalisation of the university system in the nineteenth century (Ogilvie, 1957).

Yet the grammar schools that dominated education for children were prevented from modernising by a restriction of a different nature: their founding statutes tightly defined what they could teach. As Samuel Johnson put it in *A Dictionary of the English Language* (1828), a grammar school was 'a school in which the learned languages [Latin and Greek] are grammatically taught'. For members of the growing commercial and professional classes, hoping to educate their children for careers in new fields such as law, medicine, commerce, engineering, the arts and the armed services, there seemed to be little point in sending their children to a grammar school.

During the second half of the seventeenth century, local businessmen began to take matters into their own hands, endowing their own grammar schools, some of which expressly forbade the teaching of Latin (Jones, 1938). A few of the older grammar schools, such as Bedford and Macclesfield, successfully obtained private Acts of Parliament which allowed them to enlarge the scope of their original foundations.

The older grammar schools, however, went into a decline lasting several centuries. Demand tailed off and some, such as Shaftesbury Grammar in 1780, closed for want of pupils. As late as 1805, Leeds Grammar would lose a lawsuit for attempting to introduce modern studies. This decision was finally reversed with the Grammar Schools Act of 1840, which allowed the 782 remaining endowed grammar schools to apply to substitute other subjects for Latin and Greek, but only if they had insufficient revenues, and only if the result had 'due Regard to the Intentions of the respective Founders and Benefactors' (Gillard, 2018). But by this late stage, the focus of education policy had shifted to 'rescuing' the poor, as we shall find out in Chapter 4.

Question for discussion

Is there any unchanging core knowledge that is fundamental to a liberal education? Why does a liberal education seem difficult to sustain over time?

Conclusion

The development of education has always been driven by a sense of the importance of knowledge about the world. Whether the aim was to participate in adult society, to spread the word of God, to win battles or to become *L'uomo universal*, knowledge has been the key. Schools and universities were created in order to pass on the accumulated knowledge of society in a more systematic fashion. Educators have thought about how to make this knowledge more accessible, be that Alcuin advocating the use of humanist scripts, Tyndale writing for 'the boy that driveth the plough' or Mulcaster proclaiming the utility of the English language. Knowledge created in one cultural context has struck a chord in another, and the struggles to assimilate it to these new contexts have helped drive civilisation forward. Our modern education system is the result of what some now call cultural appropriation and is all the better for it.

The potential of knowledge to enrich our lives was embraced in the ancient liberal arts. These provided an open-ended model for transmitting and, more importantly, developing knowledge, a process which led over the centuries to the Enlightenment and a far greater understanding of ourselves and the universe in which we live.

Yet for many, the open-ended nature of knowledge has threatened danger. All advances in the scope of education have been accompanied by a fear of what people might do with what they've learned, and a reluctance to extend the opportunity to everyone. As we end this chapter, with the Industrial Revolution just around the corner, formal education was still the privilege of a tiny minority. In Chapter 4 we will find out how it finally came to the masses.

Summary points

- The Ancient Greek idea of the liberal arts aimed to liberate man by enlarging and expanding his choices.
- The Romans used education to 'romanise' conquered peoples, establishing schools in Britain.
- The early Christians adapted the classical education model to their own ends following the fall of the Roman Empire in the West.
- The Gregorian mission brought Christian education to Britain in the late sixth century, and Latin grammar schools were established to teach Scripture.
- Alcuin of York updated the ancient idea of the Seven Liberal Arts for the Christian world, expanding education beyond what was necessary to learn Scripture.
- Alfred the Great revived knowledge and learning after the Viking invasions, and a grammar school education became a route to a better life.
- As knowledge accumulated, specialist universities were formed, and Oxford and Cambridge carved out a duopoly on higher education in England.
- The rigours of the scholastic method were enriched by the rediscovery of ancient thought during the Renaissance, opening the way for humanism.
- Humanism arrived in England during the late fifteenth century, bringing a new emphasis on classical studies and literature.
- The arrival of printing in England gave ordinary people direct access to Biblical knowledge and encouraged them to think about its meaning.
- The Enlightenment brought a wealth of new knowledge, which grammar schools were barred from teaching by their founding statutes.

Recommended reading

Robinson, M. (2013) *Trivium 21c: Preparing Young People for the Future with Lessons from the Past.* Carmathen: Independent Thinking Press.
Thomas, G. (2013) *Education: A Very Short Introduction.* Oxford: Oxford University Press.

References

Aristotle (1995) *Politics*, Book 8. Oxford: Oxford University Press.

Baynes, T. (1894) What Shakespeare Learnt at School. In T. Baynes (Ed.), *Shakespeare Studies and Essay on English Dictionaries*. London: Longmans, Green, and Co.

Bede (tr. L. Sherley-Price) (1955) *A History of the English Church and People*, Books 1 and 2. London: Penguin.

Bragg, M. (2017) *William Tyndale: A Very Brief History*. London: SPCK Publishing.

Burckhardt, J. (1990) *The Civilization of the Renaissance in Italy*. London: Penguin.

Bykes, J.B. (Ed.) (1976) *The Concise Oxford Dictionary of Current English* (6th edition). Oxford: The Clarendon Press.

Cresswell, J. (2010) *Oxford Dictionary of Word Origins*. Oxford: Oxford University Press.

Curtis, S.J. (1963) *History of Education in Great Britain*. London: HarperCollins.

Ferguson, E. (Ed.) (1990) *Encyclopedia of Early Christianity* (2nd edition). Abingdon: Routledge.

Gillard, D. (2018) *Education in England: A History*. Available at http://www.educationengland.org.uk (Accessed 18 October 2022).

Gutek, G.L. (1972) *A History of the Western Educational Experience*. London: Random House.

Jones, M.G. (1938) *The Charity School Movement: A study of 18th century puritanism in action*. Cambridge: Cambridge University Press.

Kersey, S. (1980) Medieval Education of Girls and Women. *Educational Horizons*, **58**(4), pp. 188–192.

Lawson, J. and Silver, H. (1973) *A Social History of Education in England*. London: Methuen & Co.

Marrou, H.I. (1956) *A History of Education in Antiquity*. Madison: University of Wisconsin Press.

Ogilvie, V. (1957) *The English Public School*. London: B.T. Batsford.

Reitz, J.M. (2004) *Dictionary for Library and Information Science*. Exeter: Libraries Unlimited.

West, A.F. (1912) The Seven Liberal Arts. In A.F. West (Ed.), *Alcuin and the Rise of the Christian Schools*. New York: Charles Scribner's Sons.

Wormald (2004) *Alfred [Ælfred]*. Oxford: Oxford Dictionary of National Biography. Available at: https://www.oxforddnb.com/view/10.1093/ref:odnb/9780198614128.001.0001/odnb-9780198614128-e-183 (Accessed 18 October 2022).

Whyte, W. (2018) *The Medieval University Monopoly*. History Today. Available at: https://www.historytoday.com/miscellanies/medieval-university-monopoly (Accessed 18 October 2022).

3 How concepts of femininity have influenced the education of girls and women in England, 1800 to 1988

Christine Eden

Introduction

At the beginning of the 1800s very few girls had access to education, and there was widespread hostility towards the idea of providing educational opportunities for girls. Over the period we are examining, education became available to all pupils, and since the late 1990s considerable publicity has been given to the fact that girls have a higher level of achievement than boys in school examinations and greater numbers proceed to university.

This chapter focuses on how the educational developments leading to this transformation were influenced by cultural beliefs about what was considered appropriate and 'natural' for girls and women, which to differing degrees affected women of all social classes. Those beliefs emphasised the role of motherhood and viewed women as physically weak and inherently intellectually inferior to men. Campaigners, who were mainly women seeking to achieve equal educational opportunities, had to challenge those beliefs, which both limited educational opportunities and defined the curriculum. At the end of the chapter, a brief summary of the current position suggests that, while education for girls has been transformed, there is a continuing discourse about appropriate masculinity and femininity which affects girls' experience within education, the family and workplace, and where women with 'better' educational qualifications are less successful than men.

The chapter explores how the cultural ideology of femininity influenced educational provision and the curriculum, and how other factors also constrained and promoted educational opportunities:

- the critical importance of social class position in determining educational experiences;
- economic, social and political changes, including cultural attitudes towards equal rights within society;
- an increasing recognition on the part of the state of its role in providing education;
- the significant role played by campaigners for women's rights.

As the state became more involved in providing greater access for formal education for girls, there were significant gains, particularly in winning access to secondary and higher education. However, education remained steeped in an ideology which emphasised the importance of the domestic sphere for women, and access to grammar schools and universities for girls remained inferior compared to that for boys (Dyhouse, 2005). It was not until the 1988 Education Act that the same national curriculum for boys and girls was established.

DOI: 10.4324/9781003039532-4

The period under discussion covers a significant number of reports and legislation, only some of which will be explored. More detail can be found in Gillard's (2018) useful resources and commentary.

Models of femininity in the nineteenth century

Nineteenth-century England was a capitalist and patriarchal society which gave men control over women's education. Femininity was defined in relation to masculinity, and the core of this meant women occupied subordinate positions, serving men (Rowbotham, 1973). At the start of the century there was a clear separation of future roles relating to the 'natural' characteristics of men and women. This placed men in the public sphere operating as the economic provider, while women were considered physically weaker but with a strong moral imperative; they belonged within the private sphere of the family, and motherhood should be the height of their ambition. Again, such attitudes were unremittingly hostile to girls' education.

Upper- and middle-class women were largely excluded from the public sphere, and their attention was expected to be focused on the private sphere of the family. When middle-class women found work necessary, they were expected to be a nurse or a governess, continuing the caring functions of women within the family. Any education was often given in the home by poorly educated governesses, designed to teach middle- and upper-class girls the skills and accomplishments that would enhance their femininity, present them as an attractive marriage option for men and equip them to be the 'perfect wife.'

Any discourse deemed 'learned' was termed 'masculine', and women who displayed learning were ridiculed. Such views ensured women were economically, physically and emotionally dependent upon men and were reinforced by scientists who argued that women were physically inferior to men, were incapable of undertaking intellectual activities for any period of time, and were biologically less intelligent (Dyhouse, 2014). Psychological models emphasised the irrationality of women and their emotional responses, which were seen as making them the weaker sex, physically and mentally. The limited paid work available for upper- and middle-class women ensured that marriage was seen as the most desirable survival strategy available.

Working-class girls were forced by economic necessity to participate in paid work, but they also had a key role in servicing working-class men as the economic providers of the family, and possibly the middle and upper classes in domestic service. Middle- and upper-class interests were served by ensuring the working class was not educated 'above their status' but available to service the needs of domestic labour. As the nineteenth-century economy expanded, working-class men also feared that women entering the labour market would depress their wages. Such cultural attitudes were located in a discourse that reflected a patriarchy where women's minds, as well as their bodies, were controlled by men. Clabaugh (2010: 166) sees this as a theme that has run through history and quotes Plato, who believed that a woman's virtue was 'to order her house, keep what is indoors, and obey her husband'. This position was supported by the Church, which saw it as part of a divine order within marriage. While there were class-specific variations, this patriarchal ideology affected all women and their access to education and, when that became available, the nature of the curriculum available to them.

There were women who challenged these expectations and argued for women's right to education, but often at considerable personal cost, as can be seen in the life of the feminist and writer

Mary Wollstonecraft (1759–1797) who died in childbirth towards the end of the eighteenth century. She campaigned for equality between the genders with equal access to education for women and, against the prevailing position, argued that the expectations of behaviour associated with different genders was socially constructed and located in the patriarchal values of her time. Her ideas were anathema to men in positions of power; her personal life was used to smear her reputation and make her a figure of fun. Like many other women campaigners she was largely 'hidden from history', until November 2020 when a statue in her memory was erected in Newington Green, Islington.

The model of 'the perfect wife' for middle- and upper-class women translated into 'the good woman' for working-class women who, it was argued, should also give priority to caring for their husbands and children. Purvis (1995) suggests that such a model for working-class women, many of whom would have had to engage in paid work for survival, was a form of class cultural control by the middle classes, trying to transmit a bourgeois family ideology by insisting that a woman's place was in the home. In effect this was an attack by the middle class upon the patterns of working-class motherhood and parenthood. It would have been influenced by the fact that the middle classes were dependent on working-class women being available to carry out their domestic tasks, and this class interest affected what education provision was available for working-class women during the nineteenth century, much of which depended on a middle-class voluntary effort.

Educational provision: 1800 to 1870

The nineteenth century was a time of social, political and economic upheaval, with industrial growth requiring the construction of factories for the mass production of goods. This led to a significant movement of the population from the country to the towns, with working-class men, women and children working long hours in the factories and living in abject poverty. There were debates about working-class conditions and the role of education, with some seeing education for the working class as a threat to the social order of society, whereas others believed that some basic education was a requirement of an industrial society.

At the start of the century, education provision was organised along gender and class lines in that it was available only to a minority of boys from affluent middle- and upper-class families, educated in the grammar and public schools and not available for the working class or for women. Some upper- and middle-class girls with progressive parents *were* educated, usually in association with their brothers, and some attending private boarding school and small day schools aimed at ensuring girls acquired the accomplishments that would enhance their opportunities for a good marriage rather than improve their intellectual capacity. There would have been no science, and only a very privileged few were taught to a high level in subjects such as mathematics (Purvis, 1991).

Concerns for the poverty of the working class and a growing awareness of the relevance of basic education to industrial growth, plus philosophers such as Jeremy Bentham arguing for political rights, led to a variety of schools being provided for poor boys and girls mainly by wealthy industrialists and philanthropists. There was a considerable variety of schools including dame schools, workhouse and parish schools, church schools, industrial schools and ragged schools where boys and girls received very basic education in reading, writing and arithmetic, with possibly some sewing for the girls and trades such as tailoring and shoemaking for boys (Gillard, 2018). Girls' attendance was lower than boys due to their involvement in domestic tasks within the home and their employment within textile factories (Purvis, 1989).

Industrialisation brought the need for better education across the population, and in 1839 the government slowly began to take some responsibility for education. It set up a Committee of the Privy Council on Education which made national funds available to build new schools and commissioned various reports and legislation (Gillard, 2018). The middle and upper classes retained their hostility to the idea of educating the working class, but the number of schools continued to grow and attendance at elementary schools increased across the first half of the nineteenth century, with the majority of children attending leaving school before they were 11.

The educational expansion which occurred across this period was still very closely aligned with the class structure, with only basic skills and vocational training for the working class. The only similarity across the social classes was a segregated learning experience for boys and girls and a differentiated, gendered curriculum. There was a gradual shift in approaches to girls receiving education during this time as the contribution of women to their children's education became apparent. But it took until the Taunton Commission in the 1860s to argue that women and men shared the same mental capacity and that more public secondary schools for girls were required.

Until the 1870s new educational opportunities for middle- and upper-class women were instigated and funded largely by women campaigners fighting against prevailing attitudes. Attitudes were slowly beginning to change, encouraged by the liberal principles emerging from the French Revolution and the eighteenth-century European Enlightenment. There were also concerns about options for unmarried women needing to seek a livelihood (Rowbotham, 1973). This enabled the development of a number of initiatives including Queen's College in London, set up in 1848 to give governesses marketable qualifications, and the Ladies College in London in 1849. The North London Collegiate School was set up in 1850 by Francis Buss, and in 1854 Dorothea Beale joined Cheltenham Ladies College. A number of Ladies' Educational Associations were set up in the 1860s which campaigned for girls to be allowed to sit for examinations and to have access to universities. In 1869 Girton College, Cambridge was co-founded by Emily Davies and became the first university college in England to educate women. These developments benefited upper- and middle-class women and had little impact on the educational experiences of the majority of working-class girls who left school at the earliest opportunity for drudgery in the home or the workplace.

The curriculum in these organisations included subjects that traditionally had been the preserve of men and was not confined to domestic subjects, but there was also a considerable number of campaigners who Bush (2005) calls 'conservative reformers'. They argued for increased educational opportunities, but within a curriculum that emphasised femininity, respectability and the importance of their role as a wife and mother. This argument for feminine respectability remained a potent force in the fight for education, even while this position was opposed by others. This tension can be seen in the writing of Emily Davies, who argued for women's rights including women's suffrage. Her writing shows she recognised that winning the argument for equality in education required paying homage to traditional notions of femininity:

> Many persons will reply, without hesitation, that the one object to be aimed at, the ideal to be striven after, in the education of women, is to make good wives and mothers. . . . Clearly, no education would be good which did not tend to make good wives and mothers; and that which produces the best wives and mothers is likely to be the best possible education. But having made this admission, it is necessary to point out that an education of which the aim is thus limited, is likely to fail in that aim.
>
> (Davies, 1886: 10–11)

These initiatives had little relevance for working-class women, but when they did have access to educational opportunities outside formal education, they also reinforced a domestic ideology. When working-class women were allowed to join the Workers Educational Association towards the end of the nineteenth century, they were offered a curriculum considered appropriate for wives and mothers. This made them subject to both class and gender power relations in that these organisations were controlled, to a large extent, by middle-class men. The Manchester Institute argued that its main aim in educating working-class women 'was to enable them to make their homes happier and more attractive to husbands and a training ground for the children' (Gerrard and Weedon, 2014: 241). The curriculum offered reading, writing and arithmetic, but neither science nor mathematics, and women were taught separately. To counter this, a female Education Institute was set up in Huddersfield in 1864, but it was again dominated by the middle classes and all the senior positions were held exclusively by men.

The Newcastle and Taunton Reports

Concerns about Britain's competitiveness with other European countries increased the attention given by the state to education, and a number of reports were commissioned in the 1860s. Both the Newcastle and Taunton Reports argued that educational opportunities for girls should be increased, but at the same time they still recommended a curriculum that located women's role within the domestic sphere. The Newcastle Report in 1861 has a discussion about the pressures on girl pupil-teachers with fears for their future without good domestic skills:

> It is a great wrong to her mother, father, brothers, and sisters, if she be prevented from bearing her fair share of the usual household work of her home, and a greater injury to herself if she be excused from this. . . . Otherwise, if she fail to obtain a Queen's scholarship, or if she marry an elementary schoolmaster, or a small shopkeeper, or a small yeoman, she will be anything but a good housewife; or if she become a certified schoolmistress, she will not be the person whom sensible thoughtful parents of humble life will care to entrust with the formation of the character of their girls.
>
> (Newcastle Report 1861, vol. 1: 104)

Similarly, the report sees the time spent on needlework as valuable for their future role as mothers: 'The girls are found extremely useful in this respect, being more apt, cheerful, and kindly teachers than boys; and they derive from this occupation a valuable preparation for becoming mothers' (ibid: 218).

The Taunton Report (1868) focused on schools for the middle classes. It advocated an increase in the number of girls' secondary schools, of which there were only 13 in England, and these were judged to be of poor quality. Concern about the quality and provision of secondary education was fuelled in part by anxieties about the future of unmarried middle-class women due to 'the great drain of the male population of this country for the army, for India, and for the colonies' (ibid: 546). The report is positive about girls' ability to learn and to a considerable degree argues for equality in educational provision and subject matter. One of its striking comments related to performance in the Syndicate Examinations: 'In almost every respect it is more satisfactory as regards the girls than as regards the boys' (ibid: 54). Yet the report continues to reflect a model of femininity linked to girls' physical frailty, referring to differences in the 'capacity of learning' between boys and girls as attributable to boys' 'greater power of endurance'.

1870 to 1899

Those 1860 Reports prompted the significant 1870 Elementary Education Act (sometimes called the Forster Act), which saw the government taking responsibility for introducing free and compulsory universal education for all children aged 5 to 13, and Local School Boards in England were created to finance and build elementary schools. This act was notable both for instigating a national system of state education in England and for promoting an education system divided by social class through the provision of public schools, grammar schools and elementary schools (see Chapter 11). Grammar and public schools pursued a classics curriculum, while the elementary schools, attended by the majority of pupils, were limited to basic skills and some vocational training. Grammar schools for girls became permissible, although this 'victory' was a belated development compared to the provision already available for boys. The right to education for working-class girls, many of whom spent their time either in domestic labour or working in the mills, frequently meant an afternoon of needlework. At the time this drew unsuccessful protests, and the practice of teaching needlework in elementary schools grew at the expense of academic subjects.

While state secondary schools for girls increased following the Taunton Report, it was women campaigners who provided girls with educational opportunities closer to that offered to boys. In 1872 one group of women launched the National Union for Improvement of the Education of Women of All Classes, which later became the Women's Education Union. This aimed specifically to establish good and cheap secondary Day Schools for all classes, and school fees were kept low (Bird, 1998). Many of these schools emphasised the need for girls to have access to the same curriculum as boys, including science subjects; but they recognised, as Emily Davies had done, that it was expedient to equip girls with the skills and behaviour necessary to reflect a traditional model of femininity. Most of the schools provided domestic science courses for girls over 17 (Bird, 1998; Bush, 2005). Schwartz (2011: 683) comments, 'as a result the women's colleges both challenged and reproduced dominant ideas of middle-class femininity without ever rejecting such norms altogether'.

The battle for access to higher education gathered momentum towards the end of the nineteenth century, in spite of claims about the threats to women's health from intellectual study. Despite passing university examinations, women were not allowed to be awarded degrees until 1878 at the University of London, 1895 at Durham, 1920 at Oxford and 1948 at Cambridge (Dyhouse, 2002). Certain universities did allow women to participate in courses, but women were not entitled to a degree. These were big steps in the fight for equal rights in education, but by 1900 it was still the case that women represented only around 16 per cent of the total number of full-time students at British universities (Dyhouse, 1995: 469). Emily Davies in the 1860s commented on her difficulties in raising money for a woman's university college by ruefully remarking that few people really wanted women to be educated.

Legal changes such as the Married Women's Property Acts, 1870 and 1882, and the Matrimonial Causes Acts changed the status of women and gave them new freedoms. But resistance continued to the idea that women should be educated outside the private sphere of the family. Where it was accepted that such education could occur, it was for many still rooted in a model that emphasised the domestic role of middle-class women. Such resistance to girls' education was reinforced at the end of the nineteenth century when 'social Darwinistic' ideas about national efficiency and social progress became popular (Dyhouse, 1976: 41). Such an approach saw intellectual education as risking infertility and undermining the priority to be given to motherhood, arguments that had been levelled at women campaigners earlier during the nineteenth century. These attitudes were particularly focused on the minority of women who aspired to university, but they also affected debates about the education required for working-class girls and led to a focus on their need for training in domestic work, resulting in the subject of domestic economy becoming compulsory by 1880 (Heggie, 2011).

Questions for discussion

What were the main characteristics of nineteenth-century patriarchy?
How did that model affect girls' access to education across different classes?

Twentieth century: 1900 to 1926

The view that education was damaging to the health of women and society increased in the early twentieth century and sustained the prevalence of domestic subjects in the curriculum for girls. This was justified by the poor physical state of war recruits revealed in a 1904 report from The Interdepartmental Committee of Physical Deterioration. This report coincided with a highly publicised colonial rugby tour defeat which together created a significant panic in the British public over the apparent deterioration of its men. The report reinforced the emphasis on working-class women's role in ensuring the health of the family, and argued that women who went out to work neglected childcare and in so doing were threatening the very moral fabric of society. The 'natural' functions of women were back and embedded in the policies of the state education system. In 1904 regulations were published that ensured girls received training in domestic subjects in secondary schools. This position was challenged by women campaigners as it threatened other areas of study, and the Girls' Public Day School Trust so objected to this approach that it chose to dispense with government grants rather than submit to such demands. The School Trust's fears were confirmed in that, in 1908, it became possible for an approved course in domestic subjects to be substituted for science in girls' schools, and in 1909 it was suggested that housework might also displace mathematics other than arithmetic. Such a move reinforced a long-held belief that girls should be excluded from studying scientific knowledge (Watts, 2003), which had a very detrimental impact on the minority of middle-class women fighting for access to universities. Without science backgrounds women could not apply to study areas such as medicine, and this barrier remained for many years with quotas on female student admissions into medicine remaining into the 1970s.

There were no barriers, however, to women entering the teaching profession, which was seen as an appropriately 'caring' profession. Teachers were needed following the introduction of compulsory education, and grants were made available to encourage recruitment. While this was not necessarily their first choice, it was one of the few opportunities for young women from both working-class and middle-class homes to gain access to some form of higher education and acquire a job at the point of graduation. This continued to be an option taken by many working- or middle-class women for the first 40 years of the twentieth century (Dyhouse, 1997). This was a significant factor in the increase of women within universities during the twentieth century, many of whom were from lower middle and working classes.

The need for female labour during the First World War had shown that women could be highly effective in contributing to the economy, but the position of women in post-war government reports continued to reflect a traditional view of women's roles in relation to marriage and the family. Although this view was moderated by an acceptance within government that the expansion of women's education was desirable, there were still powerful voices that spoke out against it.

Hadow Reports 1923 and 1926

Discussion about the sort of secondary education required for the twentieth century was debated in various reports in the 1920s. The Hadow Report in 1923 supported greater access to education for girls, but saw this occurring within a gendered curriculum which emphasised girls' domestic roles and the physical and mental differences between boys and girls. The report argued there should be greater freedom in the curriculum, especially in girls' schools, but emphasised the importance for girls of 'Domestic Subjects' at the expense of science and mathematics:

> In relation to the curriculum as regards girls, it must include practical instruction in Domestic Subjects, such as Cookery, Needlework, Laundry work, Housekeeping and Household Hygiene. For older girls (over 15 years of age) Natural Science may be wholly or partially dropped, and Mathematics may be confined to Arithmetic, in order to make room for a fuller course in a combination of Domestic Subjects.
>
> (Hadow, 1923: 46)

Hadow echoed earlier views about girls' physical frailty in that he argued, 'Girls should be protected from physical fatigue and nervous overstrain' (Hadow, 1923:139) and the report suggests that to protect girls, they should take the First School Examination a year later than boys, while concerns about their psychological vulnerability and 'sensitive constitution' led to this recommendation:

> Girls must not be admitted to the same written examination as boys, for they could not possibly reach anything like the same standard. If the bold step were taken of admitting them to such tests, the results must not be published in order of merit, on account of the more excitable and sensitive constitution of the female.
>
> (Hadow, 1923: 128)

On several occasions the report promoted the education of girls. Yet it also explicitly argues that an appropriate curriculum for girls be tied to their future domestic roles and their psychological limitations. The report is rooted in the assumption that boys and girls have different needs, attitudes and personality characteristics, with Hadow seeing a 'traditional conception of women as consisting in modesty, gentleness and willingness to follow rather than to lead' (ibid: 113) and expressing concerns about their physical limitations:

> In general, there seems to be agreement among psychologists that the physical characteristics of the feminine sex have a certain indirect effect upon the minds of women and girls . . . They are more susceptible to physical fatigue, both as a result of bodily exertion and as an indirect concomitant of mental effort.
>
> (ibid: 86)

The report includes comments from women they interviewed that presented very different perspectives, although such views did not change the overall argument of the report:

> The point to be emphasised at the outcome of this study is that, according to our present light, the psychological differences of sex seem to be largely due, not to difference of average capacity, nor to difference in type of mental activity, *but to differences in the social influences brought to bear on the developing individual from early infancy to adult years.*
>
> (Miss Thompson, quoted in Hadow, 1923: 87, author's emphasis)

The Hadow Report was written at a time when women had demonstrated their ability to take over 'men's work' during the war, and there was constant public debate about women's rights arising from the suffragette movement. Hadow knew the world was changing: he said, 'we are only on the threshold of the development of women's work and their opportunities' ibid: 125). But he never wavered from his view that women should be 'makers of homes', and schools should prepare them for this. This same approach can be seen in Hadow's 1926 Report, *The Education of the Adolescent*. The views presented on 'housecraft' echo the position at the turn of the century:

> We consider that courses in housecraft should be planned so as to render girls fit on leaving school to undertake intelligently the various household duties which devolve on most women. . . . *They should also be shown that on efficient care and management of the home depend the health, happiness and prosperity of the nation.*
>
> (ibid: 234, author's emphasis)

These government reports accepted that girls had the right to full-time education but continued to argue that the natural place for girls was within the domestic sphere, which was of such importance that the study of domestic subjects could replace science and mathematics.

1927 to 1988

The 1944 Education Act and its impact

The 1944 Education Act was highly significant in that it offered all children the right to free secondary education up to the age of 15 and led to a tripartite system of grammar, secondary modern and technical schools, thus reinforcing the existing class structure. It also resulted in priority being given to boys in the implementation of the 11+ examination which determined access to which type of school. In many local authorities the mark for boys was set at a lower level than for girls to ensure there were roughly equal numbers of boys and girls in grammar schools. Girls were 'failed' so lower-achieving boys could 'succeed'. Failure meant attending secondary modern schools where there was little opportunity to progress into the professions or universities. Although it had been argued the different schools would have parity of esteem, this was never the case, and in reality attending a secondary modern came to be seen as a mark of failure.

I have personal experience of these times in that I was one of the lucky girls for whom the 11+ opened up opportunities. I passed the 11+ and secured a scholarship to a direct grant school. Every morning I waited for my bus on one side of the road, while on the opposite side my sister and later my brother waited for their bus to take them to the local secondary modern school. I went on to university and eventually became a university lecturer, while my sister left school at 15 and went to work in Clarks' Shoe Factory and my brother became a carpenter. At the time the differences between us were slight, but the consequences were huge.

Those attending grammar schools were likely to be middle-class pupils, while secondary moderns were dominated by children from poor and working-class backgrounds. The nature of the curriculum in secondary moderns was orientated towards training in basic subjects with an emphasis on practical skills which, in the case of girls, meant domestic activities. Delamont (2013) talks of 'the domestic drudgery that dominated the curriculum of girls' secondary modern schools in England after 1944'. This was a system of education ensuring that the majority of working-class girls had little choice but to live out their destiny as wives and mothers and were encouraged to see this as desirable and inevitable (Dyhouse, 2014).

The inequalities in opportunities, funding and resources between grammar schools and secondary moderns meant that the period between 1944 and 1960 was characterised by increasing criticisms of the class inequalities perpetuated by this divide. Sociological studies focused on boys' education, access to the labour market and debates about masculinity. There was very little comment on girls' experience of secondary modern schools, and what little there was tended to continue to emphasise their future domestic roles and the nature of femininity.

The Crowther and Newsom Reports

The Crowther Report (1959) was set up with a focus on the education of boys and girls between 15 and 18, but also with a change in focus to consider women's increasing entry into the labour market. Crowther was aware that 'the wife of today has a large number of years which she can devote to activities outside her home' (Crowther, 1959: 32). But this awareness was located in assumption of the primacy of motherhood, particularly for the 'less able'. The report argues that during adolescence 'boys' thoughts turn most often to a career and only secondly to marriage and the family and that the converse obtains with girls' (ibid: 34).

While Crowther claimed to be looking for ways to increase professional opportunities for women, his underlying message reinforced women's homemaking roles and responsibilities, as is the case in the Newsom Report (1963) entitled *Half Our Future*. This report explored the education of pupils of 'average or less than average ability' between the ages of 13 and 16 and, as in the Crowther Report, these girls are all destined for their future roles as wives and mothers. The report considers what would be involved in a curriculum built around these expectations:

> One line of advance lies in courses built round broad themes of home making, to include not only material and practical provision but the whole field of personal relations in courtship, in marriage, and within the family – boy and girl friend, husband and wife, parents and children, young and old.
>
> (Newsom, 1963: 137)

The Newsom Report also found that access to science was still influenced by gender, with girls dominating in biology and boys in physics, and that mathematics was the subject in which boys' and girls' schools most clearly diverged. Both reports confirm the assumption that the rightful place of girls was first and foremost as mothers and homemakers and their education should firstly provide what was required for that future. Such assumptions helped obscure problems about girls' achievement and their opportunities in the labour market, but these were picked up by women campaigning for equal rights and better educational opportunities for girls.

Challenges to girls' education: 1960 to 1970

During the 1950s and 1960s the big debate was how the tripartite system was discriminating against working-class children and whether a comprehensive system would create a more equal society (Halsey et al., 1964). The issue of women's subordinate place in society was left to the second-wave feminist movement of the 1960s and 1970s to address by opposing the gendered curriculum most girls experienced, and exposing the limited expectations and achievements of girls (Dyhouse, 2005).

Within society there was a changing culture with an emphasis on equal opportunities which helped challenge stereotypes of traditional masculine and feminine roles. By the 1970s these concerns led to legislation such as the Equal Pay Act 1972 and the Sex Discrimination Act 1975 which made discrimination illegal across a wide range of areas, including employment and education. The development of a legal framework to challenge stereotypes and structural inequalities was very significant in society as a whole and for the education system. But within education there remained a lack of equal opportunities for girls. Tradition and teachers' attitudes directed girls away from maths and sciences and boys away from domestic science, and textbooks within state schools reflected girls' future domestic roles. Careers advice also was inadequate and sex biased, with girls encouraged to train in traditional female spheres of work. Inevitably, the subjects taken at school influenced what work options were available and what university courses girls could access (Arnot et al., 1999).

Women's groups were significant in trying to change practice as well as arguing for equal opportunities and promoting a wide range of education projects such as Girls into Science and Technology (GIST) in 1980 and Women into Science and Engineering (WISE) in 1984 which aimed to encourage girls into traditionally male subjects (Deem, 1992). Various research in the 1980s illustrated the lack of equal opportunities for girls in education and their invisibility when at work. Such research argued that a change was needed in the discourse about what was 'natural' for woman in society and its implications for the education system (Dyhouse, 2014).

From 1988 to 2022

In 1988 the Education Reform Act brought in a national curriculum which appeared to respond to the wishes of campaigners over the centuries that boys and girls should experience the same education. Under the new curriculum and forms of assessment, girls' academic attainment rose and surpassed that of boys. But research has shown that the classroom remained a place where attitudes and behaviour sexualised and objectified women and confirmed the continuing power of models of traditional masculinity and femininity (Skelton et al., 2009). Within schools and universities, recent evidence shows considerable sexual abuse and harassment, and women from ethnic minorities suffer additionally through racism (Revolt Sexual Assault, 2018; WEC, 2016). Gendered, classed and ethnic inequalities continue to limit opportunities and futures. While girls have equalled and surpassed boys in educational achievement, the subjects studied remain clearly gendered in the way they are perceived by pupils and teachers. This affects how subjects are taught and pupil choices within schools and universities (Eden, 2017). The gendered curriculum is particularly visible at the point of A-level choices. Boys choose physics, mathematics and computing to a greater degree than girls, and girls choose psychology, education and art at school and university.

The sexism leading to harassment and sexual violence in schools continues into the workplace (EHRC, 2018; UUK, 2020). Women's success in gaining access to higher education is not translated into success within the labour market, which is reflected in the gender pay gap in 2021 of 15.1 per cent among all employees and 8.3 per cent among full-time employees, reflecting that women are more likely to be in part-time work with low pay (ONS, 2022).

This is seen as due to the 'choices' made by women to reduce their commitment to full-time work and a career to undertake childcare responsibilities, reinforcing the continuation of the ideological model that prioritises women's natural functions of childbirth and care (Pedulla and Thébaud, 2015).

That these attitudes continue to be deeply entrenched in UK society was made evident during 2020–2021 when working patterns in the UK were deeply affected by the global Covid-19 pandemic. Many men and women were required to work from home, opening up the option of greater sharing of childcare roles by men and women. The social context encouraged such possibilities with evidence from social attitude surveys indicating changes to traditional stereotypical assumptions about women's responsibility for childcare, the educational attainment of women having overtaken that of men and high female workforce participation. Having both men and women at home provided favourable circumstances to enable greater parental sharing of childcare. But traditional patterns of childcare continued.

Despite both men and women working from home, research undertaken for the BBC found that traditional attitudes and behaviour about childrearing responsibilities still dominated (Goswami, 2021; Kantar, 2021). While Covid-19 increased the amount of time spent on childcare within the family, the share of childcare done by women was very similar to that pre-Covid: 71 per cent of women claimed they were most responsible for childcare or home schooling compared to 26 per cent of men. Yet surprisingly, two-thirds said that they believe that childcare should be equally shared when there are two working parents at home, and fewer than 8 per cent of people said primary parental responsibility should lie with women: a clear theory/practice dichotomy, with stated attitudes not aligning with behaviour and practice.

While women's educational achievement is higher than that of men, they have problems accessing promotion compared to men similarly qualified and do not occupy senior positions of power (Bright Horizons, 2020). While the femininity model of the eighteenth, nineteenth and early twentieth centuries has changed, it still influences the division of labour in the family as well as the culture of organisations and how they implement equal opportunities legislation (BITC, 2019). Girls achieve higher grades in school examinations and attend universities in higher numbers than boys, but the costs associated with responsibility for childcare cancel out much of those educational advantages. These responsibilities lead directly to the gender pay gap and unequal access to positions of power in the workplace. Men continue to dominate every sector of politics, public life and business, and the situation is even more problematic for women from ethnic minority groups who are under-represented in positions of power in every sector. Even in education, an area traditionally dominated by women, only 31 per cent of university vice chancellors and 40 per cent of secondary head teachers are women (BITC, 2015; Fawcett Society, 2022). There is a thread of gendered expectations running from the last two centuries to contemporary society about 'natural' responsibility for childcare which prevents educational success translating into success within the labour market.

These expectations may no longer limit women's access to education or the workplace in the explicit way they once did, but they still place limits on women's opportunities and choices resulting in gender pay and labour participation gaps. Childcare is the single most important explanatory factor of these gaps. Women's educational achievements have not fundamentally challenged the underlying assumptions embedded in the last two centuries that children's care is primarily a mother's responsibility. Yet the debates on childcare are largely conducted in terms of lack of provision and cost. This fails to challenge underlying ideologies and assumptions about gendered childcare responsibilities. Clearly better and cheaper childcare provision is needed, but of equal importance is promoting an alternative model of parental childcare by both men and women that gives all women greater choice and opportunities.

Question for discussion

Do you see any continuity between nineteenth-century views of 'women's place' and current stereotypes and expectations that affect girls and women's experiences of education and the labour market?

Conclusion

This chapter has looked at girls' education from a time when very few girls had access to education, to the current day where girls achieve better results at school and more women attend universities. The model in its ideal form initially restricted girls and women from all classes to the private sphere of the home and family. The focus has been on the way in which cultural notions of femininity, rooted in a model that emphasises natural biological functions and physical vulnerability, have influenced these educational developments.

To understand the dramatic changes that have occurred involves recognising the interrelationship of key factors such as social-class position, the overall social and economic context, the growing involvement of the state and the role of campaigners in fighting for educational opportunities for women. These various factors have all influenced the increase in the opportunities and the nature of the curriculum available for girls and women. But we have seen in various documents how, for the majority of the period under discussion, the knowledge and training relevant to domestic roles continued to be given priority, reflecting continuity with a model of femininity still embedded in the natural functions of motherhood.

In the early twenty-first century, reverberations from the past can still be seen in the gendered choices made by boys and girls within school and within the labour market, even while acknowledging that such options have been transformed. While girls' educational achievements now exceed those of boys, continuity exists over time in the discourse that frames the choices made by males and females, the experiences they encounter within educational organisations and the continuing difficulties girls face as contemporary models of femininity continue to have a negative impact on girls across classes and ethnic groups.

Despite numerous pieces of legislation, work design and organisational structures still create barriers for both men and women to participate equally in the family and childcare. Attitude surveys show significant shifts in recent years in approaches to men's and women's involvement in childcare, but the reality is that women spend much more time in childcare than men and, within employment, women's chances of promotion and attaining positions of power place them in positions subordinate to men. Recent evidence suggests that even when circumstances promote sharing childcare, it remains to a large extent the responsibility of women.

For much of the time under discussion, it seemed appropriate to argue that education reproduced gender inequalities and helped legitimise the notion of women's roles being based on their natural function as mother and wife. That position is less visible today, but cultural attitudes and a discourse that helps construct gendered choices within education still continue, and shared childcare has not been achieved. The nineteenth-century campaigners would see that progress has been made, albeit slowly, but the fight for women to be free of gendered experiences of education and how these translate into opportunities in the labour market is not yet won.

Summary points

- The nineteenth century was a time of considerable economic, social and political change which provided the context for the considerable developments that occurred in the provision of education for girls.
- Social class position was a major factor in determining the nature of educational opportunities.
- The key focus of this chapter has been how both education provision and the curriculum available to girls was influenced by the perception of femininity which placed women in a subordinate role within the private sphere of the home and gave priority to their role as mothers.
- The role of the state became increasingly significant in providing education, but for most of the period it argued that girls' curriculum should reflect their domestic roles.
- Women campaigners in both the nineteenth and twentieth centuries had a significant impact in promoting education opportunities for girls and women.
- Although girls' education provision has transformed, there is continuity over time in the cultural attitudes that still affect girls' educational experiences, the expectations of women's role in childcare and access to careers and power in the workplace.
- There has been a failure to challenge underlying ideologies and assumptions about masculinity and femininity that still affect women's educational experiences and their familial responsibilities for childcare. Society needs a new paradigm that frees women from being defined through their 'natural' function as mothers and gives them equal opportunities to translate their educational achievements into opportunities within the labour market.

Recommended reading

Dyhouse, C. (2013) *Girls Growing Up in Late Victorian and Edwardian England*. Oxford: Routledge.
Eden, C. (2017) *Education, Gender and Work: Inequality and Intersectionality* (Chs. 6,7 and 10). London: Routledge.
Purvis, J. (1989) *Hard Lessons: The Lives and Education of Working-Class Women in Nineteenth-Century England*. Cambridge: Polity Press.
Tinkler, P. and Jackson, C. (2014) The Past in the Present: Historicising Contemporary Debates about Gender and Education. *Gender and Education*, **26**(1), pp. 70–86.

References

Arnot, M., David, M. and Weiner, G. (1999) *Closing the Gender Gap? Post War Education and Social Change*. London: Polity Press.

Bird, E. (1998) 'High Class Cookery': Gender, Status and Domestic Subjects, 1890–1930. *Gender and Education*, **10**(2), pp. 117–132.

BITC (2015) *Race at Work 2015*. London: Business in the Community.

BITC (2019) *Equal Lives: Parenting and caring in the workplace*. London: Business in the Community.

Bright Horizons & Working Families (2020) *Modern Families Index 2020*. London: Working Families.

Bush, J. (2005) 'Special Strengths for Their Own Special Duties': Women, Higher Education and Gender Conservatism in Late Victorian Britain. *History of Education*, **34**(4), pp. 387–405.

Clabaugh, G.A. (2010) History of Male Attitudes toward Educating Women. *Educational Horizons*, **88**(3), pp. 164–178.

Crowther Report (1959) *15 to 18: A Report of the Central Advisory Council for Education (England)*. London: HMSO.

Davies, E. (1886) *The Higher Education of Women*. London: Alexander Strahan.

Deem, R. (1992) Feminist Intervention in Schooling 1975–1990. In A. Rattansi and D. Reeder (Eds.) *Rethinking Radical Education*. London: Lawrence and Wishart.

Delamont, S. (2013) Girl Trouble: Panic and Progress in the History of Young Women. *Gender and Education*, **25**(7), pp. 941–943.

Dyhouse, C. (1976) Social Darwinistic Ideas and the Development of Women's Education in England, 1880-1920. *History of Education*, **5**, pp. 41–58.

Dyhouse, C. (1995) The British Federation of University Women and the Status of Women in Universities, 1907–1939. *Women's History Review*, **4**(4), pp. 465–485. Available at https://doi.org/10.1080/09612029500200093 (accessed May 13, 2023).

Dyhouse, C. (1997) Signing the Pledge? Women's Investment in University Education and Teacher Training before 1939. *History of Education*, **26**(2), pp. 207–223.

Dyhouse, C. (2002) Going to University in England between the Wars: Access and Funding. *History of Education*, **31**(1), pp. 1–14.

Dyhouse, C. (2005) *Students: A Gendered History*. London: Routledge.

Dyhouse, C. (2014) *Girl Trouble: Panic and Progress in the History of Young Women*. London: Zed Books Ltd.

Equality and Human Rights Commission (2018) *Turning the Tables: Ending Sexual Harassment at Work*. London: EHRC.

Fawcett Society (2022) *Sex and Power*. London: Fawcett Society.

Gerrard, T. and Weedon, A. (2014) Working-Class Women's Education in Huddersfield: A Case Study of the Female Educational Institute Library, 1856–1857. *Information & Culture*, **49**(2), pp. 234–264.

Gillard, D. (2018) *Education in England: A History*. Available at: http://www.educationengland.org.uk/history/timeline.html (Accessed 7 November 2020).

Goswami, N. (2021) *We Need to Reflect on Why Women Still Do Most of the Childcare*. London: BBC. Available at: https://www.bbc.com/news/business-56414051.amp (Accessed 1 November 2022).

Hadow (1923) *The Differentiation of the Curriculum for Boys and Girls Respectively in Secondary Schools: Report of the Consultative Committee*. London: HMSO.

Hadow (1926) *The Education of the Adolescent: Report of the Consultative Committee*. London: HMSO.

Halsey, A.H., Floud, J. and Anderson, C.A. (Eds.) (1964) *Education, Economy and Society*. New York: The Free Press of Glencoe.

Heggie, V. (2011) Domestic and Domesticating Education in the Late Victorian City. *History of Education*, **40**(3), pp. 273–291.

Kantar Public (2021) *Women Much More Likely to Say They Were Responsible for Childcare during Lockdown in Britain*. Available at: https://www.kantarpublic.com/inspiration/thought-leadership/women-much-more-likely-to-say-they-were-responsible-for-childcare-during-lockdown-in-britain (Accessed 1 November 2022).

Newcastle Report (1861) *Royal Commission on the State of Popular Education in England*. London: HMSO.

Newsom, J. (1963) *Half Our Future: A Report of the Central Advisory Council for Education (England)*. London: HMSO.

ONS (2022) *Gender Pay Gap in the UK: 2022*. London: ONS.

Pedulla, D. and Thébaud, S. (2015) Can We Finish the Revolution? Gender, Work-Family Ideals, and Institutional Constraint. *American Sociological Review*, **80**(1), pp. 116–139.

Purvis, J. (1989) *Hard Lessons: The Lives and Education of Working-Class Women in Nineteenth-Century England*. Cambridge: Polity Press.

Purvis, J. (1991) *A History of Women's Education in England*. Milton Keynes: Open University Press.

Purvis, J. (1995) *Women's History: Britain, 1850–1945: An introduction*. Abingdon: Routledge.

Revolt Sexual Assault and the Student Room (2018) *Student Experience of Sexual Violence*. London: RSA.

Rowbotham, S. (1973) *Hidden from History: 300 Years of Women's Oppression and the Fight against It*. London: Pluto Press.

Schwartz, L. (2011) Feminist Thinking on Education in Victorian England. *Oxford Review of Education*, **37**(5), pp. 669–683.

Skelton, C., Carrington, B., Francis, B., Hutchings, M., Read, B. and Hall, I. (2009) Gender 'Matters' in the Primary Classroom: Pupils' and Teachers' Perspectives. *British Educational Research Journal*, **35**(2), pp. 187–204. Available at https://doi.org/10.1080/01411920802041905 (accessed May 13, 2023).

Taunton Report (1868) *Schools Inquiry Commission*. London: HMSO.

UUK (2020) *Tackling Racial Harassment in Higher Education*. London: UUK.

Watts, R. (2003) Science and Women in the History of Education: Expanding the Archive. *History of Education*, **32**(2), pp. 189–199.

Women and Equalities Committee (2016) *Sexual Harassment and Sexual Violence in Schools*. London: WEC.

4 Mass education

Harley Richardson

Note: This is the second of two chapters exploring the development of English education before the era of modern state funding and control. For a full treatment of the subject, read in conjunction with Chapter 2 on liberal education.

Introduction

As we learned in Chapter 2, the Ancient Greek idea of a liberal education was later put to religious ends by medieval Christians and evolved into a powerful model for learning, one that synthesised pagan and Christian thought and was imbued with a strong sense of human potential. Yet during the seventeenth century, liberal education lost its way and degenerated into a mechanical caricature of itself. What's more, formal education of any type was still only an option for a tiny percentage of children, and mostly for boys.

This chapter will explore how, over the course of the eighteenth and nineteenth centuries, education finally became a mass phenomenon in England and liberal education rediscovered its humanist spirit. Together, these advances provided the material basis for what became the State system and set up philosophical tensions that are still being played out in education policy and practice today.

Charity schools

The society for promoting Christian knowledge

The beginning of the eighteenth century saw a surge of religious and commercial philanthropy which found expression in the creation of thousands of charity schools. This philanthropy had one eye on the dangers of religious ignorance, and the other on the dangers of the poor having too much knowledge. Charity school education would go on to have unexpected consequences which neither its advocates nor its critics envisaged and, as we shall see, helped create a wider demand for liberal education.

Charity schools were not a new concept. Since as far back as late medieval times, wealthy individuals had given endowments to chantries and the schools attached to them, as we learned in Chapter 2. At a later stage, guild schools were established by the emerging Elizabethan merchant class of businessmen who had money to spare and wanted to demonstrate their public spirit.

DOI: 10.4324/9781003039532-5

What gave the eighteenth-century charity movement its particular dynamic was a reaction to the rise in poverty associated with the dramatic increase in population since the Tudor era. The motivation involved deserves some untangling. Poverty was not necessarily considered to be a bad thing in itself, since its existence was commonly understood to be God's will. Yet the now-dominant Protestant outlook believed that helping the poor and needy was an outward sign that one was amongst God's chosen. The loose morals and irreligion of the poor were also thought to threaten the stability of society, and there was the concern that if children were not educated into the established faith, they might be won over by Catholicism.

The priest and four lay persons who founded the Society for Promoting Christian Knowledge (SPCK) in 1698 believed that education was the answer to these problems. The wisdom of Solomon was their cue: 'Train up a child in the way he should go: and when he is old, he will not depart from it'. SPCK schools were described as 'little garrisons against popery' by Dr White Kenneth, one of its early members. The schools were Anglican, but their hostility to Catholicism was shared by nonconformist Dissenters, many of whom were happy for their children to attend the schools.

In May 1699 the first SPCK voluntary school was established at St George's parish in Southwark, and soon other London parishes, full of the 'Holy Zeal of Charity', rushed to follow suit. By 1729 there were 132 charity schools in the capital, teaching over 5,000 pupils. Education became the most popular form of charity in London, and the schools were treated as objects of pride by local communities. The Society did not set up or run schools, but it laid out professional requirements for teachers (mainly pertaining to religious knowledge and character), promoted subscriptions from local benefactors as the main funding model, and served as both appointment bureau and insurance society.

Charity schools were normally small, with all ages taught together in a single classroom. Lessons consisted of Bible study and moral instruction, along with the 3Rs and some handicrafts. The SPCK advocated a four-year course starting at age six, but most parents allowed their children to attend for only a couple of years until they were old enough to earn wages. The schools were conceived as preparation for apprenticeships rather than for grammar schools, and in this they were successful: over three-quarters of London pupils were placed into apprenticeships or service. Boys went into occupations as diverse as watermen, butchers, bakers, candlestick-makers, weavers, shoemakers, cheesemongers, barbers, joiners, tailors, carpenters, glovers, bricklayers, booksellers, wigmakers, linen drapers and makers of musical instruments. The options for girls, however, were far more limited, with most going into domestic service.

The SPCK's involvement in schools was remarkably productive but also short-lived, as ironically the Society fell foul of the same religious fervour that had given birth to it. During the 1710s, a rise in intolerance led to criticisms on two fronts: fresh disputes with Dissenters erupting on one side and rumours of infiltration by Jacobite Catholics on the other. The Society eventually made a public stand against both Dissenters and Jacobites, but the experience left a bitter taste, and it decided that charity schools were more trouble than they were worth, putting its energy instead into its publishing and overseas missionary work (Jones, 1938).

Nevertheless, at its height the SPCK claimed to have established over 2,000 schools in England, attended by more than 50,000 children, and many of these would continue after it withdrew from education (Curtis, 1963). Scotland, Ireland and Wales all established their own versions of the Society, adapted to their specific circumstances and needs, and schools on the English model were set up in Sweden, Denmark, Holland, Switzerland and Germany.

Sunday schools

In England, the SPCK had struggled to get a foothold outside the capital. In rural areas, farmers did not see the point of sending their children to school when they needed their help on the land, and local schools were often empty in summer and harvest months. In the new industrial towns, the problem was even worse, as many of the children were working all year round.

Demand for child labour in the factories of the Industrial Revolution was so great by the end of the eighteenth century that it kept most children away from school for six days of the week (Jones, 1938). This led to isolated experiments in schools aimed at keeping children occupied on the Sabbath. These in turn evolved into a national movement in the 1780s, thanks in large part to Robert Raikes, editor of the *Gloucester Journal*, whose outlook had been shaped by two decades as a prison reformer. Realising that inmates were often a bad influence on one another, he had attempted to introduce moral and religious instruction into prisons, but, despite his best efforts, the convicts kept reoffending, and Raikes eventually concluded that prevention, via education, was more likely to succeed than cure.

Raikes opened several very successful Sunday schools of his own in Gloucester, but the movement took off in earnest after he began to aggressively promote them in the *Journal*, which was the foremost newspaper in the West of England. Other Sunday schools rapidly sprang up around the country, funded by middle-class subscriptions and donations and offering a similar mix of Bible studies and the 3Rs to the day charity schools (Curtis, 1963). Sarah Trimmer, children's author and a founder of one such school in Brentford, had an explanation for the appeal of education on the Sabbath: the 'day of rest' was actually 'the most uncomfortable day of the week' for families living in miserable and cramped accommodation. In such circumstances, children were glad to escape to the relative order of the schoolroom, a sentiment that may have resonance with modern-day families after several months of home learning during successive lockdowns.

The schools proliferated in remarkable numbers and were welcomed by the public. Initial religious objections to teaching on the Sabbath were overcome by the improvements the schools seemed to make to the children's general conduct and the quality of their work. By the beginning of the nineteenth century there were over 5,000 Sunday schools. In helping bring education to urban and rural areas alike, Raikes succeeded where the SPCK had failed, because he took the realities of people's lives at that time into account. For several decades Sunday schools became the default form that education took for many, and inadvertently helped bring the possibility of free and universal education into the public consciousness (Kendall, 1939).

The monitorial system

Charity day schools had a second wind in the latter stages of the Industrial Revolution, when greater automation reduced the demand for children in factories. That same automation also inspired the 'monitorial system' used in the schools, described by the historian Nanette Whitbread as 'the factory system of mass production applied to instruction' (Whitbread, 1975: 6). It was developed by an Anglican, Andrew Bell, and a Dissenter, Joseph Lancaster, who independently realised that teaching duties could be delegated to pupil monitors, allowing lessons to be conducted at much greater scale than before. Classes of 250 pupils were common in monitorial schools, but Lancaster claimed as many as 1,000 boys could be taught by a single master using his version of the system (Curtis, 1963).

One surviving 'Lancasterian' classroom is preserved in the British Schools Museum in Hitchin. It has long desks, which each seated ten children and one monitor. The monitors, all aged nine or older, were the only ones taught by the master, and they would instruct the other children on their row in simple tasks and examine them periodically. All children progressed at their own pace, with those who needed the most support sitting at the front desks. The floor of the classroom was angled to place all the children in direct line of sight of the Master who, according to Lancaster, 'should be a silent by-stander and inspector' – prefiguring in some respects the view held by modern progressive educators that teachers should be a 'guide by the side' rather than a 'sage on the stage' (Jones, 1938).

The system appears to have been technically effective (not to mention relatively cheap to run), but religion was the catalyst that made it a mass phenomenon. Religious discord had brought the SPCK's involvement in education to a halt, but here it was a spur to greater activity. While Bell's educational ambitions were modest, Lancaster's talent for publicity inspired others to set up schools using his system. Sarah Trimmer, the aforementioned Sunday School founder and a committed Anglican, was alarmed at the prospect of more Dissenter schools (as she imagined them to be), and stirred up tensions between Bell and Lancaster about which of them was the true creator of the monitorial system. This led to the creation of two rival societies with the overly descriptive names common to the time – the National Society for Promoting the Education of the Poor in the Principles of the Established Church, founded in 1811 to establish Anglican schools using Bell's method, and the British and Foreign School Society for the Education of the Labouring and Manufacturing Classes of Society of Every Religious Persuasion, founded in 1814 to establish non-denominational schools using Lancaster's method. The National Society and, to a lesser degree, the British Society took over or set up thousands of charity schools, picking up where the SPCK had left off. These schools would go on to form the basis of the State system (Curtis, 1963).

Question for discussion

Consider the different motivations behind charity schools and state schools. What might be the educational impact of those different motivations?

The charity school curriculum and the working schools

The forms taken by the charity schools may have varied, but they all shared the same aim, alluded to at the beginning of the chapter – to educate the poor out of ignorance, but not *too* far out of ignorance. Sarah Trimmer, once again: 'It is not intended that the children of the poor should be instructed in the branches of a liberal education, but merely in English to enable them to read the Gospels' (Kendall, 1939: 12). No attempt was made to develop children's intellectual powers or bring about what we would now call social mobility. The purpose was to create pious and respectful members of society who would internalise the moral values expected of prospective workers of the time in which industry brought them closer to God and idleness was the worst sin.

Of the 3Rs, reading was taught first, then writing. Good-quality children's books had appeared during the eighteenth century, but the literary canon at charity schools was restricted to the Bible, the Anglican catechism and sometimes Aesop's Fables. Once pupils had mastered reading and writing, they would move on to arithmetic, but few in practice got that far. 'Liberal' activities such as music and singing were discouraged, particularly the solo performance, for its potential to encourage individual pride.

Despite the limited form of education involved, some still feared the destabilising impact on society of educating people above their station and the risk of what the essayist Cato described as '[breeding] up beggars to what are called scholars'. The philosopher Bernard Mandeville thought poverty was the only way to ensure an adequate supply of labour: 'The more a shepherd and ploughman know of the world the less fitted he'll be to go through the fatigue and hardship of it with cheerfulness and equanimity'.

The charity schools also faced persistent criticism from those who believed schools for the poor should take a more practical bent. The political philosopher John Locke had been one of several influential thinkers to advocate industrial schools for pauper children, inspired by schools in the Netherlands. Public opinion was initially sceptical, but as more factories opened, it swung round to Locke's point of view. The Workhouse Test Act, which required those who wanted poor relief to show proof of workhouse attendance, was passed in 1723, and both workhouses and working schools, which focused on education for employment rather than formation of good Christians, soon proliferated. At these schools, boys were taught crafts such as gardening, carpentry, cobbling and printing, and girls were taught spinning, knitting, sewing and strawplaiting. Their work was put up for sale and, if their income exceeded their keep, they got to keep the excess. Parents were delighted when their children, some as young as four years old, became financially self-sufficient, even if that involved a 15-hour working day.

Some high-profile early successes, such as the spinning schools at Findon and Artleborough, seemed to demonstrate the wisdom of the scheme, and existing schools began to convert to workhouses. Yet the practical limitations of the plan soon became clear. The Grey Coat Hospital had been the first to introduce spinning wheels but abandoned them in 1734 because they brought in little money and cost too much to run, and there turned out to be little market for their output. The workhouse approach was more successful in girls' schools, where learning was combined with domestic labour, but for boys the demand from artisans and tradespeople was, ironically, for those who could read and write to help with bookkeeping and commerce, which meant the pupils from the 'traditional' charity schools (Jones, 1938).

So the day charity schools did, in spite of their steadfastly narrow aims, allow some pauper children to break into professions which had previously been the domains of the middle classes. The parents who could afford to send their children to school on weekdays for a so-called 'literary education' became a superior layer within the lower classes. Here we have an irony: charity schools had been set up for moral reasons but eventually proved effective in practical terms; working schools were set up for practical reasons but proved ineffective by every criterion. They not only failed but ended up killing many children. Only 168 out of 2,339 children who entered workhouses between 1750 and 1755 survived the experience (Taylor, 1996).

Question for discussion

What relevance might the failure of workhouse schools have for skills-based education today?

The revival of liberal education

Rediscovery by the elites

Education was reaching more children than ever by the early years of the nineteenth century, but, as we have seen, quantity did not imply quality. Most children were taught a deliberately narrow curriculum, and the idea of an open-ended liberal education, where it was still practised, had degenerated into a farce, amounting to little more than an educationally moribund diet of Latin and Greek grammar.

The nineteenth-century revival of liberal education began at Rugby School which, like many of the elite public schools of the time, was known for the complacency and arrogance of its middle-class pupils. The revival's leading figure was Thomas Arnold, Rugby's earnestly religious master from 1828 to 1842, who was determined to rescue the school from anarchy and irrelevance. In common with the Renaissance humanists, he was concerned with the education of the whole person, valuing 'first, religious and moral principle; secondly, gentlemanly conduct; and thirdly, intellectual ability' (Strachey, 1918: 149). He was also a classicist who appreciated the historical, political and philosophical value of ancient writers and used them to introduce his pupils to the problems of adult life, encouraging them to read voraciously and to think about what they read. He introduced mathematics and other areas of Enlightenment knowledge to the curriculum and became the first teacher of modern history, covering contemporary European as well as Ancient history (Ogilvie, 1957).

Arnold's reforms paid off and tutors at Oxford soon realised that students arriving from Rugby were of a different ilk to those from other schools – 'thoughtful, manly-minded, conscious of duty and obligation'. Arnold is familiar to many today thanks to *Tom Brown's School Days* (1857), Thomas Hughes's fictionalised account of his own experiences as a student at Rugby, set part-way through Arnold's reforms. It paints a picture of life at the school which may be somewhat forbidding to modern sensibilities, but in its day led to a rise in demand for boarding education at a time when most upper-class education took place at home. Many of the teachers and pupils at Rugby went on to found new schools which adhered to its spirit and approach, with one new Arnoldian school opening every year for the next 40 years – schools such as Cheltenham, Marlborough, Rossall, Radley, Bradfield, Wellington, Clifton, Haileybury and Malvern (Curtis, 1963). Other alumni went on to reform older public schools such as Harrow. For many years a test of Arnold's influence was the question 'Does the school play rugby?' (the sport having been invented at the school in 1823).

These schools provided what is today known as a 'classical liberal education'. Thomas Arnold's son, the poet and school inspector Matthew Arnold, famously articulated what that meant in his collection of essays, *Culture and Anarchy* (1869). A classical liberal education was not tied to the structure of the Seven Liberal Arts, nor to the need to teach through the prism of the 'learned languages', although neither were ruled out. It simply aspired to teach children 'the best that has been thought and known' (or sometimes 'thought and said'). Depending on one's point of view, the beauty, or weakness, of the phrase is that it does not specify *what* is taught, or how. That is a question left to society to grapple with, and educators may find that a grasp of the history of education can inform their contributions to that ongoing debate. But, as we have seen, in the era we are discussing Arnold's concept accommodated modern as well as classical knowledge.

The extent to which 'teaching the best that has been thought and known' was an accurate representation of the public school education, or even of the elder Arnold's intentions, is arguable. But over time the phrase would acquire a totemic significance, providing both a rallying cry for tradition-alists and a symbol of elitist and backwards-looking education for progressive educators. It is fre-quently cited in education debates to this day, but the phrase that completes it is usually left out. Arnold argued that we should learn the best that has been thought and known so that 'we can *see things as they really are*' (Arnold, 1869, emphasis in original). In other words, the purpose of edu-cation in Arnold's eyes was to help us get to the truth. In an echo of Alfred the Great's views on knowledge and wisdom from a millennium before, Arnold saw an accurate and truthful assessment of a situation to be a necessary precursor for wise and just action.

In his time, this route to truth was mostly via the revived public schools, which soon became training grounds for the ruling classes. However, the younger Arnold used his role as an inspector to criticise the monitorial schools he visited for narrowly teaching the 3Rs, urging them to build smaller classrooms more appropriate for teaching the humanities (one of which can be seen at the British Schools Museum). He became a respected public thinker on education and advocated a primary education consisting of 'The mother-tongue, the elements of Latin, and of the chief modern languages, the elements of history, of arithmetic and geometry, of geography, and of the knowl-edge of nature', with specialisation being introduced at secondary school – 'the first great stage of a liberal education' – and university providing the 'second and finishing stage'. With the exception of Latin, this is roughly the pattern that would be adopted by the evolving State system during the twentieth century (Conway, 2010).

Liberal education for girls (See also Chapter 3)

Education for young women in the early nineteenth century was anything but liberal, as it was still restricted to the domestic skills. *The Imperial Review*'s view on education for young women was typical for the time: 'Home and home only' was the 'True College' for girls. As late as 1883, Mrs Lynn Linton, a campaigner against liberal education, still felt able to argue against opening up new career opportunities for women: 'a public and professional life for women is incompatible with the discharge of their highest duties or the cultivation of their noblest qualities'.

Nevertheless, the later stages of the Industrial Revolution brought about a number of social shifts which had an indirect but significant effect on education for girls. In working families, both parents might be away from home all day, so their daughters were sent to traditional charity or monitorial schools. Some would go on to become servants of the middle and upper classes. These girls, who had been taught the 3Rs, now had an educational advantage over the young ladies they served, an embarrassing situation that could not be allowed to stand. It became imperative for middle-class girls to be given an education in case it was discovered they were more ignorant than the servants.

This in turn created a demand for more and better-educated governesses to do the teaching. As a role that was carried out within the private home and away from public disapproval, being a gov-erness was one of the few career options open to women at the time. In 1843 the Governesses' Benevolent Institution was formed, and five years later it opened Queen's College, a new training school in Harley Street, which was open to all women over age 12, with 200 applicants in its first term and a surprisingly liberal curriculum thanks to its socialist founder, Frederick Denison Maurice. Among its first attendees was Frances Mary Buss, who would become one of the most important promoters of education for girls and of higher educational standards for all children. Buss had gained teaching experience at the age of 14, while still a pupil, and had helped her mother set up a preparatory school for young children. At Queen's she proved to be a capable student and was awarded certificates in French, German, and Geography.

On 4 April 1850, she opened the North London Collegiate School for Ladies (later amended to 'for Girls') in the Buss family home in Camden. Taking its cue from Queen's College, the school offered a liberal education, which Buss realised was the key that would open professional doors for her pupils. In public, however, she pragmatically downplayed the liberal elements of the school's curriculum in favour of 'the usual Accomplishments', not wishing to put off the wealthy and conservative local gentlemen who might support the school or send their daughters to it. The school's stated aim was to educate future mothers so that they might 'diffuse amongst their children the truths and duties of religion' and 'impart to them a portion of that mass of information placed by modern education within the reach of all'. But the school motto – 'We work in hope' – hinted, tentatively, at a greater ambition and reflected the humanist version of liberal education: a conviction that those we teach will put their knowledge to good use.

The North London Collegiate curriculum was praised for its breadth by London University's inspection team, with subjects as diverse as maths, classical studies, elementary physics, practical chemistry, French conversation classes, business philosophy, bookkeeping, cookery, preparation for the Civil Service, and dressmaking 'on scientific principles'. This was very different in composition to the classical liberal curriculum of Rugby but shared its modern character and broad outlook. NLCS grew rapidly and soon had to move to a larger site. Buss would also open the Camden School for Girls, for younger girls from poorer backgrounds, with over 700 girls attending the two schools.

When women's rights campaigner Emily Davies persuaded Cambridge University to allow girls to sit for its Senior Local Examinations, Buss supplied many of the candidates for the first exams, and the encouraging results persuaded Cambridge to carry out a further three-year trial, with girls sitting for the same subjects, syllabus and examinations as boys, a situation which became permanent in 1867. This experience convinced Buss of the value of external examinations, as they enabled her to demonstrate to the world that girls were just as intellectually capable as boys (Watson, 2000).

Nevertheless, it took another decade for universities to actually allow women to take degrees for the courses they sat. The first of these was the University of London. Colleges for girls had been established at Oxford and Cambridge, but as they did not share Buss's view that boys and girls should receive the same education, she refused to send her students to them, directing them instead to Girton College which had been set up by Emily Davies (Burstall, 1938).

NLCS pupils went on to pioneer new career choices for women, including dentistry, horticulture, pharmacy, photography, interior decorating and furnishing. Buss would help establish professional bodies such as the Association of Head Mistresses and the Teachers' Guild. And by the end of the century there were 80 endowed girls' schools whose liberal curricula were inspired to varying degrees by NLCS (Watson, 2000).

Question for discussion

Can a liberal education open up possibilities for children, regardless of social class, in the 21st century?

The working-class education movement

The clamour for a liberal education spread beyond schools, and working people began to teach themselves 'the best that has been thought and known'. This is worth reflecting on. At the beginning of Chapter 2 we learned that in the slave-owning society of Ancient Greece, Aristotle had argued that if tools could operate themselves, there would be no need for slaves and all members of society could have the freedom and leisure time necessary to benefit from a liberal education (Aristotle, 1995). Jump ahead through 2,000 or so years of philosophical and scientific advances to the Industrial Revolution, and we find that Aristotle's fantasy has become at least partial reality: the invention of automated mechanisation meant that some tools really did operate themselves.

The latter stages of the Industrial Revolution brought many working-class people a measure of free time, and some chose to spend that time learning. These 'autodidacts' (from the Greek *autos* 'self' + *didaskein* 'teach') taught themselves using the only means available: reading. Books were by this time widely available, to share if not to own, and in that context the 3Rs taught in charity schools turned out to be all that was needed to make a liberal education possible. Working people read alone and together, setting up discussion groups, evening classes and even schools. *The Intellectual Life of the British Working Classes* by Jonathan Rose (2001) documents hundreds of examples of autodidacticism in action. As the heirs of Tyndale's 'boy that driveth the plough', working people debated the morally complex stories and internal contradictions of the Bible, and also enthusiastically devoured the great works of the western canon, seeing it as their right, as rational human beings, to have access to knowledge that had previously been the preserve of the upper classes. Plays and prose such as *The Iliad*, *The Odyssey*, *Pilgrim's Progress* and the works of Shakespeare were rich in content and touched on universal concerns, revealing other possibilities beyond the mundane reality of working-class life.

This was, at least in part, knowledge for its own sake. It's unlikely that any miner read Homer under the misapprehension that it would make him a fortune, but access to a wide range of reading material was undoubtedly an enriching experience. It also helped foster a collective sense that political and social change was possible. Autodidacts read huge numbers of newspapers, political books and pamphlets, and many became politically active, at a time when socialism and communism were gripping the imaginations of people across Europe.

One striking expression of the alarm this provoked amongst the authorities can be found in an 1839 pamphlet explaining 'the intentions of H. M Government', written by Sir James Kay-Shuttleworth, the first Secretary of Education:

> We confess that we cannot contemplate with unconcern the vast physical force which is now moved by men so ignorant and so unprincipled as the Chartist leaders . . . If [the working classes] are to have knowledge, surely it is the part of a wise and virtuous government to do all in its power to secure them useful knowledge and to guard them against pernicious opinions . . . By experience and education only can the workmen be induced to leave undisturbed the controls of commercial enterprises in the hands of the capitalists.

The political mood of the time was highly sceptical of state intervention in any form, and although the material building blocks for a national system were now in place, it would be another three decades before state schools appeared in any number. It may be salutary, though, for modern readers to note that state involvement in education was initially motivated, at least in part, by the age-old fear of what people might do if given unrestricted access to knowledge. While the Chartists were defeated in the short term, Shuttleworth's concerns were borne out in the long term, with working people winning the right to vote and establishing unions and other organisations that did indeed challenge capitalism.

Whether state education went on to suppress working-class autodidacticism is a discussion outside the scope of this chapter, but the tradition thrived until the Second World War, informed the contents of the 1944 Education Act, and gave rise to adult education organisations such as the Working Men's College (founded 1854) and the Workers' Education Association (founded 1903), which continue to this day.

Question for discussion

To what extent is the autodidactic spirit reflected in modern concepts such as 'lifelong learning' and 'learning to learn'?

Conclusion

As the eighteenth century began there were only a few hundred schools in England, but by the time of the 1851 education census over 18,000 charity day and Sunday schools had been established in the scramble to influence the religious direction of society (Curtis, 1963). But despite that remarkable numerical achievement which would provide the material basis of the State system, most of the schools involved were very small and taught children for just a few hours of the week. The education they provided quite deliberately went no further than the 3Rs and familiarity with the Bible.

Nevertheless, as we have seen, even learning to read could amount to a liberal education in miniature, opening up people's eyes to wider possibilities and leading to demands for more knowledge. As social, political and technological advances gradually brought greater freedom for ordinary people, the idea that they should 'know their place' and learn only what was necessary to enter the workforce became harder to maintain. The example provided by the 'classical liberal education' of the elite public schools played an important role in widening the life chances of young women and working-class people and went on to influence state-school curricula.

The very notion of a mass education system acknowledges, to some degree at least, the idea that we all are rational beings, capable of being educated. But that is an idea we can embrace enthusiastically or reluctantly. The desire to direct education to narrow moral, political or social ends is still with us today, in calls for schools to teach 'skills for the workplace' or to promote political positions on issues such as climate change, and the idea that we can or even should attempt to educate children in 'the best that has been thought and known' remains controversial.

History shows that liberal education has played a profound role in expanding both our knowledge about the world and the intellectual and social opportunities available to people. The extent to which education has ever been truly liberal is open to question. Yet the ideal of liberal education has always existed in tension with attempts to direct education to narrow social, religious or political ends, and this remains true today. We hope these chapters have provided some perspective and insights into the underlying issues at stake.

Summary points

- A partnership of religion and commerce gave impetus to the creation of thousands of charity schools during the eighteenth century.
- Sunday schools provided a measure of education for children working in the new factories and mills.
- Industrial automation inspired the creation of monitorial schools in which hundreds of children could be taught by a single teacher, with the assistance of pupil monitors.
- Several attempts were made to establish systems of workhouse and industrial schools, but there was little demand for their output.
- The idea of a liberal education was updated in the nineteenth century to take account of Enlightenment knowledge, leading to the revival of the public schools.
- Rising middle-class demand for governesses led to the establishment of dedicated schools for girls, who demonstrated they could receive the same education as boys.
- Working-class 'autodidacts' used their new leisure time to educate themselves, and fear of a self-educated public was a factor in the state becoming more involved in education.

Recommended reading

Arnold, M. (1869) *Culture and Anarchy*. Oxford: Oxford University Press.
Hughes, T. (1857) *Tom Brown's School Days*. Harmondsworth: Penguin Books.
Locke, J. (1603) *Some Thoughts Concerning Education*. Available at: https://books.google.co.uk/books/about/Some_Thoughts_Concerning_Education.html?id=OCUCAAAAQAAJ (Accessed 18 October 2022).
Rose, J. (2001) *The Intellectual Life of the British Working Classes*. New York: Yale University Press.

References

Aristotle (1995) *Politics, Book 1*. Oxford: Oxford University Press.
Burstall, S. (1938) *Frances Mary Buss: An Educational Pioneer*. London: Society for Promoting Christian Knowledge.
Conway, D. (2010) *Liberal Education and the National Curriculum*. Civitas. Available at: http://www.civitas.org.uk/pdf/LiberalEducation.pdf (Accessed 18 October 2022).
Curtis, S.J. (1963) *History of Education in Great Britain*. London: HarperCollins.
Jones, M.G. (1938) *The Charity School Movement: A Study of 18th Century Puritanism in Action*. Cambridge: Cambridge University Press.
Kendall, G. (1939) *Robert Raikes: A Critical Study*. London: Nicholas and Watson Limited.
Ogilvie, V. (1957) *The English Public School*, Chapter 10. London: Batsford Ltd.
Strachey, L. (1918) *Eminent Victorians*. Oxford: Oxford University Press.
Taylor, J. (1996) *Joseph Lancaster: The Poor Child's Friend*. London: Campanile Press.
Watson, N. (2000) *And Their Works Do Follow Them: The Story of North London Collegiate School 1850–2000*. London: James & James Ltd.
Whitbread, N. (1975) *The Evolution of the Nursery-Infant School: A History of Infant and Nursery Education in Britain, 1800–1970*. London: Routledge & Kegan Paul.

5 The transformation of scientific and geographical education in eighteenth century England

Paul Elliott and Stephen Daniels

Introduction

This chapter examines the expansion and reformulation of the sciences and geography as educational subjects in the long eighteenth century, between 1680 and 1830, in the context of Britain's development as a dominant global power. It explores how sciences such as astronomy, natural history and natural philosophy and geographical education projected views of the nation and the participation of its subjects. The focus is primarily upon England, although the scope of geographical affiliation, including ideas of 'nation', take in other parts of Britain. These developments were also closely connected with educational ideas and practices in Europe, the British colonies and North America. The chapter explores both formal, institutional instruction and professional training in the home, schools and academies, as well as more informal kinds of accomplishment (for example, in the realm of female education) in the domestic sphere. It examines the significance of a variety of scientific and geographical skills from forming collections of objects for natural history, studies of the celestial and terrestrial globes and map-making to memorising. A central issue is the role of scientific and geographical education as an ordering framework, mediating the practical and genteel spheres of polite society, both expressing and managing the powers of a consciously imperial nation.

The chapter contributes to investigations of the cultural-historical spaces and networks of science and learning and to more geographically oriented histories of the sciences and geography, such as those undertaken by Charles Withers, David Livingstone, Miles Ogborn, Robert Mayhew and Felix Driver, which situate geography and the sciences as formal subjects within a broad range of enlightenment intellectual endeavours. Education, in its various forms, from professional training to amateur accomplishment, is assuming a central role in the expansive field of eighteenth-century studies, particularly those which address issues of improvement and enlightenment. The analysis of scientific and geographical education addresses some broad issues concerned with concepts of nation, nature, modernity, childhood, the public sphere and polite society and is affiliated to recent cultural histories of Georgian England such as those by John Brewer, John Barrell and Ann Bermingham (2000), especially as it addresses the complications of a consciously commercial society. History of education is therefore shown to be integral to the wider study of history, and that wider understanding of history is indispensable for an appreciation of educational change in this period (Livingston and Withers, 1999; Mayhew, 2001; Ogborn and Withers, 2004).

DOI: 10.4324/9781003039532-6

Geography, the sciences and the growth of English power

The expansion of the English economy, growth of global trade, development of maritime power and establishment of colonies during the seventeenth century encouraged the development of more effective commercial, charitable and governmental maritime education. Francis Bacon's famous image of the Pillars of Hercules on the engraved title page of his *Instauratio Magna* (literally, *Great New Start*) of 1620 symbolised the success of British commerce. Imperialism was believed to be driven by the advancement of learning, which was in turn stimulated by the development of colonies and naval power in a kind of virtuous circle. The successful operation of new international joint-stock trading concerns with investors pooling their risks like the East India Company (founded 1600) and Royal Africa Company (founded 1660) required effective merchant marine and naval support to protect and expand burgeoning maritime trade routes and exploit fresh resources and opportunities, utilising their heavily armed merchantmen (Figure 5.1).

Goods such as sugar, tobacco, timber, furs, textiles, raw materials for medicines, 'new' plants and spices flowed through British home and colonial ports, especially Bristol, Liverpool, Hull and, largest of all, London, which grew into the largest European hub of global trade (Carrington, 1950). Likewise, the brutal slave trade, at its height during the 'long' eighteenth century, which forcibly transported thousands of slaves across the Atlantic from Africa and carried materials like cotton and sugar to Europe, required considerable investment in seamanship and vessels (Keay, 1993).

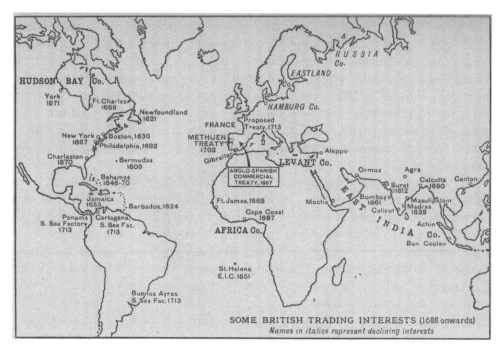

Figure 5.1 British global trading interests and companies by 1715
Source: From S. Maccoby, *Eighteenth Century England* (1931).

However, growing international competition and rivalry brought frequent wars with the Spanish and then the French and Dutch during the seventeenth and eighteenth centuries as nations fought for control of lucrative resources and global maritime trading opportunities. Whilst there were some tremendous British successes, there were also failures, such as the victories facilitated by the French during the American War of Independence (Rodger, 2006). This meant that, as Bettesworth and Fox (1782: 6–9) observed in their treatise on naval education, it was so obvious as to scarcely need saying and accepted by 'Every Briton' that the 'national Glory of England, her Dignity, Power and Opulence' and the advantages accruing from her 'extensive commerce' were fundamentally supported by her 'MARITIME Strength' which, if she ever lost her 'Superiority of the Seas', would render her insignificant and contemptible in the eye of nations. This 'critical' national imperative for the 'Preservation and Increase' of the Navy and 'Sovereignty of the Seas', which 'hostile' overseas enemies 'strain every Nerve to destroy', required that 'the 'Improvement of NAVAL Science' through maritime education be secured through provision of academies and instruction of all branches of knowledge required for 'expert and able Sea Commanders' (ibid). Despite its extensive coastlines and nautical know-how, in some respects the British Isles had disadvantages as a naval power. There were constant concerns over dwindling supplies of home-grown timber, driving campaigns to replenish national stocks through afforestation and searches for new supplies in North America and the Baltic. With prosperity and defence of the nation at stake, the practical elements of seamanship were crucial to the nation's wealth and survival, and there was also a premium placed upon innovations that would improve these. These factors meant that more effective methods of nautical navigation and better teaching of these methods were required.

Teaching navigation to naval and merchant marine officers included providing them with skills as artists and draughtsmen so they could draw geographical features of new lands like coasts and cliffs, ports and harbours, fortifications, mountains, trees, and buildings so location and harbours could be more effectively charted and identified. Effective teaching of astronomy and navigation required familiarity with equipment such as drawing tools, maps and charts, globes, compasses, astrolabes, quadrants and armillary, terrestrial and celestial spheres. Prospective officers needed to learn the elements of the sphere, how to understand, use and draw naval charts, atlases and astronomical and cosmographical information like solar cycles, the movements of tides and currents (hydrography) and plotting location (latitude) with compasses and quadrants (Figure 5.2).

There were fears that other nations, especially the French and Dutch, might overtake the British by improving their technical capabilities, quality of construction of merchant and naval vessels, navigation skills and education of seamen. For example, although it took a long time to implement in practice, Jean-Baptiste Colbert's ambitious programme to implement a *Gardes de la Marine* with its own academies and professors from 1681 in major ports teaching navigation, hydrography, gunnery, ship construction and related subjects was intended to revitalise the French navy (Turner, 2005; Levy-Eichel, 2017). Citing the example of the French *Gardes de la Marine*, in his *Essay on the Usefulness of Mathematical Learning* (1700), John Arbuthnot (1667–1735), the Scottish physician and writer, called for improvements in British naval education (Arbuthnot, 1721). Likewise, again highlighting French efforts to improve naval education, between 1699 and 1704 the writer and philanthropist Lewis Maidwell (1650–1716) sought to establish an English school for the 'sea service of the nation' to teach practical mathematics, navigation and other subjects, but the project foundered despite support from the Admiralty (Carrington, 1950; Sullivan, 1977).

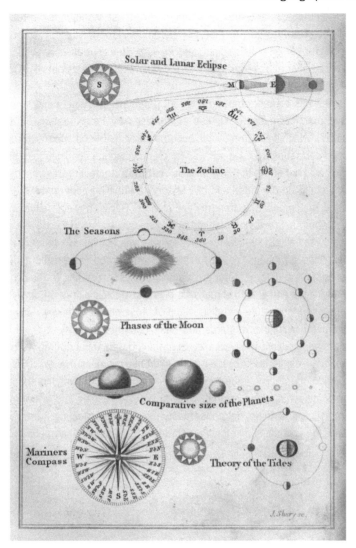

Figure 5.2 Astronomical and navigational diagrams
Source: From Rev. J. Goldsmith [R. Phillips], *A Grammar of Geography for the Use of Schools*, improved and enlarged by G. N. Wright (c. 1840).

Teaching geography and the sciences

Geography and the sciences were everywhere in eighteenth-century England as subjects of learning, in schools of all kinds and also in homes, gardens, libraries, museums, theatres, shipboard and excursions in both country and city, both within and beyond Britain. However, the two universities of Oxford and Cambridge placed a greater emphasis upon classical learning and theology during the second half of the eighteenth century. Nevertheless, as Hans and others have demonstrated using biographical information primarily derived from the original edition of the *Dictionary of National Biography* (1885–1900), whilst there was a tendency for professors appointed to scientific chairs not to lecture on their subjects at Oxford and Cambridge, these institutions did teach elements of the sciences and geography as part of their course on 'Philosophy', using textbooks such as the mathematician, geographer and theologian Rev. Edward Well's *Treatise of Ancient and Present Geography* (1701) and historical geographies of the New and Old Testament (1708, 1711–1712) (Hans, 1966; Woodley, 2009).

The general usefulness of geography to different segments of society and how it inhered with other subjects and practical endeavours was emphasised by Peter Heylyn (1600–1662) in his *Cosmographia* (1657), which was strongly influenced by Francis Bacon and much reprinted into the eighteenth century. Information from Heylyn was much recycled in cheaper books printed and marketed at those who could not afford the original lavish thick folio tome. For Heylyn, cosmography was the 'universal comprehension of natural and civil history', combining geography with natural history, civil history, practical mathematics, astronomy and climate. Geography was 'exceedingly useful' for teaching the holy scriptures, providing accounts of Biblical countries and the travels of prophets and apostles. The subject was also beneficial for astronomers who could learn different stars in different countries and their relative motions, and to physicians whose neo-Hippocratic understanding enabled them to appreciate 'the different temper of men's bodies, according to the climes they live in' and furthermore, the 'nature and growth of many simples and medicinal drugs'. Equally to 'Statesmen', the subject demonstrated the 'nature and disposition of those people with whom they negotiate' and the extent and character of their own states and other countries 'both by sea and land'. Likewise, merchants, mariners and soldiers required a 'competent knowledge in geography which presents to them many notable advantages both for their profit and entertainment' (Heylyn, 1657: 125).

There were many modes and combinations of geographical and scientific education, including exercises on globes (celestial and terrestrial), map work (both reading and drawing), rote learning, game playing, dramatic performing, field observation, specimen collecting (from rocks and minerals to plants) and topographical sketching (Figure 5.3). This was a multifarious and fluent

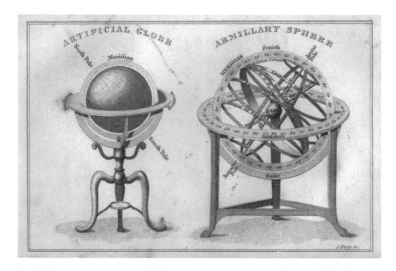

Figure 5.3 Globes

Source: From Rev. J. Goldsmith [R. Phillips], *A Grammar of Geography for the Use of Schools*, improved and enlarged by G. N. Wright (c. 1840).

geography: pupils and teachers shifted between sites, some schools were short-lived, other teaching and learning occurred on board ships or military campaigns. Some modes remained more uniform throughout the century and between different types of learning; others expressed particular pedagogical views. A crucial dimension we will explore is the material as well as intellectual aspects of scientific and geographical learning, including the making and marketing of textbooks and equipment and the design and management of places of learning.

Naval and military education

The growth of British trade and empire had a profound impact upon Georgian geographical education, most obviously by stimulating the development of an extensive network of mathematical, naval and military schools teaching navigation and related subjects such as practical mathematics, astronomy and engineering. Backed by patriotic endeavours, a premium was placed upon the acquisition of superior mathematical and geographical education to facilitate British competition with major European powers. There was considerable crossover between nautical navigation and land surveying, given the similar skills and knowledges required for each. For instance, both astronomical and mathematical knowledge were needed for determining longitude and latitude, the principles for which were the same on sea or land. Furthermore, the eighteenth-century British navy played a large role in conducting global surveys, including charting coastlines and inland and producing maps for the benefit of future naval, trading and scientific expeditions (Figure 5.4).

The distinction between military and civilian was blurred in this period. Many officers were educated in schools and academies intended for professionals. Trading concerns such as the East India Company retained naval and military forces and employed surveyors and cartographers, whilst remaining officially private companies with shareholders. The Royal Navy and trading associations like the East India Company conducted extensive maritime, coastal and terrestrial surveys such as those undertaken by the geographers James Rennell (1742–1830) in India and Alexander Dalrymple (1737–1838) across Asia and the Pacific, producing charts and facilitating astronomical observations (Dalrymple, 2020). Naval vessels for exploration and surveying, like the *Investigator* commanded by Mathew Flinders (1801), headed for the South Seas equipped with the most sophisticated sextants, chronometers and mathematical and astronomical instruments, the latest charts provided by Aaron Arrowsmith, a library, quarter-deck greenhouse to shelter living specimens, the botanist Robert Brown, astronomer John Crosley, landscape painter William Westall, plus a botanical artist, gardener and miner. Officers, the majority of whom were from the landed classes, encouraged acquisition of practical mathematical, geographical and astronomical skills for navigation and surveying. As the mapping of the Scottish Highlands and provision of forts and roads to drive forcible assimilation after the defeat of the Second Jacobite Rebellion at Culloden in 1745 demonstrates, surveying and engineering were viewed as part of military practices. Astronomical and mathematical geographical education came to be regarded as integral to British citizenship, helping to explain why study of subjects such as navigation were studied in inland locations (Marshall and Williams, 1982; Bonehill and Daniels, 2009).

Encouraged by Sir John Moore (1617–1679), a mathematician and governor of Christ's Hospital, London, a Mathematical School was established as part of the original grammar school in 1673 during the reign of Charles II to instruct 40 poor boys on the foundation and many others funded by private bequests from the ages of around 12 to 17 in navigation and arithmetic. Ten were taught until

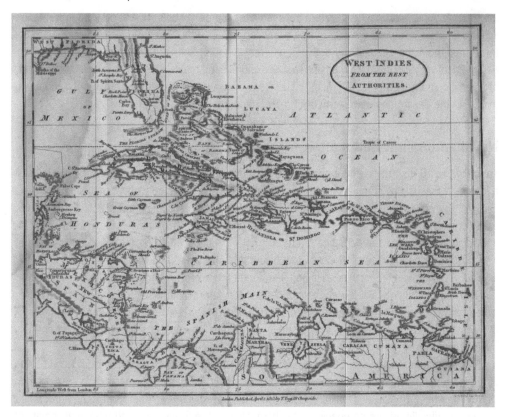

Figure 5.4 Map of the West Indies

Source: From R. Brookes MD, *A General Gazetteer of Compendious Geographical Dictionary*, 15th edition (1823).

sufficiently qualified to be initiated into the navigation practices and serve as apprentices to Royal Navy ship commanders for seven years, whilst others served on merchant ships or became tutors aboard naval vessels. Christ's Hospital School was intended to further the development of mathematical and geographical education to facilitate trade and naval competition with rival European powers. It was also promoted by fellows of the Royal Society with naval and philosophical interests, notably Samuel Pepys and Christopher Wren, and served as an excellent example of the utilitarian and patriotic value of Baconian natural philosophy to facilitate the growth of British trade and the empire.

The Mathematical School was provided with a library, globes, maps and mathematical instruments, and boys were encouraged to remain until age 16. Astronomy was taught in practical ways, with boys sitting up at night to observe the rising and falling of the moon and stars on clear nights (Pearce, 1908). Isaac Newton subsequently supported the appointment of Humphrey Ditton (1675–1715) as master of a second mathematical school at Christ's Hospital. The latter was the author of various mathematical and philosophical works, including a *New Method for Discovering the Longitude Both at Sea and Land* (1714). Masters at Christ's Hospital included prominent mathematicians and natural philosophers such as James Hodgson FRS (1672–1755); John Robertson FRS (1712–1776); James Dodson FRS, 1705–1757, author of books on navigation, astronomy and cartography; and William Wales FRS, co-navigator for James Cook between 1775 and 1799.

Subjects taught included trigonometry, geometry, astronomy, navigation, surveying and geography, and a pair of globes was purchased in 1705 at a cost of £5 with a model ship for 23 guineas. A good indication of the school's impact upon scientific and geographical knowledge and education is the number of commercial and grammar schools following a similar plan in its wake across Britain and Europe. Students included the natural philosopher James Jurin FRS (1684–1750), who became a master at Newcastle Grammar School (1709–1715) and served as Secretary of the Royal Society. Another former pupil, Thomas Crosby, published the *Mariner's Guide* (1751), a textbook on navigation and kept a mathematical school in Southwark (1710–1750) which taught mathematics, geometry, plain and spherical trigonometry, navigation and astronomy (Crosby, 1751; Hans, 1951).

Another naval school established in the latter seventeenth century which taught geography and some scientific subjects was the Greenwich Hospital School. According to the 1694 charter, the school was intended for the maintenance and education of children of injured or slain seamen, the relief and encouragement of seamen and the 'improvement of navigation', and it was organised in a similar way to Christ's Hospital Mathematical School. Although pupil numbers fluctuated from the 100 envisaged in 1712 to 60 in 1731 and 200 by 1803, the emphasis upon mathematical education was strong with training for the merchant service and the navy. The school provided master's assistants who studied for two to three years and eventually became captains, and sometimes admirals, and was sufficiently well regarded that sons of officers in mercantile marine and commissioned navy officers gained admission from 1732 onwards. Although the plan in 1728 to equip two rooms with 'Books, Maps, Charts' and models of ships for teaching mathematics and navigation does not appear to have been fully implemented, it demonstrates the direction the curriculum was taking (Macleod, 1949).

Established in 1729 and opened in 1733, the Naval Academy at Portsmouth provided a similar mathematical and nautical education to the Greenwich Hospital School for 40 young sons of nobles and gentlemen aged 12 to 15 who volunteered for the navy. Prior to this, youths either became naval officers by gaining an education aboard ship overseen by a schoolmaster, becoming one of the captain's servants; or, from 1676, by serving on board ship as volunteers-per-order. Although there were never as many pupils as originally hoped, disciplinary problems occurred and some naval officers were against shore-based education, the boys were taught navigation and other subjects by a resident master and instructors (Sullivan, 1977; Dickinson, 2007; Thomas, 2011). In 1773, reforms were implemented which saw provision expanded to boys aged 11 to 17, and the two to three years spent at the Academy counted towards qualification for the lieutenant's examination. Fifteen places were provided on a public scholarship for sons of sea officers, an innovative example of taxpayer's funding for teaching 60 years before the first government grant for education in 1833 (Lloyd, 1966).

As at Christ's Hospital Mathematical School, some of the Portsmouth Academy staff were academically well qualified to teach geography and the sciences and had considerable experience and standing as astronomers, mathematicians, navigators and natural philosophers with close links to the Navy and Royal Society. These included Thomas Haselden FRS (d. 1740), master between 1733 and 1740; John Robertson FRS (1712–1776), headmaster between 1755 and 1766; and George Witchell (1728–1785). Witchell was hired as a computer (calculator) working for the Astronomer Royal Nevil Maskelyne (1732–1811) on the first annual Nautical Almanac published by the Board of Longitude, and his work helped it to improve the accuracy of astronomical observations using better calculations of lunar distance (Sullivan, 1977). After returning from his second voyage on the *Discovery* in 1775,

James Cook sought assistance from Witchell to check his chronometer using Portsmouth Academy's Observatory equipment, and two other masters were closely involved with international astronomical observations and Cook's expeditions (Mackay, 1985). The astronomer William Bayly (1737–1810), who had been a Bristol schoolmaster and was assistant at the Royal Observatory under Maskelyne, served as master between 1785 and 1807. On the recommendation of Maskelyne in 1769, Bayly went to North Cape, Norway, for the Royal Society to observe the transit of Venus, and in 1772 was an astronomer on Cook's second voyage of discovery to the southern hemisphere. Bayly also joined Cook's third and final voyage with the *Resolution* and the *Discovery* (1776–1780), which resulted in Cook's death. Bayly's journal of the expedition across the Pacific Islands and west coast of North America is preserved in the National Archives at Kew (Bayly, 1776; Sullivan, 1977). Finally, Rev. James Inman (1776–1859) served as astronomer under Matthew Flinders on board HMS *Investigator* in 1803–1804 charting the sea around Australia. Inman published a book on nautical and navigational astronomy (1821), was Professor of Nautical Mathematics at Portsmouth from 1808 and helped initiate the first school of naval architecture there in 1810 (Inman, 1821).

Although all the masters' knowledge and experience did not automatically translate into effective learning and the school experienced some problems, the approach to teaching geographical and scientific subjects, as well as practical seamanship and navigation led by masters, boatswain and schoolmaster, was quite innovative. The mathematician John Robertson's much republished *Elements of Navigation* (1754), which was originally intended for the use of pupils at Christ's Hospital Mathematical School, provides a good indication of the curriculum there and at the Portsmouth Academy. Robertson, who also produced a book on portable mathematical instruments and their uses in geography, surveying, architecture and marine navigation, had previously served as headmaster of the Christ's Hospital Mathematical School and subsequently became clerk and librarian to the Royal Society. His *Elements of Navigation* included a dissertation on the 'Modern Art of Navigation' and chapters on navigation, arithmetic, geometry, plane trigonometry, spherics, astronomy and geography, with fold-out maps, tables and numerous diagrams. Boys practised the nautical rigging and construction demonstrated on vessels where they practised, staying for two to three years which counted towards their six years as midshipman to become a lieutenant. The curriculum included writing, arithmetic, drawing, navigation, gunnery, fortification and practical mathematics, and the Academy continued to supervise former students whilst at sea. When ships returned to Portsmouth, volunteers were required to present their journals to the Academy's Master who inspected them and reported to Secretary of the Admiralty. Volunteers continued their education at the Academy free of charge if certified by their captain for good behaviour. Aboard ship, they were required to keep their journals going, drawing maps and making sketches of coastlines, headlands, bays and other geographical features following captain's directions (Robertson, 1775, 1795; Robertson and Gwynne, 1805).

A practical geographical education intended primarily for those in the army was pursued at the Woolwich Academy. Mathematical tutors at Woolwich included Charles Hutton (1737–1823), John Bonnycastle (1750–1827) and Thomas Myers (1774–1834), all of whom published works on geography, mathematics and related subjects. Hutton's *Course of Mathematics for the Use of Cadets in the Academy* (1798–1801) and Myers's *Compendious System of Modern Geography* (1812) demonstrate the content of the curriculum and other commercial schools and tutors offered learning modelled upon that at Woolwich (Smyth, 1961; Bruneau, 2020). The Belgian Lewis Lochée (d. 1791), for instance, was proprietor and master of a military academy at Little Chelsea during the 1770s and 1780s which, he claimed in his *Essay on Military Education* (1773), operated like a 'military republic', teaching history, geography, cartography, military drawing and other components of martial sciences (Lochée, 1773).

Hundreds of tutors and private academies across the British Isles and North American colonies taught mathematical geography, astronomy, navigation and related subjects. There was, of course, a concentration of those teaching marine subjects in coastal towns. However, analysis of school advertisements and textbooks reveals that these subjects were also taught inland. Natural philosophy was taught at an academy on Little Tower Street, London, by Benjamin Worster (2009) during the 1720s, where courses in experimental philosophy with demonstration experiments were conducted to qualify 'young gentlemen' for business away from 'interruptions' in 'common schools'. Besides mathematics, French, drawing and natural philosophy including hydrostatics, the Newtonian system, optics, mechanic and pneumatics were taught (Watson, 1971). Another mathematical school was founded at Rochester by Sir Joseph Williamson and appointed John Colson (1680–1760), the future Lucasian Professor of Mathematics at Cambridge, as master. Colson translated mathematical and philosophical texts and published a work on 'the construction and use of the spherical maps' (1736). Geography, gauging, surveying, navigation and natural philosophy were taught at the Soho Academy conducted by Martin Clare FRS, the author of *The Motion of Fluids* (1735) using globes and a large library. Another mathematical school was conducted in Newcastle between 1760 and 1773 by the mathematician Charles Hutton, the author of *The Schoolmaster's Guide* (1764), who used the institution to deliver public lectures on geography and astronomy. Mathematical geography was an important feature of the education provided in the major British ports such as Bristol and Liverpool. The Irish educationist David Manson taught mathematical navigation to sailors in Liverpool until 1752, charging fees of 6d per hour (Stewart and McCann, 2017). At Kingston near Taunton, Somerset and subsequently Bristol, mathematical academies were managed by the scientific lecturer Benjamin Donn (1729–1798), a surveyor, cartographer and author of works on globes and nautical apparatus including the *British Mariner's Assistant* (1774) and *An Epitome of Natural and Experimental Philosophy* (1769) for the use of schools and 'Young Ladies and Gentlemen' (Donn, 1758, 1768, 1774).

Some geographical and scientific subjects regarded as essential for the nation's maritime success were taught on board ship. Most education for those intending to be royal naval officers was done this way by schoolmasters who also taught other young seamen on vessels. Between 1712 and 1824, some 500 to 600 schoolmasters were working on British ships, and over 1,000 warrants were issued by the Admiralty sanctioning this. Similar teaching had occurred in less systematic fashion at the expense of captains over the previous century. Henry Knight, a ship's schoolmaster recorded in 1704, was taught at Christ's Hospital and taught navigation on board the *Dorsetshire*. Future officers gained on-service training on board ship by enjoying the patronage of captains as 'servants' or following reforms undertaken by Samuel Pepys in 1676, as 'Volunteers per-Order'. Captains could have four servants per hundred crew, or eight if they were a knight or nobleman, whilst they were obliged to take on volunteers-per-order aged up to 16 who aimed to become officers. Both kinds of prospective officers had to be sufficiently skilled in the 'art and practice of navigation' and to improve their seamanship and navigation skills enough to pass their examination and be promoted from midshipman to lieutenant. From 1702, the system of schoolmasters on board vessels was formalised so 'young gentlemen' received training in the practical parts of seamanship and navigation. Schoolmasters received an additional £20 per annum above midshipman pay if on board third-, fourth- or fifth-rate ships, and eventually all rating of ships, and needed to have obtained a qualification certificate from the Trinity House Corporation (Sullivan, 1976).

Innovative methods for teaching astronomy, mathematical geography, surveying and navigation included the use of novel apparatus, topographical field-sketching, the employment of schoolmasters on military campaigns and naval vessels. There were also naval and military editions of various works. These included special editions of travel literature such as the expeditions of James Cook, gazetteers and novels intended to further geographical education (Marshall and Williams, 1982) (Figure 5.5).

Figure 5.5 Engravings of Sweden and Russia

Source: From Rev. J. Goldsmith [R. Phillips], *A Grammar of Geography for the Use of Schools*, improved and enlarged by G. N. Wright (c. 1840).

An unusual example was an edition of Daniel Defoe's *Robinson Crusoe* published in 1815, 'revised and corrected' for 'nautical education', which was 'illustrated by technical and geographical annotations and embellished with maps and engravings' by the Hydrographer of the *Naval Chronicle*, with extensive footnotes and appendices on hydrography, natural history and scientific subjects (Defoe, 1815). The *Complete Geographical Dictionary* (1787) by Rev. John Seally FRS (1742–1795) included maps and descriptions of Cook's expeditions in addition to the usual summaries of ancient and modern geography in alphabetical form with engravings of places, astronomical and chronological tables, and extracts from the private papers of one of Cook's officers. Seally established an academy at Bridgewater Square in London which taught ancient and modern languages, history, mathematics, geography, astronomy and natural philosophy, and the accounts of voyages and astronomical information were utilised in his teaching (Seally, 1787).

Domestic scientific and geographical education

In a culture suspicious of the corruptions of institutional life, the 'home' remained a model site of learning, influencing the design and management of many schools. Texts and pictures emphasised the virtues of domesticity in geographical and scientific learning, not just in and around the home but on family excursions (Figure 5.6).

Family values in geographical and scientific education took a variety of ideological forms, from the model of the royal family (both of George III and Louis XVI of France) to the international kinship networks of religious dissenters. The cult of motherhood profoundly shaped pedagogy, especially in some progressive texts, where 'the home' served not as an introverted retreat from the world but as a public vantage point for its comprehension. Key images of geography and the sciences in the home included pictorial conversation pieces and childhood primers. As the depiction of the figure

Figure 5.6 Children being taught geography

Source: From Rev. J. Goldsmith [R. Phillips], *A Grammar of Geography for the Use of Schools*, improved and enlarged by G. N. Wright (c. 1840).

of 'Geographia' herself demonstrates, there was a pronounced feminine iconography of geographical learning, also evident in the figure of the mother-educator. Evidence of geographical and scientific teaching and learning survives in archival records such as diaries and memoirs which show very well how reading, demonstration, excursions and other activities such as solving problems with globes and assembling dissected maps (or jigsaws) were often used to teach these subjects. Scientific and geographical learning took place in a variety of domestic places and spaces and different rooms around the home including nurseries, libraries and gardens.

The sciences and geography in grammar schools

The sciences and geographical education, with their mix of humanistic and commercial learning, complicated the differences between types of institution: grammar schools, commercial schools, dissenting academies, schools for boys and girls. Older scholarship in history of education understood Georgian grammar schools as conservative institutions, obsessed with ancient languages, repetitive rote learning and ossified curricula, constrained by the dead hand of ancient statutes which masters were required to follow in return for their payment. However, whilst there is some truth in this generalisation, the needs of commerce and industry, colonialism and polite society encouraged a demand for what were perceived as 'modern' subjects. In the competitive eighteenth-century educational marketplace, commercial academies and tutors marketing their services strove to compete with grammar schools by claiming that they provided a much rounder education, more relevant to the modern age with practical modern subjects such as the sciences, geography and modern languages. Jolly B. Florian in 1796, for example, argued that his academy rectified the defects of traditional grammar school education by making 'Philosophy and the sciences' the 'principal study of young persons' – that is, both boys and girls – between the ages of 7 and 17 (Florian, 1796).

Furthermore, as the research underpinning Edward Gibbon's *Decline and Fall of the Roman Empire* (1776–1789) demonstrates so well, biblical and classical scholarship and ancient history (and perceptions of these endeavours) were themselves undergoing profound changes during the 'long' eighteenth century, which impacted upon materials used for teaching these in schools such as textbooks, grammars and maps (Gibbon, 1776). Hence, although Robert Mayhew was right to emphasise that there was much continuity in the Early Modern humanist textual geographical tradition as it impacted upon grammar schools, we should recognise the variety of ways in which geography and the sciences impacted upon learning in these institutions. Whilst, therefore, in principle so-called 'modern' subjects such as geography, astronomy, natural philosophy and natural history might appear not to have featured in most grammar school classical humanist curriculums, in practice they became part of teaching in some institutions, both formally and informally. In response to both the intellectual inclinations of masters and the local demand of parents, ways were found to circumvent statutes against modern subjects (for example, by offering other subjects as an optional extra for additional charges), and innovations in teaching, included visual aids and dramatic performances, although this was a contested process which also attracted some opposition. The rhetoric against grammar schools used by some dissenting educationalists and commercial tutors, therefore, masks a much more varied and complex situation in relation to both grammar schools and nonconformist academies. In the latter, there was in many cases a continuing belief in the value of classical education even though modern subjects were key to how they marketed themselves against grammar schools.

Studies of classical geography were regarded as an essential component of classical education and must have been given in most schools, even if they could not afford expensive works such as some editions of classical geographers or the grammar school master William Hill's *Dionysius Orbis Descriptio Commentario Critico et Geographico* (*Dionysius' Description of the World with a Critical and Geographical Commentary*) of 1658, with Greek and Latin texts, notes and clear copper plate maps, which went through various editions and was used in many schools. Whilst such books and maps tended to be prohibitively expensive during the eighteenth century, the publication of abridgements and cheaper editions of popular illustrated works such as Georges-Louis Leclerc, Comte de Buffon's *Natural History* (1749–1788), Oliver Goldsmith's *History of the Earth and Animated Nature* (1774) and geographical grammars helped make geography and the sciences more accessible to grammar school pupils and wider readers (Hutton et al., 1792; Goldsmith, 1804) (Figures 5.7 and 5.8).

The general usefulness of geography to different segments of society and how it inhered with other subjects and practical endeavours was emphasised by Peter Heylyn (1600–1662) in his *Cosmographia* (1657), which was strongly influenced by Francis Bacon and much reprinted into the eighteenth century. The information was also often recycled in cheaper works printed and marketed at those who could not afford the original lavish thick folio tome. For Heylyn, cosmography was the 'universal comprehension of natural and civil history' combining geography with natural history, civil history, practical mathematics, astronomy and climate. Geography was 'exceedingly useful' for teaching the holy scriptures, providing accounts of countries mentioned in the Bible and the travels of prophets and apostles. The subject was also beneficial for astronomers who could learn different stars in different countries and their relative motions, to physicians whose neo-Hippocratic understanding enabled them to appreciate 'the different temper of men's bodies, according to the climes they live in and, furthermore, the 'nature and growth of many simples and medicinal drugs'. Equally to 'Statesmen', the subject demonstrated the 'nature and disposition of those people with whom they negotiate' and the extent and character of their own states and other countries 'both by sea and land'. Equally, for merchants, mariners and soldiers, they required a 'competent knowledge in geography which presents to them many notable advantages both for their profit and entertainment' (Heylyn, 1657).

The teaching of geography and astronomy in some grammar schools was long established and evident in their interior furnishing and decoration, with Francis Bacon remarking in the *Advancement of Learning* (1605) that 'spheres, globes, astrolabes, maps and the like' were now provided in many colleges as 'appurtenances to astronomy and cosmography, as well as books' (Bacon, 1824). According to Charles Hoole (1660), the upper story of grammar schools should have a 'fair, pleasant gallery wherein to hang maps and set globes, and to lay up such rarities as can be gotten in presses or drawers, that the scholars may know them', whilst a large map of the world was hung on the north wall of Winchester College by around 1660 (Bacon, 1824). Two eighteenth-century institutions where geography and astronomy became significant subjects were Hull Grammar School, when John Clarke was master, and Gresham's School, Holt, Norfolk, under John Holme. Both these masters promoted their views to a wider audience by authoring pedagogical treatises. At Gresham's School, which was governed by the London Fishmonger's Company, astronomy, geography and the study of the globes were introduced using practical activities, and pupils were encouraged to employ maps and their senses whilst travelling, along with globes, packs of cards and interesting stories in the classroom to help memorise the information. Dramatic performances

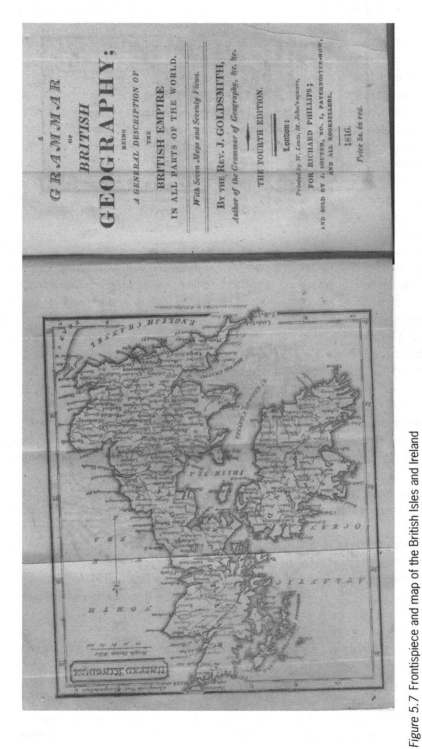

Figure 5.7 Frontispiece and map of the British Isles and Ireland

Source: From Rev. J. Goldsmith [R. Phillips], *A Grammar of British Geography*, fourth edition (1816).

Figure 5.8 Frontispiece of *Buffon's Natural History Abridged*, 2 vols., (1792), a work often recommended for use with children and young people

of 'verses declamations and orations' were presented in front of friends, family and school benefactors at Christmas and other times, with pupils personified as divine beings in costumes and wigs to celebrate their progress, with the school's geographical and scientific instruments and maps used as props (Elliott and Daniels, 2008).

The subtle ways in which natural philosophy might feature as part of grammar school education, even when not formally part of the curriculum, are evident from the achievements of Chesterfield Grammar School, Derbyshire, under William Burrow, who served as usher between 1711 and 1722 and headmaster from that year until 1752. Whilst the curriculum never formally changed in this period, the success of the school is evident from the number of boys who were sent at this time to Cambridge University, which was far more than any other in the county. Pupils included the future physician and natural philosopher and Lunar Society founder Erasmus Darwin (who proceeded to Cambridge and Edinburgh University); his older brother, the landowner and botanist Robert Waring Darwin, author of *Principia Botanica* (1787), the antiquarian Samuel Pegge (1733–); and the medical men John Stubbinge (1704–1734) and Charles Balguy, the latter of whom became a secretary of the Peterborough Gentlemen's Society and member of the Spalding Gentlemen's Society, and published classical and medical works. The inspiration that Erasmus Darwin received from Burrow and respect in which he held him is evident from surviving correspondence with him. We learn from correspondence in 1736 and 1737 concerning another pupil, William Farington, that, besides the expected Latin translation exercises and reading of classical works, Farington had a 'genius for drawing' an aptitude for poetry and discussed 'Natural Philosophy, and other ornamental studies' with one of Burrow's sons, who 'endeavoured to form in him proper thoughts and notions of em' which would make him a 'good Scholar and a fine Gentleman' (Darwin, 1750; Riden, 2017).

At Cheam School in Surrey, in the years before he found fame as the leading exponent of the picturesque movement, Rev. William Gilpin (1724–1804) strove to provide a more practical educa- tion for his pupils founded on commercial principles more adapted for 'landholders, tradesmen' and those intended for 'public officers' combining the methods of business schools with the classical learning of 'boarding schools'. Treating the school as a miniature 'state' and adopting the language of statehood, pupils were provided with garden plots to grow fruit and vegetables, whilst, in addition to the usual Greek and Latin, the curriculum included arithmetic, geography and drawing. Geography was taught using what were called 'dissected' maps of counties made into jigsaws, and in 1765 one pupil had to ask his parents for a replacement for the Flintshire piece which he had lost! Presaging Gilpin's later career as the leading English topographer, the boys were encouraged to ride and ramble around the local country, and with help from Gilpin's brother Sawrey, much emphasis was placed upon expeditions where they drew what they observed in the surrounding countryside from nature (Gilpin, 1879; Stewart and McCann, 2017).

The sciences, geography and dissenting education

Whilst there were differences between denominations, the education promoted by Protestant Dissenters or nonconformists was distinctive in supporting personal, cultural, spiritual and social development, and forms of progressive citizenship. The sciences and geography were prominent components of dissent's new map of learning. Despite civil restrictions, and the sharpening sectar- ian lines at the end of the century, Dissenters were a powerful cultural force, strongly involved in local government, especially of expanding commercial towns. They networked internationally, espe- cially with Scotland, Holland, Switzerland and America. This geographical context, and its culture of natural enquiry, helped to establish geography as a key discipline. The writings of Isaac Watts, and later, if more contentiously, Joseph Priestley, were widely influential in Protestant culture at large. Hackney College and Warrington Academy had an influence well beyond their catchments. As Priestley's career demonstrates, Presbyterian and Unitarian ministers took a keen interest in the sciences, partly because of the belief that in doing so they celebrated divine glory and the power of creation, but also because of the perceived practical advantages that the sciences were believed to have and the number of merchants, industrialists, businessmen and medical men in their congre- gations. One intellectual aspect that informed Unitarian theology and the approach to education was associationism. This resulted in curricula which valued the classics but emphasised the need for a good education in other subjects, such as modern languages, geography and the sciences, for clergy as well as professionals. For instance, Rev. James Pilkington, minister of the Friargate Chapel at Derby, provided much information concerning natural history, geology and hydrology in his *History of Derbyshire* (1789), whilst Rev. William Wood, Priestley's successor at Leeds, was a fellow of the Linnean Society, taught natural history to the girls in his school and wrote articles on the subject for Arthur Akin's *Annual Review* and Abraham Rees's *Cyclopaedia* (1802–1820)

(Wellbeloved, 1809/2010; Watts, 1998). Two of the most influential Unitarian educationists were John Aikin, tutor at the Warrington Academy who taught natural history and practical sciences, and his sister Anna Barbauld who had a wider impact with their voluminous educational and other writings (Watts, 1998).

Another striking example of a dissenting school in which the sciences and geography were taught in an imaginative, integrative and experiential manner was the Laurence Street Academy run by the Welsh educationalist David Williams. Williams offered a wide range of subjects in the curriculum including mathematics, geography, history, modern languages, moral and political philosophy, natural history, astronomy and other sciences such as chemistry. Older boys about the age of ten or so were encouraged to pursue studies in chemistry, hydrostatics and pneumatics and critically read articles in the *Transactions of the Royal Society*, the French *Encyclopedia* and transactions of European scientific societies. Williams emphasised that natural history was the 'first pursuit of the human mind' for which young children in particular had a special aptitude, and pupils were encouraged to collect plants and other objects from the house and their locality, including different types of wood, rocks and minerals. These were used as a means of introducing different words and concepts (Williams, 1789; Stewart and McCann, 2017). As well as these expeditions, students were encouraged to do gardening and horticultural activities. Unlike many schools and the more common methods of teaching 'the globes', geography was not so much introduced with astronomy but through close observations of immediate domestic life, the local district and excursions further afield. The boys then used these observations to make further investigations, of the weather and climate, the oceans and the solar system, which were supported by the creation of maps and the construction of globes and other mechanical devices such as clocks (Williams, 1789; Simon, 1976).

Other very influential dissenting educationists who encouraged the teaching of geography and scientific subjects were John Aikin (1747–1822) and Anna Laetitia Barbauld (1743–1825), the son and daughter of John Aikin (1713–1780), tutor at the dissenting Warrington Academy. They made their names as published writers, essayists, poets and educationalists, commanding a wide, highly respectful readership in polite society; in the 1790s their work became politically contentious. In a range of writings, they extended the scope and moral seriousness of geography, to consider relations of land and life, and the comparative development of the habitable world, raising its status as a subject of learning for both children and adults. They focus on the place of geographical education in both child development and adult citizenship, in particular the interaction of people with the natural world as well as each other, and the relation of things to words, and objects to representations. Two institutions have a strong presence in Aikin's writings, Warrington Academy and Palgrave Academy, Suffolk where, for a period, Anna Laeititia Barbauld developed her ideas in teaching practice, giving prominence to geography as a way of developing citizenship. An expanded idea of the home and the domestic sphere is the pivot of her vision. In a series of best-selling texts (both in the United States and Britain), including teaching books, children's stories, guidebooks and magazine articles published under his editorship, John Aikin developed what he called 'the philosophy of geography', a wide-ranging, liberal vision of the world and its workings, with a strong sense of the physical environment. The geographical pedagogy of both Barbauld and Aikin was developed and popularised from the early nineteenth century in the works of John Aikins's children Lucy and Arthur Aikin. The family's enterprise was known as 'the Aikin School' (Daniels, 2011).

Girls' education

A well-documented example of geographical and scientific education pursued in a girl's school is the work of Margaret Bryan at Bryan House, situated at Blackheath between 1795 and 1806, and subsequently Hyde Park Corner, London, and then Margate from 1816. We know something about the curriculum because of Bryan's publications based upon her lectures, especially her *Compendious System of Astronomy*, *Lectures on Natural Philosophy*, *Conversations on Chemistry* and *Comprehensive Astronomical Class Book* (1815). All the diagrams and illustrations were drawn by her and presumably used in teaching, and having sent the manuscript to Charles Hutton at the Woolwich Royal Military Academy, she was praised for demonstrating how even 'learned and more difficult sciences' were 'beginning to be successfully cultivated by the extraordinary and elegant talents of the female writers'. Bryan's books demonstrate that astronomy, mathematics, natural philosophy and chemistry were being taught to girls, and her works were subscribed to by some of her current and former female students, the lectures of natural philosophy by 157 women (Bryan, 1787; Hans, 1951; Kamm, 2010). Some more information about the stages in which geographical and scientific subjects were taught at this time, and the methods used, comes from the evidence of a girl's academy conducted by Mrs Florian at her boarding school for girls at Leytonstone, Epping Forest. According to an advertisement for 'Female Education' placed in her husband J.B. Florian-Jolly's *Course of the Sciences and Philosophy* (1806), the subjects and methods were designed to make female education 'keep pace with the general diffusion and rapid progress of useful knowledge' that distinguished the current age. From the ages of around 8 or 9 to 12, young ladies were taught English, French, geography and history. Geometry and trigonometry were covered to enable understanding of astronomical principles and the 'geographical knowledge of our globe and of Natural Philosophy . . . illustrated by experiments and machines', whilst geographical maps formed by pupils were used to illustrate different historical periods (Florian-Jolly, 1806; Hans, 1951).

'Opening the Book of Nature': Pestalozzi and the teaching of geography and natural history

The idea of using the immediate environment as a tool for teaching was hardly new, and Comenius, for example, in his *Schola Infantiae* (*School of Infancy*) emphasised that young children began to learn geography as they perceived the spaces around them, discovering domestic life, fields, mountains, forest meadows and rivers. Similarly, the schoolmaster Hezekiah Woodward (1590–1675) observed that lessons could be constructed using everyday places and events, including observing agriculture and domestic economy and horticulture, even if this was primarily to instil moral values. However, in the wake of Rousseau, it was the influence of Johann Heinrich Pestalozzi (1746–1827) that led to a turn to experiential learning using the environment in British schools from the early nineteenth century. His ideas on British education became pronounced after the end of European wartime hostilities in 1815, and reformers visited Pestalozzi's model school of Yverdun and his disciple Fellenberg's school at Hofwyl. He authored texts and set up schools based on Pestalozzian ideas and practice. In turn Pestalozzi considered Britain to be constitutionally and culturally the country where his ideas could be best realised. Some key aspects of Pestalozzi's pedagogy were changed in translation, for example principles of 'spontaneity' (self-activation) in Phillip Pullen's *The Mothers Book* and Pestalozzi's *System of Practical Geography*; and the role of the local environment in Elizabeth Mayo's writings on object lessons, which became incorporated in commodity-centred colonial geographies. Some schools in and around London, for example at Cheam and Ealing Grove, incorporated Pestalozzian practice (Elliott and Daniels, 2006). An influential exemplar is the Worksop Institution, Nottinghamshire, run by husband and wife Beatus and Adele Heldenmaier. Beatus Heldenmaier had attended Pestalozzi's Yverdun School and studied for a doctorate in Berlin where he was taught by the German philosopher Georg Wilhelm Friedrich Hegel and the geographer Carl Ritter. The Worksop Institution attracted pupils from progressive families throughout the Midlands and North of England, and some from overseas, and included field trips to both industrial and agrarian sites. There is (for schooling at the time generally) a rare collection of letters to home by two Worksop pupils, William and Charles Marling, which offer an alternative view of this highly praised institution (Elliott and Daniels, 2005). The school became a model for later nineteenth-century educational writing, notably in Herbert Spencer's *Education: Intellectual, Moral and Spiritual*. Spencer's father William George was secretary of the Derby Philosophical Society, which Heldenmaier joined (Elliott, 2004).

Conclusion

The lessons of geography, the sciences and citizenship in eighteenth- and early nineteenth-century England have implications that extend beyond this period and place. They had legacy for succeeding periods of imperialism and post-imperialism in Britain and beyond, and subsequent kinds of geographical and scientific education, both as formal disciplines and informal modes of learning. They framed such issues as progressive education, vocational training, nature appreciation, child development and cultural policy.

Summary points

- Many aspects of geographical and scientific education were transformed between c. 1680 and 1820 in the context of Britain's development as a dominant commercial and naval global power.
- Engagement with geographical subjects and Enlightenment sciences like astronomy, natural history and natural philosophy projected views of the nation.
- Geographical and scientific subjects were taught and encountered in formal settings like schools and universities and in wider culture and society, for example, through print culture, public lectures and literary and scientific associations.
- Some geographical and scientific endeavours were pursued in informal contexts, for example, as a form of accomplishment in the realm of female education in the domestic sphere.
- Encouraged by the spread of ideas and market competition, innovative methods were introduced to teach geography and the sciences including the use of maps, globes and jigsaws in schools, employment of scientific apparatus and forms of experiential learning like natural history walks, gardening and teaching on board merchant marine and naval ships.

Acknowledgement

Some of the research which informed this chapter was undertaken as part of a major study of Georgian geographical education undertaken at the University of Nottingham funded by AHRC Research Grant, 'A Place in the Nation: Geographical Education and Citizenship in England

1700–1830' Grant No. B/RG/AN6156/APN12558 directed by Professor Stephen Daniels, and the authors would like to express their gratitude for this assistance. We would also like to thank Professor Keith McLay of the University of Derby for providing materials on the history of naval and military education.

Recommended reading

Elliott, P. and Daniels, S. (2008) 'No Study So Agreeable to the Youthful Mind': Geographical Education in the Georgian Grammar School. *History of Education*, **39**(1), pp. 1–18.
Hans, N. (1966) *New Trends in Education in the Eighteenth Century.* London: Taylor and Francis.
Livingstone, D.N. and Withers, C.J.W. (Eds.) (1999) *Geography and Enlightenment.* Chicago: University of Chicago Press.
Porter, R. (Ed.) (2003) *The Cambridge History of Science: Volume 4: Eighteenth-Century Science.* Cambridge: Cambridge University Press.

References

Arbuthnot, J. (1721) *Essay on the Usefulness of Mathematical Learning* (2nd edition). Oxford: Printed at the Theatre.
Bacon, F. (1824) The Advancement of Learning (1605). In *The Works of Francis Bacon* (10 vols.). Cambridge: Cambridge University Press.
Bayly, W. (1776) *Log Kept by William Bayly (Aug 1–1779 Dec 3).* London: The National Archives, Kew, ADM 55/20.
Bermingham, A. (2000) *Learning to Draw: Studies in the Cultural History of a Polite and Useful Art.* New Haven: Yale University Press.
Bettesworth, J. and Fox, H. (1782) *Observations on Education in General but Particularly on Naval Education.* London: Matthew Hesse.
Bonehill, J. and Daniels, S. (Eds.) (2009) *Paul Sandby: Picturing Britain.* London: Royal Academy of Arts.
Bruneau, O. (2020) The teaching of mathematics at the Royal Military Academy: Evolution in continuity. *Philosophia Scientiæ*, **24**, pp. 137–158.
Bryan, M. (1787) *A Compendious System of Astronomy in a Course of Familiar Lectures* (2nd edition). London: H.L. Galabin.
Carrington, C.E. (1950) *The British Overseas: Exploits of a Nation of Shopkeepers.* Cambridge: Cambridge University Press.
Crosby, T. (1751) *The Mariner's Guide: Being a Compleat Treatise on Navigation.* London: J. Hodges.
Dalrymple, W. (2020) *The Anarchy: The Relentless Rise of the East India Company.* London: Bloomsbury.
Daniels, S. (2011) 'Outline Maps of Knowledge': John Aikin's Geographical Imagination. In F. James and I. Inkster (Eds.), *Religious Dissent and the Aikin-Barbauld Circle, 1740–1860.* Cambridge: Cambridge University Press.
Darwin, E. (1750) Letter to W. Burrow 11 December 1750. In D. King-Hele (Ed.), (2007) *The Collected Letters of Erasmus Darwin.* Cambridge: Cambridge University Press.
Defoe, D. (1815) *Robinson Crusoe.* London: Joseph Mawman.
Dickinson, H.W. (2007) *Educating the Royal Navy: Eighteenth – and Nineteenth-Century Education for Officers.* Abingdon: Routledge.
Donn, B. (1758) *A New Introduction to the Mathematics, Being Essays on Vulgar and Decimal Arithmetic.* London: Kessinger.
Donn, B. (1768) *The Schoolmaster's Repository . . . Designed for the Use of Schools.* London: Gale ECCO.
Donn, B. (1774) *Epitome of Natural and Experimental Philosophy Including Geography and the Use of the Globes . . . Designed for the Use of Schools.* London, 1769; *The British Mariner's Assistant.* London: Gale ECCO.
Elliott, P. (2004) Improvement, Always and Everywhere: William George Spencer (1790–1866) and Mathematical, Geographical and Scientific Education in Nineteenth-Century England. *History of Education*, **33**, pp. 391–417.
Elliott, P. and Daniels, S. (2006) Pestalozzi, Fellenberg and British Nineteenth-Century Geographical Education. *Journal of Historical Geography*, **32**(4), pp. 752–774.
Elliott, P. and Daniels, S. (2010) 'No Study so Agreeable to the Youthful Mind': Geographical Education in the Georgian Grammar School. *History of Education*, **39**(1), pp. 1–18.

Florian, J.B. (1796) *An Essay on an Analytical Course of Studies*. London: Gale ECCO.

Florian-Jolly, J.B. (1806) *Elementary Course of the Sciences and Philosophy*. London: J. Sto.

Gibbon, E. (1776) *The History of the Decline and Fall of the Roman Empire* (6 vols.). London: Penguin.

Gilpin, W. (1879) *Memoirs of Dr. Richard Gilpin . . . Together with an Account of the Author by Himself*. Edited by W. Jackson. London: Forgotten Books.

Goldsmith, O. (1804) *A History of the Earth and Animated Nature* (4 vols.). York: Blackie and Son.

Hans, N. (1951) *New Trends in Education in the Eighteenth Century*. London: Taylor and Francis.

Heylyn, P. (1657) Cosmographie: Containing the Chorography and History of the Whole World (1657). Cited in F. Watson (Ed.) *Beginnings of the Teaching of Modern Subjects*. London: S.R. Publishers.

Hoole, C. (1660) New Discovery of the Old Art of Teaching School (1660). Cited in F. Watson (Ed.) *Beginnings of the Teaching of Modern Subjects*. London: S.R. Publishers.

Hutton, W., Leclerc, G.-L. and de Buffon, C. (1792) *Buffon's Natural History Abridged* (2 vols.). London: R. Griffin.

Inman, J. (1821) *Navigation and Nautical Astronomy: For the Use of British Seamen* (1st edition). London: R. and J. Rivington.

Kamm, J. (2010) *Hope Deferred: Girls' Education in English History*. Abingdon: Routledge.

Keay, J. (1993) *The Honourable Company: A History of the English East India Company*. London: HarperCollins.

Levy-Eichel, M. (2017) 'Suitable to the Meanest Capacity': Mathematics, Navigation and Self-Education in the Early Modern British Atlantic. *Mariner's Mirror*, **103**, pp. 450–465.

Livingstone, D. and Withers, C.J.W. (Eds.) (1999) *Geography and Enlightenment*. Chicago: Chicago University Press.

Lloyd, C. (1966) The Royal Naval Colleges at Portsmouth and Greenwich. *Mariner's Mirror*, **52**, pp. 45–156.

Lochée, L. (1773) *An Essay on Military Education*. London: Printed for the Author.

Mackay, D. (1985) *In the Wake of Cook: Exploration, Science and Empire, 1780–1801*. London: Croom Helm.

Macleod, N. (1949) History of the Royal Hospital School. *Mariner's Mirror*, **35**, pp. 182–202.

Malham, J. (1790) *Navigation Made Easy and Familiar to the Most Common Capacity: Or the Young Sailor's Sure Guide, and Scholar's Best Instructor in the Art of Navigation*. London: Gale ECCO.

Marshall, P.J. and Williams, G. (1982) *The Great Map of Mankind: British Perceptions of the World in the Age of Enlightenment*. London: Dent.

Mayhew, R. (2001) *Enlightenment Geography*. London: Springer.

Ogborn, M. and Withers, C.J.W. (Eds.) (2004) *Georgian Geographies: Essays on Space, Place and Landscape in the Eighteenth Century*. Manchester: Manchester University Press.

Pearce, E.H. (Ed.) (1908) *Annals of Christ's Hospital*. London: Methuen and Company.

Riden, P. (2017) *The History of Chesterfield Grammar School*. Chesterfield: Old Cestrefeldian Society.

Robertson, J. (1775) *A Treatise of Such Mathematical Instruments as Are Usually Put into a Portable Case* (3rd edition). London: T. Heath, J. Hodges and J. Fuller.

Robertson, J. (1795) *Elements of Navigation* (2 vols., 4th edition). London: Hansebooks GmbH.

Robertson, J. and Gwynne, L. (1805) *Elements of Navigation, and a Treatise on Marine Fortification . . . for Use of Children in the Royal Mathematical School* (2 vols., 7th edition). London: J. Nourse.

Rodger, N.A.M. (2006) *The Command of the Ocean: A Naval History of Britain, 1649–1815*. London: Penguin.

Seally, J. (1787) *A Complete Geographical Dictionary, or Universal Gazetteer of Ancient and Modern Geography* (2 vols.). London: Gale ECCO.

Simon, B. (1976) *The Two Nations and the Educational Structure, 1780–1870*. London: Lawrence and Wishart.

Smyth, J. (1961) *Sandhurst: The History of the Royal Military Academy, Woolwich, the Royal Military College, Sandhurst, and the Royal Military Academy, 1741–1961*. London: Brigadier Sir John Smyth.

Stewart, W.A.C. and McCann, W.P. (2017) *Educational Innovators*. London: Macmillan.

Sullivan, F.B. (1976) The Naval Schoolmaster during the Eighteenth Century and the Early Nineteenth Century. *Mariner's Mirror*, **62**, pp. 311–326.

Sullivan, F.B. (1977) The Royal Academy at Portsmouth 1729–1806. *The Mariners' Mirror*, **63**, pp. 311–326, 312–313.

Thomas, J.H. (2011) Portsmouth Naval Academy in the Age of Nelson: A Reassessment. *International Journal of Maritime History*, **23**, pp. 111–144.

Turner, A.J. (2005) Advancing Navigation in Eighteenth-Century France: Teaching and Instrument Making in the Port of Rochefort. *Mariner's Mirror*, **91**, pp. 531–547.

Watson, F. (1971) *Beginning of Teaching Modern Subjects*. London: S.R. Publishers.

Watts, R. (1998) *Gender, Power and the Unitarians in England, 1760–1860*. Abingdon: Routledge.

Wellbeloved, C. (1809/2010) *Memoirs of the Life and Writings of the Late Rev. W. Wood FLS*. London: Nabu Press.

Williams, D. (1789) *Lectures on Education* (3 vols.), Vol 2. London: John Bell.
Woodley, S. (2009) Oh Miserable and Most Ruinous Measure: The Debate between Private and Public Education in Britain, 1760–1800. In M. Hilton and J. Chefrin (Eds.) *Educating the Child in Enlightenment Britain: Beliefs, Cultures, Practices*. Abingdon: Routledge.
Worster, B. (2009) *A Compendious and Methodical Account of the Principles of Natural Philosophy*. London: Kessinger Publishing.

6 The Lax family of Staindrop and the making of a teaching dynasty

Claire Tupling

Introduction

This chapter follows the life of the Lax family who lived in Staindrop, County Durham, and who were involved with elementary school teaching. Examining occupational reproduction, the chapter traces three generations of this family as they move in and out of school teaching from the mid-nineteenth century until just after the First World War. This focus on one family brings a unique perspective to understanding the history of elementary education in the nineteenth century, offering an insight into the experiences of individuals and the influence of family, a feature under-examined in the history of education.

The chapter begins by considering how the lives of teachers have been studied by historians, and it outlines how the study of this family was approached. Introducing Joseph Lax of the first generation of teachers in this family, the chapter provides a contextual overview of the emerging elementary school system of the nineteenth century. The chapter then explores the lives of Joseph's children and grandchildren, highlighting issues of gender, death and economic misfortune that prompted and punctuated the teaching careers of this family.

Studying Teachers

Studying the lives of teachers contributes to understandings of the history of education, offering accounts of how education was experienced by those working within educational institutions at the time. Revisionist and new cultural history approaches have provided a much-needed focus on the lives of 'ordinary' people who experienced education in the past, particularly women, who were often overlooked by more traditional approaches to the study of the history of education (Larsen, 2011). Several studies have examined the class, gender and social and occupational mobility of elementary school teachers in the nineteenth century which provide a useful context for this study of the Lax family.

Horn (1980) used census returns and other archive material to trace a growth in the proportion of teachers under the age of 25 across the nineteenth century. Highlighting an increase in the numbers of uncertificated teachers working in elementary schools around the turn of the twentieth century, this study indicates an increasing feminisation of the teaching workforce. Other studies have also used a range of documentary evidence to examine gender and social class and their links to the professionalisation of teaching and the occupational mobility of pupil-teachers and teaching (Bergen, 1982; Coppock, 1997). Some studies have focused specifically on the experiences of women

DOI: 10.4324/9781003039532-7

teachers. These include Widdowson's (1980) study which examined the ways in which the pupil-teacher scheme that offered professional training opportunities enabled women to progress through a teaching career to the extent that they made up around 75 per cent of the elementary teaching workforce by 1914. Studies tracing the careers of women teachers are needed as much of the scholarship on the profession of elementary school teaching has focused on the schoolmaster, ignoring the experiences of women elementary school teachers (Burstyn, 1970). The experience of women and their career mobilities is particularly significant for this study as, while the starting point for this study is a schoolmaster, Joseph Lax, it is his daughters who appear as key agents in the occupational reproduction of teaching into a second generation and beyond. This is not simply a case of the Lax children inheriting an occupation by following in their father's, or grandfather's, footsteps to become teachers. Rather, there is a gendered pattern of occupational reproduction, which may signify individual decision-making in choosing elementary teaching as an occupation.

This study of the Lax family uses an archival case study to present a family-history narrative of occupational reproduction across three generations of one family associated with elementary school teaching in Staindrop, Durham, in the second half of the nineteenth century. A range of historical records, such as census returns, newspaper articles and records of births, deaths and marriages, is used to construct this account. Staindrop, the village in which Joseph Lax raised his children, was the epicentre of this family's elementary teaching experience. Additionally, the 'family occupation' was practised elsewhere as the family grew. One significant source, the school logbook (a legal requirement for schools introduced as a result of the Revised Code in 1862) for Staindrop National School is missing from County Durham's archive and therefore cannot be drawn on in this study. Potentially, this would have provided a valuable first-hand account of the daily life of the school during the time Joseph Lax was headmaster. It may have provided an insight into Joseph's attitudes and approach to teaching, including his relationship with assistant teachers, pupils and pupil-teachers. As it does not appear to have survived, we will never know. There are, then, no first-hand accounts from members of the Lax family. The sources used in this study represent traces of the existence of members of the Lax family as recorded in 'objectified communications' required by the state or as reported in newspapers and other documents. These are 'relics' and are 'a limited selection of all that could have survived' (Goldthorpe, 1991: 213). Doubtless, there may be other relevant records which have not yet been discovered. The documents used for this chapter are not assumed to offer 'the truth' about the Lax family but are interrogated in order to produce a narrative of one family over time.

This chapter brings the 'richness of an individual family narrative' to more generalised understandings of teaching and occupational mobility during the nineteenth century (Marsden, 1997: 353). Why has the Lax family been chosen for this study? They are but one family worthy of investigation, and there is no basis for assuming them to be either typical or atypical of other families associated with elementary school teaching during this time. Focusing on another family would likely illuminate other aspects related to elementary school teaching. The Lax family does, however, provide a specific case upon which to focus, particularly in relation to gender and occupational reproduction, and the unpredictable circumstances of this reproduction. Occupational reproduction is chosen as the term used to explore how teaching is practised across three generations, as it draws on Bourdieu's (2004) theory of capital in exploring how the socio-economic context and social networks may have shaped members of the Lax family's decision to be elementary school teachers (Smith, 2002).

The Lax family were uncovered in census returns whilst researching my own family history, and their history is intertwined with my own family history. My great-great-grandparents, Timothy and Mary Leonard, lived in Staindrop, raising a family at the same time as Joseph and his second wife. The census returns of the late nineteenth century do not record any of Timothy and Mary's children as 'scholars', though it is likely they attended the National School at some point in their childhoods. My great-grandfather, Robinson Leonard, aged 12, was rewarded with a Bible for good attendance at Sunday School in 1882. The schoolmasters of National Schools were expected to encourage attendance at Sunday School, and so it can be inferred that Robinson and his siblings attended Staindrop National School when Joseph Lax was headmaster. It is inevitable that the Lax family interacted with my ancestors. Timothy Leonard, some years younger than Joseph Lax, grew up in nearby Barnard Castle, as did Lax. In 1851 Timothy is recorded as a scholar, potentially attending Barnard Castle National School whilst Lax was attending that school in his role as a pupil-teacher. By the end of the nineteenth century, in 1894, Timothy Leonard and Joseph Lax are both candidates for election to the newly created Staindrop Parish Council (Teesdale Mercury, 1894a). Joseph was elected, Timothy wasn't (Teesdale Mercury, 1894b).

Another 'relic' from my own family history that connects to the story of the Lax family survives in a school photograph from Staindrop in 1907 (Figure 6.1).

My grandmother, unidentified, is amongst a group of schoolchildren with a schoolmaster. By this date Joseph Lax had retired, and so it is likely that the schoolmaster pictured is Alfred Edwards, who is introduced later in this chapter.

These 'relics' of history enable a focus on the teaching careers of Joseph Lax and his family, but the status of these artefacts that have recorded aspects of the Laxes' lives are contingent on understanding the context in which they were created, including the motivations for their creation, and the purpose for which they were created. In order to provide an understanding of the social

Figure 6.1 School photography from Staindrop, dated 1907

context in elementary education in which they were created, the chapter now provides an overview of the changing shape of elementary education in the nineteenth century.

Questions for discussion

- Is it helpful or misleading to draw parallels between the use of unqualified teachers at the beginning of the twentieth century, and the use of unqualified teachers today?
- Is it significant that the historian has a personal connection with the Lax family? Do we need a sense of personal relevance to motivate us to engage with history?
- Is it important that educationists do their own historical research? Why?

Elementary schooling and schoolteachers in the nineteenth century

In England and Wales prior to the 1870 Education Act, schooling for working-class children was provided through a variety of school types, including those run by religious organisations. The Government increasingly concerned itself with the state and supply of elementary schooling, responding to a series of surveys conducted on behalf of Education Select Committees. An 1818 survey of parochial returns listed a mix of schooling types in Staindrop, including endowed schools and 'other institutions' consisting of five day-schools and 'four schools kept by mistresses', concluding that the '[t]he means of education for the poor are not greatly deficient' in this parish (Select Committee on Education of the Poor, 1818). By the early 1830s two new infants' schools had been established in Staindrop. (Abstract of Answers and Returns on State of Education in England and Wales, 1835) A National School was established in Staindrop in the 1840s.

From the 1830s, as the Government increasingly concerned itself with elementary education and the provision of elementary schooling expanded, inspection reports expressed concern over poor-quality teaching, including the 'ignorance' of monitors, a characteristic feature of both the National and British and Foreign Schools Society schools. In response, James Kay-Shuttleworth, secretary to the Committee of the Privy Council on Education, proposed a new pupil-teacher system to replace the inadequate monitorial system.

The new pupil-teacher scheme instigated through new regulations in 1846 introduced an apprenticeship and examination route into elementary school teaching. The new system enabled elementary school children between the ages of 13 and 18 to be trained and paid as pupil-teachers. From there they could compete for a Queen's Scholarship, tenable at a teacher training college where they would complete their training to become certificated schoolmasters or mistresses. Competitive examination was primarily associated with the universities and its application within elementary school teacher training, 'an occupation that was not considered respectable in middle-class opinion . . . [seemed] 'culturally incongruous' (Knudsen, 2016). Thus, this new system can be seen as an attempt to create a professional workforce of elementary teachers and, along with the stipend awarded to certificated teachers employed in schools, helped to fuel the expansion of the elementary school workforce. The pupil-teacher scheme operated from 1846 throughout the remainder of the nineteenth century.

In introducing the scheme, Kay-Shuttleworth (1862) recognised that the occupation of 'schoolmaster' (the scheme was open to women, but he refers primarily to the schoolmaster) was not attractive, with an income 'very little greater than that of an agricultural labourer' and which was also subject to fluctuating pupil attendance. Schoolmasters relying on a precarious income, Kay-Shuttleworth argued, was 'to condemn the poor to ignorance'. The pupil-teacher scheme was therefore an attempt to raise the status of elementary school teaching:

> Their Lordships desired to render the profession of schoolmaster honourable, by raising its character, by giving it the public recognition of impartially awarded certificates or diplomas, and by securing to well-trained or otherwise efficient masters a position of comfort during the period of their arduous labours.
>
> (p. 475)

Kay-Shuttleworth envisaged that recruits to the pupil-teacher scheme would come from members of the manual classes, for whom the scheme enabled a career that otherwise would not be possible. The scheme was not, however, conceived as a means by which candidates could enter a middle-class profession. A status comparable to professions in medicine or the law was not intended to be conferred on the position of the schoolmaster. Indeed, Kay-Shuttleworth did not see the position of elementary school teacher as one that would attract candidates from the middle class:

> It cannot be expected that members of the middle class of society will, to any great extent in this country, choose the vocation of teachers of the poor.
>
> (p. 481)

It was through this pupil-teacher scheme that Joseph Lax progressed to be become a certificated schoolmaster.

Questions for discussion

- What is the social status of the school teacher today? Does it even make sense to ask that question?
- Do you think recent government action has tended to raise or lower the professional status of teachers?
- Do you think professional status is related to social status? If so, how?

Joseph Lax

Joseph Lax was born in Barnard Castle, Durham, in 1834 and was baptised on 28 December that year. He was the eldest of six children born to John and Mary Lax. In the 1851 census his father John Lax was recorded as auctioneer and Sheriff's officer. By the 1861 census, an additional position of clerk to the local board of public health was added to his listed occupations. Joseph Lax, then, did not come from the manual classes, but neither was this a family where entry to a middle-class profession could be assumed. Joseph's brother John became a butcher and later a farmer. His next youngest brother, Thomas, moved to nearby Darlington and became a printer. The youngest brother William Parkin, following in his father's footsteps, was an auctioneer's clerk, later becoming an auctioneer after his father's death. William was summonsed to Barnard Castle Police court in 1883 for failing to send his children to school, reflecting resistance to compulsory schooling amongst some working-class families (Teesdale Mercury, 1883). This event also suggests that schooling was not automatically embraced by the wider Lax family. William died in 1884 aged 43, and his children's illnesses and absences from school feature in entries in the Barnard Castle School logbook. Joseph's sisters have no occupation of their own recorded on an any of the nineteenth-century censuses, reflecting either the absence of employment or an under-reporting of the paid work of married women at the time (Higgs and Wilkinson, 2016).

In 1851 the family lived in Barnard Castle and the 16-year-old Joseph was a pupil-teacher at Barnard Castle National School (Teesdale Mercury, 1875). As a pupil-teacher, Joseph would have received training and payment under Kay-Shuttleworth's scheme and would have then been awarded a Queen's Scholarship to complete his training to become a certificated schoolmaster. He is recorded as having received a third class, third division certificate of merit from the Oxford Diocesan Training School after examination by Her Majesty's Inspectors (HMI) at Christmas (Committee of Council on Education, 1854). Joseph Lax would have been 19 when he became a certificated schoolmaster, and he secured the position of headmaster at Staindrop National School at this time (Teesdale Mercury, 1908). Examination of the records of Culham College, the Oxford Diocesan Training College that Lax attended, suggests it was not unusual to be become a headmaster directly upon leaving the training college (Horn, 1980). Neither was it unusual to be appointed to headship at the age Joseph Lax was when he became a headmaster. In securing this position on completing his training and at such a young age, Joseph may well have benefitted from a rising demand for certificated schoolteachers at this time (Horn, 1980). Additionally, in securing a position at Staindrop, only a few miles from his home town of Barnard Castle where his father was still an auctioneer and clerk to the board of public health, it is possible that Joseph benefitted from levering social capital in obtaining this position.

As a condition of government funding, the National School at Staindrop was subject to inspections from Her Majesty's Inspectors (HMI). Inspections by the Rev Moncrieff, HMI are reported in the *Teesdale Mercury* on several occasions, typically commending Mr. Lax, 'for the unwearied interest he takes in the advancement of his pupils' (Teesdale Mercury, 1859). In particular, the local newspaper was keen to report on the success of pupil-teachers, supervised by Lax, in their progress towards achieving a Queen's Scholarship (Teesdale Mercury, 1858).

As the headmaster of Staindrop National School, Lax became involved in activities beyond the immediate required tasks of any schoolmaster. Assuming roles in addition to teaching was not unusual for National Schoolmasters. As Smith discusses, the National Schoolmaster was considered by the National Society as an assistant to the vicar and expected to take on Sunday duties, including acting as organist and choirmaster to the extent that the schoolmaster was sometimes described as the 'parson's fag' (Smith, 2002). Joseph Lax was a member of the church choir whose performances at concerts were highlighted in the local newspaper. In later years he is recorded as choirmaster, whilst his son Fred is organist (Teesdale Mercury, 1881).

The role of the parish clerk was often reserved for the National Schoolmaster, and often the schoolmaster was a lonely position subordinate to the clergy and other positions, such as farmers in the local community who viewed the schoolteacher as a tradesman (Smith, 2004). The social position of the schoolmaster was noted as such in the report to the Newcastle Commission of 1861:

They are isolated beings, beneath the educated portion of the community in social rank, and unwilling to lower themselves to that of mechanics.

(Newcastle Commission, 1861)

Whilst there is no evidence that Lax was appointed parish clerk, based on the evidence of his involvement with church life, it could be assumed that Lax was a schoolmaster servant of the church (Smith, 2002). However other sources indicate that Joseph Lax did not experience the isolation identified in the Newcastle Commission report (1861). The *Teesdale Mercury*'s reporting suggests Joseph was an enthusiastic and much appreciated contributor to local concerts. Other reports reveal his involvement in a range of civic activities. In April 1866 the *Teesdale Mercury* reports that Lax had been appointed an overseer of the poor, in 1894 he came top of the poll in the election to the newly created parish council, becoming its first chair and, in 1899, is reported to be foreman of the jury for a coroner's inquest. In 1901 he was elected vice-chairman of the Staindrop Conservative Association, whilst his son-in-law and fellow schoolmaster who was soon to succeed him as headmaster, Alfred Edwards, was elected honorary secretary (Teesdale Mercury, 1901a). Lax was also initiated into the Rose of Raby Lodge of the Freemasons in 1877 (Ancestry.com). With admission to Freemasonry by invitation, Lax would have been far from isolated and, by joining this group, would have opportunities for networking (Burt, 2003). Freemasonry was a means by which the middle classes could reinforce their class identity through a network of alliances (England, 2007). Along with Lax's political affiliation, this indicates he aligned himself with the establishment and distanced himself from the working classes whose children he educated. Lax may also have been involved in professional networks, as he is reported as amongst a deputation of Durham teachers at a presentation to a former HMI. Professional self-organisation was a practice that many teachers engaged in during the nineteenth century, even if this was not always encouraged by government (Knudsen, 2016).

Although there is no way of knowing for certain how Lax viewed his class identity, Bergen notes that 'elementary teachers seemed to view themselves as having risen above the working class', having achieved the status of a certificated teacher via the pupil-teacher route (Bergen, 1982). Lax's involvement in this wide range of activities, beyond those roles that might be seen as typical of the 'parson's fag', could suggest that Lax considered himself as socially and professionally distant from his working-class pupils. However, for other members of the Lax family, becoming a schoolteacher was not a direct route to becoming middle class; rather, becoming a teacher may have involved leveraging opportunities where there were few alternatives. Joseph Lax remained as headmaster at Staindrop National School for 47 years until ill health forced his retirement in 1901 (Teesdale Mercury, 1901b). He died in 1908 and is buried at Staindrop.

Questions for discussion

- The professional role of a twenty-first-century teacher is acknowledged to be very varied, going well beyond academic tuition. To what extent is it reasonable to liken the varied duties of a teacher now, to the nineteenth-century position of a 'parson's fag'?
- Do duties that go beyond teaching strengthen or undermine the professional identity of a teacher?

Raising the second and third generation of teachers

In 1855 Joseph married Phoebe Lodge, the daughter of a plantation worker and a laundress. They had a daughter who died in infancy in March 1856, and Phoebe died the following year. Joseph married Jane Ingram in 1858, and between 1860 and 1876 eleven children were born. A son, Alfred, born in 1869, died in infancy, but ten survived to adulthood. Census records reveal at least five of the surviving children were enrolled as pupil-teachers, employed as assistant teachers, or became teachers at various points between 1871 and 1911.

This chapter cannot consider the educational and occupational lives of all the Lax family, but it presents a brief portrait of three of Joseph and Jane's children, Frederick John, Harietta Emily and Helena Jane, and their families to illustrate the occupational reproduction of teaching into a second and third generation.

By the time the Lax children began teaching, the state's involvement in the funding, provision and monitoring of elementary education had intensified. In 1858 the Newcastle Commission was formed by Parliament with the task of inquiring into providing an 'extension of sound and cheap elementary instruction to all classes of the people' (Newcastle Commission, 1861: 1). The desire to find a cheap means of providing elementary education came in the context of rising costs since the introduction of the pupil-teacher system in 1846 (Midgley, 2016). Additionally, there was a need to reduce government spending after the Crimean war (Coppock, 1997). The Newcastle Commission report, published in 1861, identified poor attendance and low standards of literacy and numeracy. Making a number of recommendations, it aimed at extending instruction in and raising standards of literacy and numeracy. The report also recommended changing the way schools were funded and schoolteachers were paid.

Following these recommendations, Robert Lowe, vice-president of the education department, introduced a 'Revised Code' in 1862 (Committee of Council on Education, 1862). Key revisions included a payment-by-results system with inspectors examining pupils in the 3Rs of reading, writing and arithmetic. Payments to schools were made according to attendance, and the stipend for certificated teachers was removed. The 'Revised Code' reformed the pupil-teacher system that had supported Joseph Lax to embark on his teaching career. The Queen's Scholarships were removed, and as a result there were fewer enrolments to teacher training colleges, and fewer pupil-teachers, though numbers increased again following the 1870 Education Act (Trouvé-Finding, 2005). Pupil-teachers now had to be paid for by school managers from the school grant (Maguire, 2000). In appointing his children as pupil-teachers in the context of this revised system, Lax may have used a cost-effective source of pupil-teachers. For existing certificated elementary teachers, the Revised Code 'signalled a major – and abrupt – reversal of fortune' (Knudsen, 2016). One suggested motivation Lowe had for reducing the conditions of schoolteachers was his belief that elementary school teachers were arrogant, 'protected by an indulgent state' and so had become lazy and ineffective. The payment-by-results system was seen as a way to raise standards whilst lowering costs (Midgley, 2016).

A significant consequence of the Revised Code included 'disappearing male pupil teachers' which contributed to a feminisation of elementary school teaching (Robinson, 1997: 366). Men were discouraged by the payment-by-results system and the lack of a guaranteed income, especially when they could secure higher wages in industry (Coppock, 1997; Jabbar, 2013). However, for young women, elementary school teaching offered an occupational opportunity amongst few alternatives, other than domestic work (Coppock, 1997). For the daughters of Joseph and Jane Lax, and possibly the granddaughters, elementary school teaching offered a means of securing an occupation and income when other options for a professional role were not available. Whilst women may have taken up opportunities offered by an expanding elementary schooling system, government also benefitted from feminisation of the teaching workforce. Women teacher salaries were around two-thirds that of men and so offered a 'cheaper, more pliable and captive workforce' (Knudsen, 2016: 525). This trend towards feminisation of elementary school teaching provides the context in which the Lax children embarked on elementary school teaching.

Questions for discussion

- Can twenty-first-century educational practice be compared with 'payment by results'? If so, do you think the same assumptions lie behind it ('that teaching was not a complex job and that a payment-by-results system would act as an incentive to raise standards')?
- Is there still a relationship between gender and status within the teaching profession? Why?

Harietta Lax

Harietta Emily Lax was born in 1863 and, at the age of 7 in the 1871 census, is recorded as a scholar. In the 1881 census she is a pupil-teacher, and in the 1891 census she is married to Robert Holliday, an estate office clerk, and has no occupation recorded for herself. Robert died in early 1893, leaving Harietta widowed with a baby daughter, Florence Margaret Annie (Teesdale Mercury, 1893a). By the 1901 census Harietta is recorded as an elementary school teacher and was living with her daughter Florence, father Joseph and older sister Katherine Mary. If the lack of occupation in 1891 is accurate, it suggests that Harietta returned to teaching following the death of her husband. The reasons for Harietta's decision to return to teaching remain as speculation, but it is likely the death of her husband resulted in a change of financial circumstances as well as living arrangements. With her father Joseph still the headmaster in 1901, Harietta may well have been well placed to take advantage of employment opportunities as an elementary school teacher.

Both Harietta and her daughter Florence are recorded as being employed as schoolteachers with Durham County Council (the Local Education Authority having been created by the 1902 Education Act) on the 1911 census. In 1918, Harietta's daughter Florence married Frank William Lupson, who was appointed as assistant master to Staindrop 'Church' School in 1909 (Teesdale Mercury, 1909). Marriages between teachers are likely where job opportunities bring teachers into a locality where their immediate social circle tends to be other teachers (Steinberg, 2009). This appears to be the pattern followed by Frank Lupson who moved to Staindrop to take up the position of assistant master. In 1911 Frank was lodging in Staindrop, and in 1912 he was admitted to the Rose of Raby Lodge of the Freemasons, as was Alfred Edwards and Joseph Lax in previous years (Ancestry.com, 2015). In marrying Florence Margaret 'Daisy' Holliday (now a piano teacher) in 1918, Frank Lupson joined a family network of teachers.

Helena Jane Lax

Helena Jane Lax, born 1868, is the final child of Joseph and Jane Lax to be considered. Helena herself left few records. However, it is her role in connecting the Lax family to another teacher, specifically Alfred Edwards, the schoolmaster introduced earlier in the chapter who succeeded her father as headmaster, that is of interest.

In 1891 Helena is recorded as an 'assistant schoolteacher'. In 1898 she married Alfred William Collier Edwards, assistant master at Staindrop National School. Alfred was appointed to this role around January 1893 and assumed the headship on the retirement of his predecessor and father-in-law Joseph Lax in 1901 (Teesdale Mercury, 1893b). Helena, like her sister Harietta, may have been well placed to be employed as an assistant schoolteacher because of her father's position. In marrying Alfred, she was not only the headmaster's daughter, but additionally a schoolmaster's wife, establishing another link to the family teaching network. Like the other married women already referred to in this chapter, Helena had no occupation of her own recorded in the 1901 census. On the retirement of her father, Joseph Lax, Alfred became headmaster. However, this is not simply a case of passing on an occupation to the son-in-law, thus keeping teaching as a family business. The reproduction of occupation in this case is reliant on Helena as a key agent in that occupational reproduction. It was by marrying Helena that Alfred became part of the Lax family and was then able to inherit his father-in-law's position. This is not to suggest that Alfred could not become headmaster without marrying into the Lax family, but through that marriage, he joined the second generation of the Lax family in elementary school teaching. In 1909 Alfred was joined by Frank William Lupson, as assistant master who then later married Helena, and Alfred's niece, Florence 'Daisy' Holliday, thereby extending the family network of elementary school teachers within a third generation.

As with Joseph Lax, Alfred was also admitted to the Rose of Raby Lodge of the Freemasons, and his involvement with the Staindrop Conservative Association has already been noted (Ancestry.com, 2015). It appears he was also involved in professional networks, as he was a delegate to the National Union of Teachers annual conference in 1913 (Teesdale Mercury, 1913). He was also organist and a chorister in Staindrop parish church, fulfilling the role of 'parson's fag' (Smith, 2002). As was the case with Joseph Lax, Alfred appeared to consider himself to be more than just a schoolmaster, seeking status through professional and social networks.

Conclusion – learning from the Lax family

Joseph Lax benefitted from Kay-Shuttleworth's pupil-teacher scheme, becoming a certificated schoolmaster and securing the position of headmaster at Staindrop National School where he remained for his entire working life. Elementary school teaching became a family occupation over the course of three generations, and this family provides an example of occupational reproduction. However, unlike the study by Marsden who also traced a 'teaching dynasty' over three generations, there was no father-son reproduction of a teaching career (Marsden, 1997). Joseph Lax's sons did not follow him into elementary school teaching, and it cannot be said that his daughters inherited elementary school teaching, either.

Even if Joseph Lax considered himself 'above the working class', this did not mean his children were able to enter a profession, or lower-middle-class occupations such as clerking (Bergen, 1982). However, the three children of Joseph Lax that this chapter has focused on, Frederick John and his daughter Kate Maria, Harietta Emily, Helena Jane and their famlies were active agents in the reproduction of teaching in to a second, and even a third generation. This is not to claim that members of the Lax family deliberately set out to reproduce teachers by becoming teachers themselves or by marrying them, but that they were agents in this reproduction. For example, Harietta Emily appeared to return to teaching following her husband's death, and this may have been a decision taken in the context of a need to support herself and her daughter. Additionally, she was able to find employment as a teacher because her father was a headmaster. Coppock discusses how the lower-middle classes 'hijacked' elementary school teaching for their daughters, because of the prospects it offered particularly for women, contributing to a feminisation of elementary school teaching (Coppock, 1997: 184). Whether the Laxes actively hijacked elementary school teaching cannot be determined, but the trace evidence suggested that they did avail themselves of opportunities offered by the expansion of elementary schooling.

Summary points

- The social status of elementary school teachers was unclear, precarious and contested.
- An increasingly female workforce reflected government policy of deliberately lowering the status of elementary teaching.
- Teaching remained a source of financial and social security, favouring those with family connections within the profession/occupation.
- A case study of one family reveals the importance of personal agency in shaping the social significance of teaching as an occupation.

Recommended reading

Midgley, H. (2016) Payment by Results in Nineteenth-Century British Education: A Study in How Priorities Change. *Journal of Policy History*, **28**(4), pp. 680–706.
Trouvé-Finding, S. (2005) Teaching as a Woman's Job: The Impact of the Admission of Women to Elementary Teaching in England and France in the Late Nineteenth and Early Twentieth Centuries. *History of Education*, **34**(5), pp. 483–496.

References

Ancestry.com (2015) United Grand Lodge of England Freemason Membership Registers, 1751–192. Online. Available at https://www.ancestry.co.uk/search/collections/60620/ (Accessed 21 December 2022).
Bergen, B.H. (1982) Only a Schoolmaster: Gender, Class, and the Effort to Professionalize Elementary Teaching in England, 1870–1910. *History of Education Quarterly*, **22**(1), pp. 1–21.
Bourdieu, P. (2004) The Forms of Capital. In S.J. Ball (Ed.) *The RoutledgeFalmer Reader in Sociology of Education*. London: RoutledgeFalmer. 15–29.
Burstyn, J.N. (1970) Women's Education in England during the Nineteenth Century: A Review of the Literature, 1970–1976. *History of Education*, **6**(1), pp. 11–19.
Burt, R. (2003) Freemasonry and Business Networking during the Victorian Period. *The Economic History Review*, **56**(4), pp. 657–688.
Committee of Council on Education (1854) Minutes, Correspondence, Financial Statements, and Reports of H.M. Inspectors of Schools, 1853–54. *19th Century House of Commons Sessional Papers*, 1854. Online. Available at https://parlipapers.proquest.com/parlipapers/docview/t70.d75.1854-030576 (Accessed 21 December 2022).
Committee of Council on Education (1862) Minute Establishing Revised Code of Regulations. *19th Century House of Commons Sessional Papers*, 1862. Online. Avalable at https://parlipapers.proquest.com/parlipapers/docview/t70.d75.1862-038498 (Accessed 21 December 2022).
Coppock, D.A. (1997) Respectability as a Prerequisite of Moral Character: The Social and Occupational Mobility of Pupil Teachers in the Late Nineteenth and Early Twentieth Centuries. *History of Education*, **26**(2), pp. 165–186.

England, J. (2007) Unitarians, Freemasons, Chartists: The Middle Class in Victorian Merthyr. *The Welsh History Review*, **23**(4), pp. 35–58.

Goldthorpe, J.H. (1991) The Uses of History in Sociology: Reflections on Some Recent Tendencies. *The British Journal of Sociology*, **4**(2), 147548507.

Higgs, E. and Wilkinson, A. (2016) Women, Occupations and Work in the Victorian Censuses Revisited. *History Workshop Journal*, **81**(1), pp. 17–38.

Horn, P. (1980) The Recruitment, Role and Status of the Victorian Country Teacher. *History of Education*, **9**(2), pp. 129–141.

Jabbar, H. (2013) The Case of 'Payment-by-Results': Re-Examining the Effects of an Incentive Programme in Nineteenth-Century English Schools. *Journal of Educational Administration and History*, **45**(3), pp. 220–243.

Kay-Shuttleworth, J. (1862) *Four Periods of Public Education as Reviewed in 1832, 1839, 1846, 1862*. London: Longman, Green, Longman, and Roberts.

Knudsen, A.T. (2016) Profession, 'Performance', and Policy: Teachers, Examinations, and the State in England and Wales, 1846–1862. *Paedagogica Historica*, **52**(5), pp. 507–524.

Larsen, M.A. (2011) *The Making and Shaping of the Victorian Teacher*. London: Palgrave Macmillan.

Maguire, M. (2000) The State Regulation of United Kingdom Teacher Education in the Nineteenth Century: The Interplay of 'Value' and 'Sense'. *International Studies in Sociology of Education*, **10**(3), pp. 227–242.

Marsden, B. (1997) Training, Careers and Lives: A Longitudinal Study of a Teaching Dynasty. *Cambridge Journal of Education*, **27**(3), pp. 343–354.

Midgley, H. (2016) Payment by Results in Nineteenth-Century British Education: A Study in How Priorities Change. *Journal of Policy History*, **28**(4), pp. 680–706.

Newcastle Commission (1861) The Royal Commission on the State of Popular Education in England. *Parliamentary Papers*, 1861, XXI. pp. 293–328.Online. Available at https://parlipapers.proquest.com/parlipapers/docview/t70.d75.1861-037189 (Accessed 21 December 2022).

Robinson, W. (1997) The 'Problem' of the Female Pupil Teacher: Constructions, Conflict and Control 1860–1910. *Cambridge Journal of Education*, **27**(3), pp. 365–377.

Select Committee on Education of the Poor (1818) Digest of Parochial Returns, Volumes I., II., and III. (England, Wales, Scotland and British Isles). *19th Century House of Commons Sessional Papers*, 1819. Online. Available at https://parlipapers.proquest.com/parlipapers/docview/t70.d75.1819-005977 (Accessed 21 December 2022).

Select Committee on Education of the Poor (1835) Abstract of Answers and Returns on State of Education in England and Wales, Volumes I., II., III. *19th Century House of Commons Sessional Papers, 1835*. Online. Available at https://parlipapers.proquest.com/parlipapers/docview/t70.d75.1835-015804 (Accessed 21 December 2022).

Smith, J.T. (2002) 'The Parson's Fag': The Schoolteacher as the Servant of the Church in the Second Half of the Nineteenth Century. *Journal of Educational Administration and History*, **34**(1), pp. 1–22.

Smith, J.T. (2004) Merely a Growing Dilemma of Etiquette? The Deepening Gulf between the Victorian Clergyman and Victorian Schoolteacher. *History of Education*, **136**(2), pp. 157–176.

Steinberg, N. (2009) From One Generation to the Next: Teachers and Teaching in the German Colonies in South Russia 1804–1914. *Paedagogica Historica*, **45**(3), pp. 329–353.

Teesdale Mercury (1858) Local and General News: National School, Staindrop. *Teesdale Mercury*, 1 September 1858.

Teesdale Mercury (1859) Local and General News: Staindrop National School. *Teesdale Mercury*, 24 August 1859.

Teesdale Mercury (1875) Barnard Castle National School. *Teesdale Mercury*, 7 July 1875.

Teesdale Mercury (1881) Concert at Staindrop. *Teesdale Mercury*, 9 March 1870.

Teesdale Mercury (1883) Barnard Castle Police Court. *Teesdale Mercury*, 6 June 1883.

Teesdale Mercury (1893a) Staindrop. *Teesdale Mercury*, 11 January 1893.

Teesdale Mercury (1893b) Hospitality at Raby: Lord Barnard's Treat to the Children. *Teesdale Mercury*, 4 January 1893.

Teesdale Mercury (1894a) The New Local Govenment Act: The Polling, Some Surprises. *Teesdale Mercury*, 19 December 1894.

Teesdale Mercury (1894b) The New Local Government Act: Complete List of Candidates. *Teesdale Mercury*, 12 December 1894.

Teesdale Mercury (1901a) Conservatism at Staindrop. *Teesdale Mercury*, 3 April 1901.

Teesdale Mercury (1901b) Mr Lax. *Teesdale Mercury*, 18 September 1901.

Teesdale Mercury (1908) Death of Mr Joseph Lax of Staindrop. *Teesdale Mercury*, March 1908.

Teesdale Mercury (1909) Teesdale Matters Educational: Appointed. *Teesdale Mercury*, 27 January 1909.

Teesdale Mercury (1913) National Union of Teachers: Delegates from This Neighbourhood. *Teesdale Mercury*, 19 February 1913.

Widdowson, F. (1980) *Going Up into the Next Class: Women and Elementary Teacher Training, 1840–1914*. London: Women's Research and Resources Centre Publications.

7 Quintilian's educational impact

W. Martin Bloomer

Introduction

The Roman educationalist Quintilian, active in Rome at the end of the first century CE, presents a graduated programme of education, with a clear starting point, a goal and a series of steps to get from one to the other. This is not always the case with the practice of education today. Often the good of education or the purpose of today's exercise, or that test in two weeks, is not explained to students. Sometimes explanations are not convincing, and student and teacher trudge along in a curriculum set by someone else, or perhaps just fill time as we think of what we would rather be doing. Quintilian would not have approved: education cannot arise from external commands which only encourage internal evasions. Education must include its own protreptic, its own inner motivation. Even before students can consciously motivate themselves to learn, a teacher attentive to the child's capacities, including the disposition to play and to compete, will ensure the successful pre-training of the-soon-to-be-rational student. In his 12-book work Quintilian has communicated influential ideas, implicit and explicit, about learning, teaching, the student, teachers, venue, materials and the importance of education.

The confidence of this work and author are extraordinary. He believed that he had established the proper, single course of education, and his education was the best education, the only education which would make a Roman child a free, mature citizen, in fact a governor of the world. He constructs an ideal of the educated citizen who is an orator of the republic. On the one hand, in his contemporary Roman world, the collective elite decision-making of the republic had been replaced by a single emperor. Quintilian does not admit to the fact that the empire was governed by an emperor. Instead, he sticks to that old-fashioned tendency of education to present texts and ideas that were supposedly current and potent in our grandparents' time. On the other hand, it has to be said that it does not concern him that his ideal, the good orator able to sway to the people to correct action, never really existed. His text does not notice the mud-slinging, money and violence of politics. There is a sense that society can go wrong, but he asserts that the art and practice of rhetoric, alone, can discern the public good and persuade the citizens to action.

He had been the most famous teacher of the centre of the world, and at the time of the publication of his monumental work he was the official educator of the children of the Roman emperor's family. He enjoyed both a position of authority and an astonishing cultural relevance (astonishing to us for whom there are alternative kinds of education and alternative routes to adulthood or success in society and, it must be said, for whom the teacher is not often held in such high esteem). He lays out an education that seems to imagine the Roman boy (girls are in school, too, at least to the age

DOI: 10.4324/9781003039532-8

of puberty, but he writes as if they were not there) on his way to becoming an orator, a lawyer and politician/statesman for the republic. Thus, the imagined end is the free man who moves his peers to a verdict or public policy simply by addressing them.

Quintilian's text delineated a step-by-step programme, in reasonable doses, to move the child through a learning process which was socially, culturally and politically necessary and constitutive. But since Quintilian's work is so large, and since it presents all of rhetorical theory (the science of persuasive speaking), it has often been read piecemeal, e.g. for a definition of metaphor (the substitution of a word from a different semantic field for the regular word), or for a history of oratory or what he thought about extemporaneous speaking (better to prepare; only use in emergencies). It does have this handbook quality – for it rearranges, synthesizes and homogenizes a wealth of books and approaches from the time of Plato (fourth century BCE) through the Hellenistic scholars and onto Roman writers, especially Cicero (pertinent dialogues are the *On the Orator* [55 BCE] and the *Brutus*, a history of Roman orators [46 BCE]). However, Quintilian means to present all that a student must learn (and how he is to learn it) in order to become an orator. The programme of this education is outlined in the *Institutio Oratoria* (*The Formation of the Orator*), and its final exercises are modelled in two collections, the *Major* and the *Minor Declamations*, both ascribed to Quintilian, although modern scholarship has shown that the so-called Major Declamations are not his. No matter. They were believed to be his, and the three texts together can be thought of as Quintilianic education.

Contents

Full outlines of the 12 books of *The Formation of the Orator* can be found online; the introduction to each book by Donald Russell in his Loeb edition are excellent guides to Quintilian's intellectual background and to recent scholarship. The books begin with grammatical schooling (learning the alphabet, spelling, reading, writing) in Book 1, and in Book 2 proceed to rhetorical schooling, from preliminary exercises such as reading and composing fables up to training in mock diplomatic and mock legal speeches. Book 2 also introduces the definition of oratory. Here too come arguments that rhetoric (the academic discipline) and oratory (the social-political institution) are valuable and beneficial. Once rhetoric has been thoroughly introduced, Books 3 to 10 present detailed, synthetic accounts of the scholarship on the science of speech and the particular elements of speech making (it is easy to get lost in the rhetorical forest here). In Book 9 Quintilian offers detailed accounts of the various figures of speech and an account of prose rhythm. Books 10 and 11 move on to the various exercises that train up a student to use all the stuff described in such detail in the earlier books so as to make a speech. These building blocks of writing begin with a long list of what to read, with the stated purpose that wide reading in the various genres of ancient literature, Greek and Latin, will supply the student with words, techniques of argument, and moral ideas. He scarcely acknowledges any other purpose for reading (pleasure, distraction, meditation, understanding of human motivation or social and political change). He is on a mission to develop the orator and notices what the student should take from different writers. This profound utilitarianism is a great part of his achievement. He is seeking to make the student an alert, active, selective and creative imitator of the old writers. He proceeds in this book to give practical directions: stay healthy, get enough rest, take notes. Book 12 returns to the grander subject of the adult orator in society.

Questions for discussion

Clearly not everybody could be a grand orator. Does asserting that there is a single ideal for education serve a communicative or social purpose?

What is today's ideal (or ideals), and how much of an ideal or of a fiction is it?

Quintilian has a highly structured approach, and in these books the student learns how to think about the fundamental issues of a case, how to build up a speech from outline to full text, memorise and deliver it, along with such details as how to use a syllogism and full instruction on style, the manner of speaking, dependent not just on clarity and the fit of words to content but also the proper use and understanding of figured speech, including metaphor and simile but also direct address to the audience and speech in character. The importance of all these details for the history of education cannot be overstated: here is a compendium of ancient language science, a theory of composition and practical hints, such as a guide to what to read. Even when mock legal cases ceased to be a curricular exercise in the Middle Ages, composition on set themes, advice on the use of examples, stylistic recommendations more generally continued to affect student training and adult writing and speaking.

The point

All of this education is to make the boy into an orator. That, at any rate, is the stated purpose. Quintilian wants the boy to come to school, not to be home-schooled, for this is the only way in his judgement for the boy to become a *vir bonus dicendi peritus*, 'a good man skilled at speaking'. He is reusing a definition from the elder Cato (239–169 BCE), who had written educational texts dedicated to his son and was for the Romans something of a sage, himself a great soldier, statesman, censor of morals and expert on agriculture, and on education. The definition begs for explanation. Quintilian in fact makes no sustained defence of his ideal. That the science of speaking (rhetoric) and expertise in speaking (oratory, eloquence) could be used to bad ends was clear. Yet, like Cicero and Isocrates before him, Quintilian does not posit some morality as a precondition for learning the skills of communicative persuasion. Rather, the skills in speaking will moralise the individual. Lies and deceit are perfectly real, but persuasion, he thinks, is different, in moral worth but also in methods, from deceit. Persuasion uses arguments based on commonly received values, with an audience which is itself expert, or at least well experienced. It needs to be stressed that the speaker with Quintilianic virtuosity of language does not charm or seduce his untutored subjects (like the hope of capitalist advertisers with subliminal messaging and the inflation and manipulation of basic appetites). He persuades, but not simply by an algorithm of appropriate arguments appropriately delivered. He has authority. Quintilianic education will build these dual aspects: high linguistic competence with judgement of what needs to be said, when, where and how, and the presentation of the persona of a commanding orator – a moral practical intellectual with deep cultural competence who has the common good at heart.

The process

Quintilian begins with the boy at home. He insists on a pure linguistic community – parents, slave teachers, slave peers should all speak proper Latin and Greek. The boy should be started on speaking Greek because he will naturally learn Latin. A love of learning must be fostered by praise. Names and letter forms are to be learned together. The child is to be helped in writing by having a wooden tablet with the shapes of letters incised; wax is then put over the tablet and the child traces the letter shapes. Next comes a procedure rightly abandoned by modern pedagogy (but used for millennia): all possible syllables are to be learnt before advancing to the reading of words. This seems incredibly tedious. Try making a child repeat *ba, be, bi, bo, bu* throughout the alphabet, then close the syllables, *bab, bac*, etc. The only thing to be said in defence is that the ancients devoted far more time and resources, including slave labour, to this stage. Quintilian believes all are educable, but he means all Romans with resources. Some or all of these exercises might have taken place at home, but about the age of seven or eight, the boy must go to school because home schooling lacks the necessary community in which speaking performance, both that of teacher and student, must occur. The school is in miniature and in ludic mode Roman (elite, male, political) society. The young student cannot quite motivate himself; he is not yet at the age of reason – and Quintilian sees the proof of reason as the desire and power to educate oneself. Hence games are necessary. These train necessary constituents of schooling: competitive performance among peers before a single teacher who evaluates, through public praise or censure. Other relationships, those to parents or the slave tutor, the pedagogue, or affective relationships to fellow students are ignored. Further, the child is not to be beaten. Quintilian opposes the ubiquitous practice of corporal punishment, not because violence is wrong or here ineffective for achieving the desired compliance, but because of its long-term effect. The child's spirit will be broken or sullied; in fact, Quintilian thinks beating will reduce the child to the mentality of a slave. Instead of forcing the child to learn, Quintilian establishes the venue and the disposition to learn. In considering the latter he comes close to what we might call the psychology of the learner. While he acknowledges that children have individual capacity, he does not imagine different kinds of learners. All are capable; only the speed of learning varies. Some are slow, but even the fast cannot rely on talent alone. Learning comes from *ingenium*, *ars* and *usus* – innate capacity, instruction and practice. And we learn through imitation. Considerable thought in antiquity, originating in Plato and especially Aristotle, had investigated imitation, especially in its cognitive dimension. Quintilian means something much more restricted, and also does not follow Plato's lead in thinking about learning as recollection or as a result of dialectic. Because the child imitates, he must associate with speakers of good Latin, with his age mates and not with the older boys; he must read the right books; he must be given sample texts and be told to paraphrase, reduce, amplify – all in a social context, for he is by nature competitive. Imitating in a group and trying to be recognised as the best is learning. Imitation does not ultimately lead to the exact reproduction of what has come before, since the child is being taught selection and discernment (in Latin, *iudicium* judgement). The desire to excel impels a certain variation, and this variety – a clear relation to prior models with individual distinction – is what marks the accomplished speaker as a *vir bonus dicendi peritus*. Such is the theoretical movement of the boy to the educated man. In practice the child performs the following exercises. 'Performs' seems the apt word since the student receives instruction by listening and reading, repeats by speaking and writing, all out loud and in the presence of the teacher or pedagogue, the personal slave tutor and, finally, before the school body in competition.

Quintilian describes the preliminary exercises in his first book (1.9) (in Greek *progymnasmata*, in Latin *praeexercitationes*). (On the range of these exercises throughout antiquity see Penella in Bloomer, *Blackwell Companion*). At this point Quintilian imagines that the boy can read, but reading means more than elementary literacy. The grammar school teacher has read to the boy from the poets and explained the meaning and grammar of the passages. A certain amount of content, history and mythology, has been learnt. Grammatical terms would have been introduced and grammatical analysis modelled. At this point Quintilian turns to the long series of exercises in composition that will lead eventually to the formation of an orator. The series begins with fable, sententia – a one-line wisdom saying – and chreia. The chreia is an attributed saying – at the most developed a sayings tale of the form when X said A to Y, Y replied with B, where B is a withering sententia. Importantly, Quintilian writes that the students begin by retelling fables in good, simple language. They then wrote such fables. Next, they seem to be working from written poetic fables and recasting these as prose (apparently keeping the diction), then they vary the diction, then they play with the treatment by expanding and contracting particular details.

All of this play with a literary text shares formal techniques with a great deal of the ensuing curriculum, which restates a given text with strong concentration on the student's active variation of stylistic features, without invention of new details and without changing the received plot. The student does not come up with his own stories. Quintilian explicitly says that the next exercises – sententia, chreia and ethologia – are to be taken from the boy's reading. These exercises increase in narrative complexity. The first is a simple sentence of wisdom. Attributing the bit of wisdom to a sage makes the sententia into a chreia: for example, 'Isocrates used to say that the root of education was bitter, the fruit sweet'. The more complex chreia adds narrative frame: 'When Alexander the Great asked Diogenes [the philosopher in his barrel in the middle of Athens] what he could do for him, Diogenes said, "Stop blocking my sunshine"'. The ethology, more commonly known as prosopopoia, gives the speaker additional sentences. Quintilian refers at the conclusion of this section (1.9.6) to short narratives taken from the poets. The unstated connection is that all of these first writing and speaking exercises are building the student's capacity to tell a story. He is working on making narratives (short, simple, with one main speaker), and Quintilian wants nothing else to interfere.

Thus, he makes a split here – against a common practice of the day. He wants the aforementioned curriculum and nothing more to be the work of the grammar school teacher, with the student passing on to rhetoric at perhaps the age of 12. Quintilian does not set an age. He simply wants the boy to move on when competent. The problem was that the teachers of the next stage, rhetorical school, had neglected the subsequent exercises so as to focus on speech making. Quintilian wants the boy to study these at his next school and not to rush to making full-scale speeches. Before treating these (Book 2), Quintilian considers what else the boy should learn: there is so much enthusiastic recommendation of music, acting, geometry and dancing that one suspects these subjects had fallen away or were not so commonly taught. On several occasions Quintilian seems to worry that education is being rushed along to the practice of speeches (declamation) without sufficient attention to preliminaries. At times Quintilian argues for their pedagogic value in themselves: geometry does more than sharpen young minds, it is a practical and advanced science, necessary for figuring out how to enclose property and how to understand Plato. For the most part he keeps coming back to the training of voice and gesture so important to the ancient speaker. The modern correlate of the orator must be the opera star who is able to stun by voice and movement and hold our attention for sustained periods without amplification or subtitles. Book 2.4 takes up the next exercises, without expansive treatment, as Quintilian feels forced to argue for the moral purpose of the art of rhetoric (2.11 ff.). Nonetheless, the student of education can see the interests of the ancient school in developing an advanced argumentative and narrative competency. The rhetorician is to teach narrative, refutation and confirmation, praise and censure, commonplaces, theses and laws. These are for the most part training in argument. Commonplaces are common in that they are arguments against the vices of a kind of person such as a drunkard. Theses are likewise general since they are not tied to a specific person or occasion; for example: 'Is country life better than town life?', and not 'Should we move from Rome to Naples this November?'. Quintilian also mentions general passages that could be inserted into a speech: 'Should we trust witnesses?'. As with praise and blame of historical figures, the student is building a kind of ethics-light or philosophy-light series of speech pieces which he could adapt by putting in his client's or opponent's name or circumstances. With the treatment of law we see the most advanced analytic training of this curriculum. Legal particulars are all but ignored, for as Quintilian says, the elementary student is not concerned with real laws and real legislators or historical circumstances. Instead, in this pre-legal training, the student learns to question the law's form (is the language clear?) and content (is it self-consistent?). Is the law right and expedient? Again, our rhetorical student has a small lightly philosophical toolkit, where community advantage and ethical consistency seem paramount.

For a detailed account of what was taught at the highest level of schooling, we turn to declamation, mock forensic and deliberative speeches. Quintilian treats these in his work *On the Orator's Formation*, but his practice is more clearly demonstrated in two collections that were attributed to him, the larger and the lesser declamations. This latter collection seems to have stemmed directly from his school. It may well reflect notes taken down during his classes or the teacher's own notes. Declamation was about a century old, though there were earlier similar methods of speech training, by the time Quintilian offered his directions and exemplary performances. The *suasoria* was a speech of advice at some critical moment to a historical or mythological figure. The dynamic is here important since (as with the *controversia*) it is an imaginative projection of the student's status and situation. The student adviser must persuade his elder to recognise his talent and value his advice. This dynamic of male adolescence within the school of a traditional society is dressed in a historical imagination. The student intervenes to counsel Alexander the Great to stop (or not) at the shores of India, or to tell Cicero to burn his writings so as to avoid death at the hands of his political enemy Marc Antony. Facts of history or investigation into the many extant sources on these topics were not necessary. Rather, the student was charged to make a compelling speech of persuasion, arguing essentially from persona; the present course of action is presented as consonant with the character of the great man and as maintaining his good reputation.

The more demanding, final exercise was the *controversia*. Here a mini plot and a law were presented to the student. The student is to develop a speech pro or contra, i.e. either accusing or defending the named perpetrator. The fantastic quality of the *controversiae* has often been remarked: characters include pirates, stepmothers, tyrants. A rape victim is given the choice to marry or kill her rapist. A blind son is accused of planning to poison his father. A cross-dressing youth is gang raped. In the *Minor declamations* the situations are not so consistently lurid. A typical example is no. 270 with this law and plot (translation from the Loeb volume of Russell):

> Let him who is the cause of a death receive capital punishment. A young man raped a girl, one of twins. She hanged herself. The father brought the other before the magistrates and instructed her to opt for the rapist's death. The young man thought that she was the one he had raped. The magistrate ordered him to be executed. Later it came out what had happened. The father is accused of having been the cause of a death.

The student must now compose and deliver a speech to indict or exculpate the father. Included in the extant collection are the instructions given the student (the *sermo*, not always very full or helpful). Repeatedly the teacher directs the student to consider the law by defining a crucial term in the law. In this case the teacher focuses on the difficult part; he says that emotion and equity are easy here, but 'cause' from the wording of the law must be defined so as to shift responsibility away from the father. Often responsibility is shifted. Declamation seems to have its students trapped in a literal application of a law. If the letter of the law cannot be shaken through redefinition, equity or intention of the law can be invoked. The student declaimer is also being instructed in how to arouse sympathy. The declamation sticks to the strict confines of the given plot. Niceties of actual law, any question of evidence or witnesses are not allowed. The student seeks arguments from the (recurring) personae provided and must work within a standard emotional universe. Whereas the plot may seem a rather bizarre, imagined situation, in fact the commonality is simply that something dreadful has happened to the household – a father has been killed, a daughter of the house raped, a son disinherited – and the student must speak to restore the house. He is of course symbolically restoring or replicating Roman social order. There is not much plumbing of why the world has gone awry. A rich man or tyrant or stepmother or overly suspicious or severe father or a young rapist threatens the family. Into this breach of Roman morals (of piety and fidelity and self-control) comes the young speaker to save the family. That there is no final solution, that declamation keeps going on and on, generation after generation of student, is not a problem if we consider that the purpose of this education is to insist that the Roman social order is good and in need of the next generation's protection and replication.

Questions for discussion

How violent is today's reading and writing curriculum? And do the student's school activities play at ending or righting this violence?

How does education seek to influence the student's sense of duties? Why has modern education given up on such rhetorical exercises?

Summary points of the major legacies of Quintilian's thinking

Quintilian is a well from which people keep drawing. Even those making a radical break from his system, such as Jean-Jacques Rousseau with his *Émile* and its ideas of a natural childhood, are still drawn by his earnest mode of prescribing an ideal childhood so as to make the child into the adult. On a large scale his legacies for educational theory and practice are these.

- Education needs a program and a manifesto. The institution of education needs modes of persuasion directed to parents, child-minders, patrons, teachers and students. Quintilian's treatise presents a fusion of Greek science and Roman experience that he believes to be a single adequate education. This needs only to be followed by parents and educators. Their acceptance of the project is more difficult than the children's pursuit of this long process. Quintilian thinks that the child is naturally suited to (and thus must follow) this essentially linguistic and stylistic formation.
- Rhetorical education is the necessary and nearly sufficient preparation of the individual for life. Education begins with the taking of the child into school and ends with delivering the youth as

a competent defender and prospective leader of society. The moralizing enterprise takes place at school; home life is acknowledged as an important precondition, but the educational manifesto treats its own institution as the crucial one: a child grows biologically at home, culturally, and not simply cognitively, at school.

- Quintilian insists that rhetoric has a moral disposition and that rhetorical education will make the person good. Undergirding these assertions and his work is a supposition that rhetoric provides an etiquette of thought, speech and action. Rhetorical education will provide a consistency of self and speech, transparently good and effective at achieving the (common) good.
- Education is of paramount importance for the health of state, society, family and individual. From Aristotle and from Roman tradition, Quintilian believes that human beings are political animals. We are meant to live in society and to serve and guide it. Quintilian does not describe an education in politics, but his education is composed in a way to form the young 'political animal', or given the nationalist tinge to Quintilian's thinking, the 'Roman political animal'. Through education the elite child learns to behave as a mini-Roman, playing as head of a family, pleader in the courts, resolver of familial and civil conflicts. This ambitious project of making a governing class begins with the individual student understanding relations to families and friends, with duties as Cicero had put it. Literature is studied in part to find examples and encouragement for such behaviour. These duties (*officia*) are moral, social and political, since they are acted out in the public eye, in the city and especially in the lawcourts. Declamation in particular considers and resolves apparent contradictions in social and familial roles and relations.
- Education involves activating a child's engagement and strength of mind. Quintilian has thus given a proto-theory of the psychology of the learner. In this slimly conceived theory of mind, an innate disposition to learn must be cultivated, by a teacher, exercises and a learning community. The learning mind is imitative and hence must be given good positive models and kept from bad (diction, texts, teachers, students, gestures, enthusiasms, passions). The child is a blank slate who must be set things to copy, in writing and in memory, before developing his own judgement and motivation.
- For all the recommendation of holistic education and all the liberal arts, language has pride of place. The student's life is a progress through literacy skills, memorisation of texts, oral delivery, literary study. At the end, the student is something like a talking book – steeped in literary traditions and now able to compose and perform as a literary master. This rhetorical education teaches that style of speech and writing makes the man.
- Education has the aim of producing conflict managers for society. Quintilian does not call for military or political training, nor does he imagine his students becoming generals or being senators. (These leaders at this point in Rome would have had a rhetorical education, but they are not seen, by Quintilian and the traditional education, as the goal of this education). Quintilian has prepared the student to become a lawyer (in modern terms), a powerful patron who can defend his clients in the Roman courts. The leadership which his education imagines is that of a leader who can speak for others, subordinates, especially slaves, freedmen, children, women, the poor. The conflicts to be calmed, as presented in the plots of declamation, are a symbolic threat to the Roman order that arises from a conflict of roles and duties within the extended Roman family.

Questions for discussion

How does contemporary education attempt to shape the students' sense of their prospective
   adult role?
Does such an education communicate a sense of social responsibility, duty or entitlement?

Recommended reading

Bloomer, W.M. (2011) *The School of Rome*. Berkeley, Los Angeles, London: University of California Press.
Bloomer, W.M. (Ed.) (2015) *A Companion to Ancient Education*. Chichester: Wiley-Blackwell.
Cribiore, R. (2005) *Gymnastics of the Mind: Greek Education in Hellenistic and Roman Egypt*. Princeton, NJ:
   Princeton University Press.
Marrou, H. and Lamb, G. (1956) *History of Education in Antiquity*. Madison, WI: University of Wisconsin Press.
Russell, D.A. (Ed. and trans.) (2001) *Quintilian: The Orator's Education*. Vols. 1–5. Cambridge, MA: Harvard
   University Press.
Shackelton Bailey, D.R. (Ed. and trans.) (2006) *Quintilian: The Lesser Declamations*. Vols. 1 and 2. Cambridge,
   MA: Harvard University Press.

8 Imperialism and English schools
Education for, about, and because of empire

Jody Crutchley

Introduction

It has not been the nation state, but empires that have been the predominant organising structure of the world over the last few centuries. Defining empire is a tricky task, not least because it is emotive and can mean wildly different things to different people. In the colonies or the 'periphery', empire was frequently characterised by conquest, violence, land dispossession, political domination, oppression and even genocide. Whereas, in the 'core' or 'metropole' – the ruling state of an empire – imperial expansion was often reframed as a 'civilising mission', an attempt to export values, peace, democracy or religion to foreign lands, perceived as something to celebrate, stimulating patriotism and invoking national pride. Yet, despite these differences, it is possible to provide a basic definition. Identifying something as an empire requires two essential components: unequal power relations exerted by one entity over another, and the incorporation of distant, diverse and multi-ethnic territories that was not merely an annexation of adjoining lands. Imperialism is the related practice of extending empire through conquest, economic domination or exportation of culture. However, as new imperial historians have shown recently, the artificial and reductive separation of 'metropole' and 'periphery' obscures the complexity of how interlinked, transnational imperial 'networks' of empire operated in practice. For instance, it downplayed the extent to which practices and ideas in the colonies influenced the core; imperialism was not something that simply happened 'out there', it also came back home to roost. This means that empires have had a profound and sustained impact on the metropolitan development of social, cultural, political, economic and, of course, educational phenomena.

This chapter will explore the impact of empire on education through the case study of the British Empire and its influence on schooling. The British Empire was the largest empire that there has ever been, both in terms of land mass and population. At its apogee in 1922, it covered more than 1.3 million square miles and ruled over 450 million people. Yet, the familiar, uniform, red-painted map of the British Empire disguises the diversity and disparity of colonies ruled disjointedly and with varying degrees of control. The empire was actually a collection of settler colonies, colonies of direct rule, protectorates, mandates, treaty-ports, strategic fortress colonies, informal colonies and spheres of influence (Darwin, 2009). In recent decades there has been an increased focus on those involved in imperial rule. For instance, control sometimes depended on the involvement, or 'collaboration', of native peoples. Governors and rulers were largely drawn from the British elite, but there has been significant historical debate over the extent to which the working classes were involved in, or even aware of, the imperial project (MacKenzie, 1986; Porter, 2006). Consequently, one of the

DOI: 10.4324/9781003039532-9

key sites for exploring knowledge of and participation in imperialism has emerged in the study of British schooling. The following sections will engage with this research to emphasise the depth of the relationship between empire and education. The first section will examine the imperial content of school curricula, the second section will interrogate the purposes of English education by focusing on examples of education *for* empire, and the final section will illustrate how colonial activity affected the development of metropolitan schooling.

Questions for discussion

Think about your own schooling. What, if anything, were you taught about empire? Why do you think you were taught about it in this way?

Education *about* the British Empire

Lessons about empire and imperialism were never homogenous. Curricula, and therefore the imperial content taught, varied depending on age, social class and gender. In part, this was because education was not universal for the majority of English people in the nineteenth century. Before the 1870 Education Act, access to schools was patchy; working-class institutions were provided by voluntary, religious or philanthropic bodies. Most schools cost money. Although this was not an obstacle for those wealthy enough to attend grammar schools or the ancient public schools, for the poor, education was what would now be called a 'postcode lottery' with increased opportunities to benefit from cheaper, charitable options in London or other large, urban areas. Rural schooling was harder to come by, especially owing to chronic teacher shortages in the countryside (Pigott, 1987). If a child did make it to a school, it would not be for long. Legislation favoured the factory owners and industrialists' requirements for child workers, and even after the 1833 Factory Act and 1842 Mines Act, it was legal to work from the age of ten. The absence of any systematic substantial provision during this period has therefore been called 'the great Victorian omission' (Young, 1953: 165). Yet, even after the introduction of a formal state system of schooling from 1870, education remained differentiated. Secondary education remained largely the preserve of the British elite until 1944, while girls received different lessons to boys. For example, even by the turn of the twentieth century, it was obligatory for needlework to be taught to female pupils. From 1907 there were also expectations that girls would learn dairy work, cookery and laundry work. Thus, a child's social class, gender and age were key determinants of the kind of schooling they experienced, and this, accordingly, altered the kind of messages they received about the British Empire.

Imperial content and social class differences

The kinds of lessons about empire that children were taught were affected greatly by their social class. This section will start by exploring the direct link between elite education in the public schools, intended to equip the future governors and administrators of the British Empire for their future roles in public service abroad, and imperialism. At this time, the English upper classes tended to follow an educational pathway from preparatory (prep) school to public school, before attending the universities of Oxford or Cambridge. Actually, the term 'public school' is a misnomer, as these schools are still the most elite schools in England and include famous institutions such as Eton, Harrow and Rugby School. The name is a legacy from a time when the lack of geographical catchment areas or religious restrictions warranted the term 'public' (see Chapter 10, this volume). Studies of the recruits to the colonial service have credited the public schools with developing a 'distinctive governing ethos' (Kirk-Greene, 2000: 9–22). This is borne out in numerous studies that have shown that the content of public school education was rife with imperial propaganda. Hamad S. Ndee (2010), for instance, has called the public schools a 'powerful instrument of indoctrination' in upperclass society whose ethos helped provide pupils with an 'imperial mentality'. Features of this kind of imperial education included the use of religion as moral restraint to guard against the supposed perils of 'going native' once in situ; while the development of a games ethic through team sports such as rugby and cricket produced the prized British characteristic of individual resilience, or a 'stiff upper lip', and was also intended to stimulate team spirit. Together the simultaneous aims of fostering athleticism and physical development alongside the promotion of Christian ideals, morality and patriotic duty was known as 'muscular Christianity' (Mangan, 1981). In addition to this, public schools predominately followed a classical curriculum featuring Latin, Greek and Ancient History. Unlike the more vocational courses offered in many of the state-provided schools for the working classes, these syllabuses offered more opportunity for the study of the empires of the Romans and Greeks. Classics was thought to be relevant to a future career in the empire at the time: the child's mind would be trained without 'being weighed down with too much useless information' (Pearce, 1991: 47). Thus, much of the research suggests these were imperially steeped curricula, but it is important to remember that these schools were independent and did have diverse programmes of study.

Imperial content was relatively prevalent in schools for the working classes, too, but it took alternative forms to that of the elite schools. In the latter half of the nineteenth century, the 'payment-by-results' system that had made teachers' incomes dependent on only the 'three Rs' of reading, writing and arithmetic, and needlework for girls, curtailed the expanse of the elementary curriculum. Nevertheless, imperial topics were still taught through the use of reading material in English lessons. Stories about colonial peoples offered a way to make the text appeal to children's imagination, but the pejorative and simplistic presentations of other races also bolstered assumptions of British superiority (Castle, 1996). Elementary schools for the working classes emphasised loyalty and patriotism through obedience and civic duty (Chancellor, 1970). Classroom texts therefore taught the responsibilities of a child towards the nation and the imperial project in their position as a citizen of the British Empire, but drew on an exclusionary historical narrative of Anglo-Saxonism to shore up notions of English exceptionalism (Yeandle, 2006). In 1900 the *Code of Regulations for Day Schools* introduced a 'block grant' payment system for teachers to replace the grants by individual subject. This meant that the curriculum was now, effectively, enlarged. From 1904, explicit reference was made to the teaching of 'the growth of the British Empire' in the Board of Education guidelines for subjects such as History and Geography. Yet, not all schools adopted these subjects, and so the teaching of empire was more limited as it often lost out in the timetable to the demands of more prioritised subjects. Notwithstanding these constraints, it has been shown that content concerning the British Empire had a definitive place in the curricula for the working classes, albeit in a different way to those of the upper classes. The next section will highlight how these lessons on the empire were further differentiated by gender.

Research focus: Prep schools as the cradles and crèches of empire

In the nineteenth and twentieth centuries, prep schools prepared their pupils for entry to the public schools. They emerged as 'feeders' to the English public schools at the time of the Clarendon and Taunton Commission reports, and grew in popularity from the 1860s. They therefore played a key role in the continuation of social class division and reinforced class privilege (Benson, 2014). However, more recent research into prep schools has shown that they were also orientated towards the maintenance of the British Empire. Boys were moulded from their early days into their future roles in imperial service. For instance, in the 1920s, over 200 prep schools prepared their pupils for entry into the Royal Navy and the naval-entrance examination. Pupils from St. Cyprian's prep school ended up in careers that included the Indian Civil Service and the Colonial Service in countries such as Nigeria (Pearce, 1991). These institutions helped instil an imperial consciousness into their 8- to 13-year-old pupils through fostering physical fitness and through inculcating an imperial character. The imperial focus was acknowledged at the time, too. For instance, the memoirs of its headmaster, William Pearson, refer to the Temple Grove School in London as a 'cradle of empire'. Yet the prep school fulfilled another function in the British Empire as well. Men running the empire, serving with regiments in India or administrating vast tracts of African lands, needed to put their children into boarding while both father and mother were abroad and, thus, prep schools also became the necessary 'crèches of empire' (Leinster-Mackay, 1988).

Imperial content and gender differences

Lessons about the empire in British schools were subject to contemporary gender prescriptions for girls' and boys' education (Turnbull, 1994). First, the content of the lessons both sexes received in subjects such as Science and Mathematics was gendered. Girls learned about hygiene and nutrition in their Science lessons, while boys were taught more imperially minded, commercial science. In Mathematics, girls concentrated on learning the finances of the household, while boys dealt with trade-related, financial arithmetic. Similarly, in History, the commercial topics were largely intended for just the boys. Second, owing to the requirements in England for girls to learn Domestic Subjects, each sex had different timetabled quantities of subjects that contained imperial content, such as Geography. This meant that girls often missed out on the commercial, industrial and physical geography lessons, where much of the specific information about the different colonies, climates and trade routes within the empire might be taught to their male counterparts (Hunt, 1991). Overall, this meant that, owing to its location inside certain subjects, boys would receive more explicit instruction on the empire and its commerce than girls. However, this does not mean that girls missed out on imperial lessons entirely; instead, they learned about empire differently and experienced distinctive kinds of imperial content.

Girls were required to learn an expanded range of Domestic Subjects in the elementary schools from the early twentieth century. Subjects such as Cookery were deemed more important because infant mortality and children's health took on a new significance in public rhetoric. After the disaster of the malnourished and physically inept volunteers from the working classes for the South African

Wars, widespread concern to stimulate mothering skills grew out of anxieties about the future of the empire and for the 'English race'. Similarly, in the face of mounting international and imperial competition, particularly from Germany, imperial enthusiasts sought to address declining birth rates through promoting motherhood so that there would be a greater white population to help maintain and expand the territories of the British Empire. Anna Davin's (1978) study has shown that the conscious desire by educationalists to stimulate the development of hard-working and conscientious girls, who would go on to be wives and mothers, was justified at the time through the rhetoric of 'imperial motherhood'. An illustration of the contemporary educational link made between empire and mothering is evident in the report of the Interdepartmental Committee on Physical Deterioration in 1904, which called for a greater teaching in schools of household management to girls. Similarly, contemporary teachers of Domestic Subjects justified their profession through the rationale of the courses helping to prepare girls for their future roles as mothers of an imperial people (Copelman, 1996). Boys and girls therefore received different imperial messages to one another, especially as the teaching of empire to young women was bound up in ideas connected to the promotion of imperial motherhood.

Imperial content and age differences

Age was another way in which teaching about the British Empire was differentiated in English schools. Graduated courses of instruction became an increasing feature of education in England. In History and Geography, different levels of knowledge were required as children progressed through various learning 'standards' (Marsden, 1977). Younger children were taught less imperial content. Their historical and geographical courses focused on local topics, and their lessons about empire were filtered through the framework of imperial citizenship. Young pupils were encouraged to emulate the imperial heroes or 'Great Men' from their stories (Yeandle, 2015). As they grew, children began to learn specific imperial content about the colonies of white settlement, such as Canada, or interlinked trade, like the food supply. This meant that, either consciously or unconsciously, older pupils learned a version of empire that stressed 'sameness' and kinship, rather than difference (Barnes, 2011). For instance, in the curricular guidance issued by the Board of Education between 1909 and 1914, reference was made almost exclusively to British dominions – the colonies of white settlement that included Australia, Canada, South Africa and New Zealand – even though these colonies did not comprise anywhere near the majority of the empire. Contemporaries perceived dominions to be different to dependent colonies and more similar to England. Thus, they were represented disproportionately in imperial rhetoric in order to emphasise the cultural similarity of the British Empire. Overall, then, imperial content was taught predominately to older pupils in this period, and it was intended to emphasise kinship and connection.

One further way in which historians have shown that imperial content was differentiated by age concerns the presentation of colonial races and English superiority in school texts. School books helped to foster and perpetuate myths about the empire through the selective presentation of historical events (Glendenning, 1974). These texts bolstered assumptions of superiority by supplying racial stereotypes that helped justify claims that indigenous populations were 'an awkward and recalcitrant people who refused to accept the benefits of European commerce' (Chancellor, 1970). However, recent research has emphasised the crucial distinction between school reading books or 'readers' that were meant to teach reading skills to younger audiences and textbooks intended for older and more advanced pupils (Heathorn, 2000). Distinct imperial messages are evident in each. In the textbooks, the presentation of colonial peoples, such as Africans and Asians, showed them as barbaric and savage. The language that was used to describe these people to children emphasised difference so that the youth might be secured into the imperial ethos by distancing them from undesirable others (Castle, 1996). Textbooks for older children constructed other peoples as inferior and irredeemable; authors claimed that colonial races were incapable of advancement. Conversely, readers for younger children presented an alternative 'childlike and unsophisticated' portrayal of colonial peoples. These texts 'treated African and Asian as immature, that is, akin to the early English at the onset of their path towards "civilisation"' (Yeandle, 2015: 97–98). Despite these differences, it is important to note that both kinds of books presented essentialised and racialised views of the world. Marika Sherwood (2001) has argued that the books used in schools have not improved much since, and that the pervasiveness of these educational messages has contributed to the development of the racist attitudes (personal and institutional) still evident today.

Questions for discussion

Calls to decolonise the curriculum in Britain have been given fresh impetus in more recent years by movements such as Black Lives Matter. Why do you think it might be important to understand the way empire and race were taught in the past in order to contribute to the decolonising project?

Education *for* the British Empire

Schools were a vital part of the imperial project. The previous section has shown that the supply of English manpower for the imperial service came from elite public schools such as Haileybury College, which mainly supplied India (Prior, 2013). However, as the English electorate expanded, especially after the Second and Third Reform Acts, more people had a say in government. Imperialists concerned about the impact this would have on imperial decision-making felt that working-class voters needed instruction to enable them to understand the best future governance of the empire (Stedman Jones, 1983). Children in the elementary schools were taught imperial content so that they would be able to vote with the needs of the colonies in mind. Similarly, the military requirements of the British Empire affected education. In the public schools, battles – including those organised on Wednesday afternoon as cadet training, the spontaneous mortal combats among boys and the violent stand-offs between pupils and staff epitomised in the Marlborough College rebellion – were a regular feature of daily life (Mangan, 2010). Compulsory military training was part of many public-school curricula, while rifle practice with mock guns occurred at some prep schools. Militarism was part of the ethos of elite education and helped to equip pupils for their future roles as officers. In the elementary schools, the subject of Military Drill had been prevalent since 1870 (Penn, 1999). These lessons were intended to teach pupils about their duty to participate in military service to safeguard the security of the British Empire. Subsequently, these exercises have been shown to have promoted a prescriptive form of masculinity tied explicitly to perceived imperial need (Horn, 1988). Thus, the demands of manning and controlling an empire clearly had an impact on English schools because imperial governance structures required educational apparatus to sustain them.

By the turn of the twentieth century, fears about the continuation of the empire had heightened in England. Military failures in the South African Wars, alongside the poor treatment of Boers by the army and the atrocious condition of the English-run concentration camps, brought both the strength and the morality of the British Empire into question (Krebs, 1999). Simultaneously, there was international pressure on England's commercial interests, especially from Germany. One consequence of these growing fears was the identification of schools as a site where the widespread transmission of patriotic messages might rekindle support for the empire and provide a possible solution to its longer-term stability. The rallying slogan of 'empire and education' drew imperialist organisations, such as the Navy League, the Victoria League, the League of the Empire and the Primrose League, which sought to promote imperial patriotism and to strengthen ties of kinship (Hendley, 2012). In his seminal study, James Greenlee (1987) termed this group the 'imperial studies movement'. Further impetus was given to this movement from the 1920s, when the Royal Colonial Institute became the main custodian of its agenda (MacKenzie, 1984). This organisation helped diversify the media through which pupils were taught about their familial bonds to the empire. Lantern slides, which could be lent to schools through the post, were created to pique children's interest. The potential value of cinematography was explored, as well as interest expressed in the use of the Empire Marketing Board's posters in schools. These examples therefore highlight how diverse educational materials were utilised to promote imperial unity and cooperation to help ensure the continuation of the empire.

A potent example of a similar kind of education designed to promote imperial unity and patriotism was the celebration of Empire Day in English schools. The holiday was the brainchild of the 12th Earl of Meath, Lord Reginald Brabazon. He was an imperial ideologue who wanted to promote enthusiasm for the empire and imperial pride among young people (Springhall, 1970). Although Empire Day had begun in the colonies, it was celebrated in England from 1902, and annually thereafter, on 24 May, the birthday of the late Queen Victoria. In schools, the day often took the form of morning lessons on the empire and then a half-holiday, pageant or parade in the afternoon. According to Meath (1906: 96), the purpose of the instruction given on the holiday was to engender 'loyalty, obedience, self-sacrifice, courage and devotion to duty'. The event gradually gathered tremendous momentum. By 1915, the day was observed by over 25,000 schools and had an average attendance of just over five million people (English, 2006). Children waved flags, dressed up to represent the various colonies and sang songs about England's prowess and greatness. Although it is difficult to ascertain the extent to which children were affected by this kind of propaganda, it is certainly the case that the holiday had considerable longevity. It began to lose popularity only after being renamed Commonwealth Day in 1958. Empire Day is an important case study of the ways in which English schools promoted imperial sentiment. The holiday sought to stimulate a greater enthusiasm for empire amongst the youth and, in this way, helped to support wider imperialist aims.

Research focus: Teacher exchange schemes

In the interwar period there was a variety of informal educational tours and exchange programmes for teachers that also strove to promote political and cultural unity within the British Empire. Major Frederick Ney, a Canadian imperialist, organised empire rallies and tours for young people, as well as educational exchanges. Whilst on these tours, teachers were on a kind of imperial pilgrimage. They were expected to act as ambassadors for imperial unity by fostering understanding and generally acting as 'advertisements' for the imperial relationship (Harper, 2004). In contrast, the teacher exchange scheme promoted by the League of the Empire was envisaged to have a longer-term propaganda role. In this exchange, a metropolitan teacher would spend 12 months in a school in the empire, taking the place of a colonial teacher who would, in turn, teach back in England (Crutchley, 2015). The value of these programmes was thus perceived to be in the imperial outlook of the returned teacher who would promote closer association with empire to their pupils.

Education *because of* the British Empire

In the previous section, the ways in which education sought to promote metropolitan, imperial aims have been demonstrated, but it is important to note that the relationship between schools and empire was not a one-way street. Instead, developments in the colonies affected the evolution of education in England, and, similarly, educational shifts were often imperial rather than national. For instance, the House of Commons approved a grant for £20,000 to the main two religious societies that ran English schools in 1833. This was the first time that any parliamentary assistance for the provision of education had been given. Yet, only two years later, an equivalent grant of £20,000 was made to island colonies such as Jamaica, Barbados and Mauritius, in order to provide for the education of children of recently freed slaves. It is important to note that the sums granted in each region were of equal value. This demonstrates that the rhetoric about schools in the nineteenth century was changing simultaneously across the British Empire, not just in England, as education increasingly came to be seen as the government's responsibility (Swartz, 2019). The expansion of the English state education system from the late nineteenth century coincided with a period of rapid imperial expansion, notably through the partition of Africa. One of the clearest examples of imperialism affecting the development of education in England is the passing of the 1902 Education Act, which was influenced by the South African Wars. Geoffrey R. Searle (1971) has shown that a group of reformers concerned by the colonial difficulties in the battles with the Boers, epitomised by the sieges of the garrisons of Ladysmith, Mafeking and Kimberley, sought to overhaul English institutions like schools. This 'national efficiency' movement was in the belief that it would revitalise the state's sources of strength. These ideas, stemming from colonial losses, can be found in the wording of the 1902 Act, which sought to streamline national education by bringing all schools in England, those provided for by the state and those run by the religious bodies, within the same national system for the first time.

In the twentieth century, colonial educators had a greater input into the development of imperial education, especially those from the self-governing dominions of Australia, New Zealand and Canada. From 1907, the League of the Empire inaugurated and convened Imperial Education Conferences that brought together people working in education departments around the British Empire. Representatives from the Board of Education in England were in attendance, and resolutions from the conference had a wide impact as they were circulated in the Board's annual reports and suggestions to teachers. Initially, these conferences strove to promote the formal federation of imperial education through initiatives like common curricula, shared textbooks and empire-wide certificates that would allow greater teacher mobility. However, progress in this direction was interrupted when the conferences were suspended by the outbreak of the First World War. When they resumed in 1923, the increased influence of dominions limited the original aims (Greenlee, 1987). Instead, concerns from the old colonies of white settlement dictated the agenda. In this context, it is interesting to note that the conference held in 1927 dealt with issues of inaccurate information about Australia presented in classroom materials, which seems to have rankled with delegates from that dominion. In particular, the Australian Agent-General Sir Edward Lucas was disgruntled because a titled English lady had asked his wife whether Brisbane was the capital of Melbourne (Stephenson, 2010). The grievances raised here dispel any illusions that there was a greater interest in empire in England after the Great War. Dominions' concern for parity of treatment as they fought for greater recognition and legal freedoms is therefore evident here in their desire for school pupils in the metropole to be taught correct geographical information. Thus, the imperial desires of colonial educationists were having some effect on the content of English curricula.

Questions for discussion

What were some of the issues with the teaching of imperialism in English schools in the past? What reasons can you come up with for why the empire might not be taught as much in schools today?

Conclusion

This chapter has demonstrated that imperialism had a diverse range of effects on both the content and development of English schools. Debates over the complex and various ways in which the British Empire affected metropolitan education are ongoing. Therefore, there is a need for further research to be conducted in this area, not least because the legacies of lessons on race, Anglo-Saxon superiority and imperialism still impact education today (Marsden, 1990). In the case studies examined here, we have seen that imperial content taught in the classroom was not always explicit. Furthermore, lessons might differ for boys and girls, for older and younger pupils and for the upper and working classes, as each was expected to fulfil different roles in the empire in their futures. Concerns about the security and stability of the British Empire impacted on schools directly so that the schooling system can be shown to have been simplified, at least in part, as a response to the colonial pressure exerted by the South African colonies. In addition, the patriotic celebration of Empire Day, and the efforts of the 'Imperial Studies' movement, represented attempts to inculcate imperial pride among the English youth, even if it is difficult to determine the ultimate success of their endeavours (Rose, 2010). Perhaps the most direct link between the schools and the empire is in the training of the personnel needed to staff the administrative posts and the armies of the colonies. Indeed, links between some public schools and the Indian Civil Service were particularly strong. In the final analysis, it is evident that there was a significant and symbiotic relationship between empire and education. However, the impact was not even and homogenous, but patchy (Thompson, 2005). Certainly, it seems as if the elite public schools were the institutions most fervently affected by imperial sentiment (Porter, 2006). Nonetheless, what is clear from the preceding discussion is that the impact of the British Empire cannot be ignored. Any thorough consideration of the history of English schools *must* consider the influence of imperialism.

Summary points

- The British Empire was not something that affected just the colonies: it had a profound impact on the development of metropolitan ideas and practices, and this included education.
- The imperial content taught to children depended on their social class, gender and age.
- Education for empire included the inculcation of imperial pride and patriotism so that children's future participation in the imperial project might be assured.
- Schools helped to prepare some children for roles as imperial officers and soldiers.
- It is important to note that the colonies also affected the development of English schooling.
- Although the impact of the empire on English schools was uneven and diverse, with a greater influence on the elite public schools, it was still significant. This means that imperialism cannot be ignored in the history of education.

Recommended reading

Betts, R. (1990) A Campaign for Patriotism on the Elementary School Curriculum: Lord Meath, 1892–1916. *History of Education Society Bulletin*, **46**, pp. 38–45.

Mangan, J.A. (Ed.) (1988) *Benefits Bestowed? Education and British Imperialism*. Manchester and New York: Manchester University Press.

McCulloch, G. (2009) Empire and Education: The British Empire. In R. Cowen and A.M. Kazamias (Eds.), *International Handbook of Comparative Education*. Dordrecht: Springer.

Ploszajska, T. (1990) *Geographical Education, Empire and Citizenship: Geographical teaching in English schools, 1870–1944*. London: Historical Geography Research Group.

References

Barnes, F. (2011) 'Thinking from a Place Called London': The Metropolis and Colonial Culture, 1837–1907. *Journal of New Zealand Studies*, **12**, pp. 107–123.

Benson, J. (2014) 'Get a Blue and You Will See Your Money Back Again': Staffing and Marketing the English Prep School, 1890–1912. *History of Education*, **43**(3), pp. 355–367.

Castle, K. (1996) *Britannia's Children: Reading Colonialism through Children's Books and Magazines*. Manchester: Manchester University Press.

Chancellor, V. (1970) *History for Their Masters: Opinion in the English History Textbook, 1800–1914*. London: Adams & Dart.

Copelman, D. (1996) *London's Women Teachers: Gender, Class and Feminism*. Oxford: Routledge.

Crutchley, J. (2015) Teacher Mobility and Transnational 'British World' Space: The League of the Empire's 'Interchange of Home and Dominion Teachers', 1907–1931. *History of Education*, **44**(6), pp. 729–748.

Darwin, J. (2009) *The Empire Project: The Rise and Fall of the British World-System, 1830–1970*. Cambridge: Cambridge University Press.

Davin, A. (1978) Imperialism and Motherhood. *History Workshop Journal*, **5**(1), pp. 9–66.

English, J. (2006) Empire Day in Britain, 1904-1958. *The Historical Journal*, **49**(1), pp. 247–276.

Glendenning, F.J. (1974) Attitudes to Colonialism and Race in British and French History Schoolbooks. *History of Education*, **3**(2), pp. 57–72.

Greenlee, J. (1987) *Education and Imperial Unity, 1901–1926*. New York: Routledge.

Harper, M. (2004) 'Personal Contact Is Worth a Ton of Text-Books': Educational Tours of the Empire, 1926–1939. *The Journal of Imperial and Commonwealth History*, **32**(3), pp. 48–76.

Heathorn, S. (2000) *For Home, Country, and Race: Constructing Gender, Class and Englishness in the Elementary School, 1880–1914*. Toronto: University of Toronto Press.

Hendley, M. (2012) *Organised Patriotism and the Crucible of War: Imperialism in Britain, 1914–1932*. Montreal: McGill-Queen's University Press.

Horn, P. (1988) English Elementary Education and the Growth of the Imperial Ideal. In J.A. Mangan (Ed.), *Benefits Bestowed? Education and British Imperialism*. Manchester and New York: Manchester University Press.

Hunt, F. (1991) *Gender and Policy in English Education: Schooling for Girls, 1902–1944*. Hemel Hempstead: Harvester Wheatsheaf.

Kirk-Greene, A. (2000) *Britain's Imperial Administrators, 1858–1966*. Basingstoke: Palgrave Macmillan.

Krebs, P.M. (1999) *Gender, Race, and the Writing of Empire: Public Discourse and the Boer War*. Cambridge: Cambridge University Press.

Leinster-Mackay, D. (1988) *The Rise of the English Prep School*. Lewes: Falmer Press.

MacKenzie, J. (1984) *Propaganda and Empire: The Manipulation of British Opinion, 1880–1960*. Manchester: Manchester University Press.

MacKenzie, J.M. (1986) Introduction. In J.M. MacKenzie (Ed.), *Imperialism and Popular Culture*. Manchester: Manchester University Press.

Mangan, J.A. (1981) *Athleticism in the Victorian and Edwardian Public School: The Emergence and Consolidation of an Educational Ideology*. Cambridge: Cambridge University Press.

Mangan, J.A. (2010) Images for Confident Control: Stereotypes in Imperial Discourse. *International Journal of the History of Sport*, **27**(1-2), pp. 308–327.

Marsden, W.E. (1977) Historical Geography and the History of Education. *History of Education*, **6**(1), pp. 21–42.

Marsden, W.E. (1990) Rooting Racism into the Educational Experience of Childhood and Youth in the Nineteenth and Twentieth Centuries. *History of Education*, **19**(4), pp. 333–353.

Meath, R.B. (1906) The 'Empire Day' Movement. In M.J.B. Meath and R.B. Meath (Eds.), *Thoughts on Imperial and Social Subjects*. London: Wells, Gardner, Darton & Co.

Ndee, H.S. (2010) Public Schools in Britain in the Nineteenth Century: The Emergence of Team Games and the Development of the Educational Ideology of Athleticism. *The International Journal of the History of Sport*, **27**(5), pp. 845–871.

Pearce, R.D. (1991) The Prep School and Imperialism: The Example of Orwell's St. Cyprian's. *Journal of Educational Administration and History*, **23**(1), pp. 42–53.

Penn, A. (1999) *Targeting Schools: Drill, Militarism, and Imperialism*. Oxford: Routledge.

Pigott, D. (1987) Problems of Staffing the Nineteenth-Century Rural School in England: A Regional Case Study. *History of Education*, **16**(1), pp. 29–48.

Porter, B. (2006) *The Absent-Minded Imperialists: Empire, Society and Culture in Britain*. Oxford: Oxford University Press.

Prior, C. (2013) A Brotherhood of Britons? Public Schooling, 'Esprit de Corps' and Colonial Officials in Africa, c.1900–1939. *History*, **98**(2), pp. 174–190.

Rose, J. (2010) *The Intellectual Life of the British Working Classes*. New Haven, CT: Yale University Press.

Searle, G.R. (1971) *The Quest for National Efficiency: A study in British politics and British political thought, 1899-1914*. Berkeley, CA: University of California Press.

Sherwood, M. (2001) Race, Empire and Education: Teaching Racism. *Race & Class*, **42**(3), pp. 1–28.

Springhall, J.O. (1970) Lord Meath, Youth and Empire. *Journal of Contemporary History*, **5**(4), pp. 97–111.

Stedman Jones, G. (1983) *Language of Class: Studies in Working Class History*. Cambridge: Cambridge University Press.

Stephenson, M. (2010) Learning about Empire and the Imperial Education Conferences in the Early Twentieth Century: Creating Cohesion or Demonstrating Difference. *History of Education Review*, **32**(2), pp. 24–35.

Swartz, R. (2019) *Education and Empire: Children, Race and Humanitarianism in the British Settler Colonies, 1833–1880*. Basingstoke: Palgrave Macmillan.

Thompson, A. (2005) *The Empire Strikes Back? The Impact of Imperialism in Britain from the Mid-Nineteenth Century*. Harlow: Routledge.

Turnbull, A. (1994) An Isolated Missionary: The Domestic Subjects Teacher in England, 1870–1914. *Women's History Review*, **3**(1), pp. 81–100.

Yeandle, P. (2006) English in Retrospect: Rewriting the National Past for Children of the English Working Class, c.1880–1920. *Studies in Ethnicity and Nationalism*, **6**(2), pp. 9–26.

Yeandle, P. (2015) *Citizenship, Nation, Empire: The Politics of History Teaching in England, 1870–1930*. Manchester: Manchester University Press.

Young, G.M. (1953) *Victorian England: Portrait of an Age*. Oxford: Oxford University Press.

9 Documentary visions of the secondary modern school

Claire Tupling

Introducing the secondary modern school

This chapter examines two short documentary films, *The Three A's* (Central Office of Information, 1947) and *Our School* (Krish, 1962), made to celebrate the contribution of the secondary modern school to secondary education in England and Wales. The two films bookend the life of the secondary modern school. *The Three A's* was produced in the immediate aftermath of World War II as the 1944 Education Act, which reformed secondary education in England and Wales, was being implemented. The second film, *Our School*, was produced in 1962 just as popular and political support for secondary modern schools was ending and comprehensive schools were replacing the selective system that had dominated post-war secondary schooling for two decades.

Increasingly unpopular by the time *Our School* was made, the secondary modern school has received limited attention by historians of education, in contrast with the grammar schools existing alongside them. Post-war grammar schools are associated with excellence and opportunity. Associated with consigning those who failed the 11+, mainly children from the working classes, to a limited, vocationally focused curriculum and eventually to limited career choices, the secondary modern school has come to represent inferior education. In those parts of England where selection remains, such as Kent and Buckinghamshire, grammar schools are some of the highest-rated state schools. A nostalgic view of the grammar school persists which fuels calls for their widespread re-introduction, including proposals to allow new grammar schools outlined by the then prime minister, Theresa May, in 2016 (Morris and Perry, 2017; Baldi, 2022). Such appeals to return to this 'golden age of grammar schools' are rarely met with a corresponding celebration of the secondary modern school, yet the two schools co-existed within a selective system.

This focus on grammar schools obscures secondary modern schools. Yet there is historic evidence of an alternative vision of the secondary modern school that was being promoted during their lifetime. Both the films examined in this chapter reveal an imagined vision of the secondary modern school, a school where the majority of children would be educated through a broad curriculum and developed into productive citizens.

The next section of this chapter offers an overview of the history of the secondary modern school in order to place the films into their social and political context. The chapter then outlines a case for doing history through documentary films before examining the vision of secondary modern schooling presented in each of the films.

DOI: 10.4324/9781003039532-10

Secondary modern schools

After World War II and the 1944 Act, secondary modern schools provided schooling for the majority of 11- to 15-year-olds in England. They continued to do so until comprehensive schools became a more common feature of the secondary school landscape in the wake of shifting public attitudes against selection, coupled with government support of the reorganisation of secondary provision. Despite dominating the secondary school landscape in England, there is minimal history of the secondary modern school (McCulloch and Sobell, 1994) . Histories of post-war secondary education are dominated by a focus on the grammar school and subsequently the comprehensive school. In popular discourse, the apparent success of the grammar schools has been given considerable attention, whilst secondary modern schools have been highlighted only for their failure to provide working-class children with sufficient opportunities. Yet, the success of the grammar schools is arguably relative to the secondary modern schools' apparent failure.

There are notable exceptions. Taylor's (1963) study reviewed images of secondary moderns in the press. Hargreaves's study of social relations in a secondary modern school remains a key work and has made a significant contribution to sociological understandings of the culture of schooling (Hargreaves, 1967). Offering an 'internal and particularized account', it remains one of a small number of ethnographic studies of a single school (McCulloch and Sobell, 1994: 76).

The secondary modern school became a key part of educational provision following the 1944 Education Act (sometimes known as the Butler Act) which reformed secondary education across England and Wales. The act represented a significant shift in secondary school provision in that it legislated for free and compulsory secondary education and raised the school-leaving age to 15. A similar act was passed in Scotland in 1945 and in Northern Ireland in 1947, specific to the education systems of these constituent parts of the United Kingdom. The 1944 Act was not very radical in its ideas, however, as it was built on beliefs about the importance of secondary education that had developed over the first half of the twentieth century. Secondary schooling existed before the 1944 Act, but the provision varied between local authorities. Grammar schools offered either non-competitive places obtainable via fees, or competitive places achieved through successful completion of an 11+ examination. Secondary schooling for a limited number of working-class children had been available from the end of the nineteenth century. However, before 1944 a majority of children received only an elementary education, leaving school at 14.

The principle of secondary education for the majority of children, though less so the practice, had been established in the 1918 Education Act (known as the Fisher Act). This Act, relating to England and Wales, was significant legislation coming at the end of World War I. Raising the school-leaving age to 14, the Act also abolished the practice of 'half-time' whereby pupils were permitted to work half time as well as attend school. The removal of this provision can be seen in the context of the end of the war, when troops returning from the front would need to find employment. Most significantly, in the context of establishing the principle of secondary school education was the requirement for local education authorities to provide day continuation schools for pupils aged 14–18 who were not in full-time education. These schools, had they been widely implemented, would have offered young school leavers the opportunity to attend a school one day a week whilst working (Dean, 1970). The Day Continuation schools failed to be delivered, though there were some local education authorities (LEAs) who did make provision for mass secondary attendance at a local level. In 1921 another Education Act reaffirmed existing educational provision, and attitudes to secondary education continued to progress throughout the 1920s and 1930s.

The publication of *Secondary Education for All* in 1922 (Tawney, 1922) was a statement of policy advocating a variety of secondary school types of equal status. Its author, R.H. Tawney, a historian and Labour Party activist, intended it as a policy statement for the Labour Party. The ideas presented were then developed through the Hadow committee, of which Tawney was a member. Under the chairmanship of Henry Hadow, this consultative committee was establishment by the government's Board of Education, the equivalent to today's Department for Education. Between 1923 and 1933 the committee produced numerous papers on all stages of schooling in what became known as the Hadow Reports. The reports covered topics such as the differentiation of the curriculum for boys and girls (see Chapter 3) and psychological testing to assess 'educability'. The Hadow (1926) report on the education of adolescents recommended that schooling be differentiated into primary and secondary phases. Following the Hadow recommendations, many local education authorities had reorganised their schools to expand secondary provision, and a trend in extending school life was already evident by the time of the 1944 Act (Loukes, 1959).

Another Board of Education committee under William Spens published a report on secondary education in 1938. Known as The Spens Report, it built on the recommendations of the Hadow report for a differentiated secondary curriculum and outlined a tripartite system of schools with equal status. The types of school proposed were modern, technical and grammar (Board of Education Consultative Committee, 1938). This proposal for a tripartite system was further developed by the *Committee of the Secondary School Examinations Council* reporting to the Board of Education and chaired by Cyril Norwood. The Norwood committee reinforced the principle of a tripartite secondary schooling system, crucially rejecting suggestions of multilateral schools, or schools where all three types of curriculum would be taught. Norwood's report proposed three types of school: grammar, technical and modern to meet the needs of three categories of pupils. Entry to the different school types would be based on teacher recommendation as well as testing. The report suggested that the majority of pupils would be suited to a modern school with a broad curriculum. Departing from the recommendations of the Spens, and earlier Hadow reports, parity of esteem was not expected between the school types (McCulloch, 2007).

Rather than representing radical new ideas, the 1944 Act (and the accompanying Acts applying to Scotland and Northern Ireland) was a response, delayed by war, to the recommendations of the Hadow, Spens and Norwood reports (Jones, 2016). Implementation of the Butler Act became part of a post-war restructuring of education alongside wider welfare policies that included health and housing reforms. The 1944 Act did not sweep aside the existing system but complemented and absorbed new provision into the already-existing and expanding secondary school system.

A tripartite system was supported by the new Act, and indeed followed on from the recommendations of the committee reports of the 1920s and 1930s. The tripartite system was not prescribed, however, and the Act placed responsibility upon local authorities to make provision for secondary schooling according to local context (Tomlinson, 1991). Most LEAs opted to retain their existing grammar schools with an 11+ examination used as a selection process to identify those children deemed most suitable for such schools (Peterson, 1965). Some LEAs preferred multilateral schools where all three types were included in one school site, and there were some notable pioneers of comprehensive schooling, including parts of London and Anglesey (Crook, 2002). Neither was the proportion of children attending the three types of school equal across England and Wales. Wales, for example, had developed a more extensive network of grammar schools in the pre-war years with these being retained post 1944 (Elwyn Jones, 2002). In reality, the tripartite system was never fully realised, with only small numbers of technical schools in urban areas and even fewer in county areas (McCulloch, 2002).

The tripartite, or more accurately, the bipartite system and the 11+, remained in place in most parts of England and Wales until a growing dissatisfaction with the social class inequalities associated with selection, as well as political inclination, favoured a comprehensive system.

By 1963 the secondary modern had come to signify an inferior form of schooling (Carter, 2016). It had a limited curriculum in contrast to the grammar schools, which were seen as superior. In addition, there was the accumulation of evidence that grammar schools favoured children from the middle classes whilst secondary modern schools catered overwhelmingly to children of the working classes and offered them few opportunities for social mobility (Halsey et al., 1980). Most LEAs drew up plans for comprehensivisation by the late 1960s and the majority of secondary schools were comprehensive by the late 1970s (Rao, 2002).

The minimal history of the secondary modern school noted earlier in the chapter serves to marginalise the secondary modern, and this reinforces its historical status as an inferior school (Carter, 2016). In popular discourses, including documentaries, greater attention has been given to the grammar school, highlighting its success and lamenting its downfall. A BBC documentary, *The Grammar School: A Secret History*, used archive footage and interviews with former grammar school pupils to celebrate the contribution this type of school made and the opportunities it provided to children of 'modest' backgrounds (BBC, 2016). In positioning the secondary modern school as inferior, it would seem unlikely that a similar documentary could be produced celebrating this category of secondary school. Yet the two documentaries under consideration in this chapter did celebrate the secondary modern school, presenting a vision of what secondary moderns were envisaged to be.

Visions of schooling in documentary films

Historians of education have privileged the written text, for example diaries, documents and other written material, as sources of data about the past, but films also offer us an understanding about the past (Cohen, 1996). Films, including documentaries such as *The Three A's* and *Our School* are historical sources of education. Not only are they artefacts of the past, but as films, they present a contemporary vision of what the secondary modern school is, or what it was believed it should be.

Some forms of documentary film include propaganda films supported in their production by national governments, as in the case of *The Three A's*, or by other organisations such as trade unions, as in the case of *Our School*. These films were produced to promote a particular perspective that the government or organisation had an interest in. The British Documentary Film Movement produced a series of documentaries in the 1930s and 1940s. The films present a 'national projection' with an optimistic tone that imagines a better future for the nation (Chapman, 2015). A literate population and schooling systems that enable this are symbols of national identity, and these have been the subject of documentary films since at least the 1930s. In this tradition *The Three A's* presents secondary schools as sites contributing to national renewal, whilst *Our School* emphasises the secondary modern as a site focused on providing high-quality education, although in the shadow of the more highly regarded grammar schools.

The films are concerned with the real life of secondary modern schools. However, it is important to note that they are a representation of real life, rather than constituting an objective account of reality (Aufderheide, 2007). The process of film production is important in constructing the story told, as hours of filming are condensed into these short documentaries of less than half an hour.

Employing direct observation, the films hold an illusory power for viewers, giving us a sense of witnessing events such as the everyday life of a secondary modern school, whilst also being a cultural artefact that has been constructed to invite us to see that reality in a certain way. The films invite us to see the secondary modern school in a positive way, one that is providing high-quality education and is responsive to the needs of all its pupils. Documentaries of schooling have played a 'salient role . . . in depicting schools and schooling since the 1930s', but these films are under-researched as a source of history about education (Warrington et al., 2011: 458). In examining *The Three A's* and *Our School*, this chapter contributes to a history of the secondary modern school, not because the films provide a factual account of the secondary modern school, but because they provide a contemporary vision of what secondary modern schools should be.

The Three A's

The Three A's is a documentary film produced by the Central Office of Information (COI). Released in 1947, it observed everyday life at the Allertonshire County Modern School in Northallerton, North Yorkshire. Describing the Allertonshire as 'one of the pioneers' of secondary modern education, this new type of school is introduced with a sense of hope for the future, one that offers a 'better world' for children than the one their parents have experienced. This is reflective of national renewal with a reformed education system positioned as the vehicle for this. The relevance of this new type of schooling system is made immediately apparent by the narrator: 'A great majority [of children] will move up to receive the newest type of secondary education at a county modern school'.

Outlining the recent 1944 Act which granted secondary education to all children, the film emphasises the newness of the 'modern' school, still in the 'experimental stage'. The three A's of the title are explained from the outset, these being age, ability and aptitude. These three A's were ideas outlined in the 1944 Act underpinning how education should be organised (Tomlinson, 1991). Significantly, the film identifies these as characteristics of modern education, in contrast to the 3Rs which satisfied the expectations of the previous schooling system. The message being conveyed is that the present system is an improvement on the last, where most children would receive only an elementary education. Selection at age 11 is downplayed, and the pupils are certainly not positioned as 11+ failures. Instead, the film presents the secondary modern as a school that is applicable to most pupils because of its broad curriculum. There is minimal reference to the existence of other types of secondary school with references to grammar schools coming towards the end of the film, and only in terms of parity. The applied curriculum of the modern school is even implied to be superior to that of 'other' secondary schools which rely on knowledge tested through examinations. In reality, this view was not universally held. The lack of examinations, and therefore qualifications available, contributed to the status of the secondary modern as an inferior form of education, with some reputation being gained in subsequent years when these school routinely started offering public examinations (Southern, 2016).

The film suggests to the viewer that there is consensus around secondary modern schools. However, reality is more complex. The Ministry of Education did not insist on a tripartite system and expected LEAs to draw up their own plans. By 1947, the year this film was released, a survey of LEAs revealed over half intended to open at least one non-selective school (Simon, 1991). Plans to create comprehensive schools were already in place in several LEAs in England and Wales (Crook, 2010).

The film is observational in style, and we see children engaged in a variety of lessons; many are practical as well as gendered and include gardening, farming, sewing and cooking. Narration is provided over observations of children enthusiastically engaged in these activities, emphasising that the curriculum provided relates to what the pupils know and what areas of work they will likely move into. For example, the rural location of the Allertonshire school is highlighted for the rationale of a curriculum focused on 'country pursuits'. The narrator points out that the curriculum provided in other modern schools will differ according to the local industries surrounding the schools.

The modern quality of the school is emphasised throughout, and references to selection are avoided; yet the film does make an explicit attempt to claim parity of esteem between the secondary modern and grammar schools. The narrator states: 'The modern school teacher has the same training as the grammar school teacher and the same rates of pay'.

Presented as a factual statement, this reference concerning the comparable training and remuneration for teachers in the different school types may, arguably, be seen as an attempt to allay criticism of a segregated system. Yet selection and the division of schools was not universally accepted before or after the implementation of the 1944 Act, with this division in attitudes leading eventually to a popular movement towards comprehensive education (Tomlinson, 1991). Comprehensive schools were an option provided by some LEAs in the post-war years 'when the Secondary Modern School was still in search of its soul'. In this context *The Three A's* might be seen as an attempt to project a vision of what that soul might be (Dent, 1971: 135).

In the closing scenes of *The Three A's*, the viewer sees children gathering for assembly as the narrator concludes with the following statement:

> The Allertonshire children are already enjoying the happier childhood and the better start in life that the new scheme of secondary education has planned for them. When they grow to be men and women they will repay the country for its wisdom.

This statement reflects the belief in education as an investment for the future and reminds the viewer that this new form of schooling is better than what was available previously. This can be seen as an attempt to claim and convince viewers, including parents of children likely to experience such schools, that the secondary modern school is visionary and forward thinking. It would be unfair to dismiss *The Three A's* as mere propaganda in presenting such a message. Carter (2016) notes that there are limited studies focusing on the practices within different secondary modern schools in the post-war years, and that secondary moderns were often sites of experimental education, as claimed in the early scenes of *The Three A's*.

Whilst government-sponsored documentary films in the 1940s may have sought to promote an acceptance of selection by 11+ and a schooling system differentiated by ability, this did not mean that all were convinced of its argument. The secondary modern school competed for its reputation against the higher-status grammar schools, but also the early comprehensive schools. *The Three A's* is a film about the birth of the secondary modern school, but in spite of the enthusiasm of the film, 'the enthusiasm for the tripartite system was short-lived' (Southern, 2016: 23).

Our School

If *The Three A's* is about the birth of the secondary modern school, *Our School* might be seen to be about the death of the secondary modern school, not that it is fatalistic in its tone. Sponsored by the National Union of Teachers (NUT), the film, directed by noted documentary maker John Krish, was released in 1962. It presents direct observations of everyday life in a secondary modern school, and we are invited to believe we are witnessing real-life events. In reality the scenes were 'deliberately constructed' using the pupils and teachers of the school (Russell, 2011).

Filmed at the Francis Coombe Secondary Modern school in Hertfordshire, the film is celebratory of the secondary modern school at a time when the secondary modern was in decline and the number of comprehensive schools was increasing (Rao, 2002). *Our School* was released in the same year that the Conservative government–sponsored film *Comprehensive School* was released (Munden, 1962). *Comprehensive School* was filmed at Holland Park school in London, once dubbed 'socialist Eton' in reference to the number of Labour politicians whose children attended the school (Crook, 2013). The release of both films in the same year during a period of 'acceleration' of the 'comprehensive experimentation' is significant (Crook, 1993). The existence of secondary modern schools was being challenged by increasing numbers of comprehensive schools, with this move receiving cross-party support (Crook, 2002). Just as the secondary modern was in search of its soul when *The Three A's* was released, *Our School* could be said to be an attempt to reclaim that soul.

The opening title of the film is a clear statement about the quality and value of this type of this school:

> A Secondary Modern School is, in a sense, three schools in one. It must create an academic atmosphere, supply a technical and commercial training and care for those who learn with great difficulty. This film is an impression of a few hours in such a school.

Despite overt claims that secondary modern schools would have 'parity of esteem' alongside grammar schools, they were perceived to have lower status. Following the outcomes of the 11+ examination 'parents and pupils alike regard[ed] relegation to the modern school as a sign of failure' (Banks 1998: 224). Nevertheless, individual schools could respond in a variety of ways, and many secondary modern schools offered externally examined courses alongside the expected practical and vocational courses (Brooks, 2008). It is this kind of provision that is demonstrated in *Our School*.

The 'three schools in one' is a theme that runs through the film, and the viewer is shown how this school provides education suitable for the diverse needs of its pupils. This is an interesting claim to be made by a secondary modern school, given that comprehensive schools were increasingly positioning themselves as an alternative and, by definition, offering a school for a diverse pupil body. Sponsored by the NUT and as such representing its teacher members, the film can be seen as a statement in defence of the work of secondary modern schools and their teachers in trying to achieve what the advancing comprehensives were claiming to offer.

Most of the film is without narration, and the viewer is provided with a sample of lessons from a typical school day. Condensed into 27 minutes, the scenes take us from lesson to lesson, covering the range of subjects on offer, the diversity in the abilities of pupils and the different teaching styles provided. A key focus is the teacher-pupil relationships, and in a series of scenes we see teachers as encouraging, supportive and dedicated, but also firm. For example, the film shows us a technical drawing class where the teacher moves between pupils before focusing on one pupil who is offered suggestions for improving work. The director wants us to see a demonstration of the qualities of the teaching staff at Francis Combe. The direct observation style of the film invites us to see this for ourselves and to be convinced of the quality of the school.

There are other visual clues about the quality of the school. As the audience enters a classroom, there is a sign displayed on the wall which reads: 'Miracles are performed here daily. The impossible takes a little longer'.

This can be viewed as a deliberate attempt by director Krish to project a vision of a secondary modern school as a place where all can succeed in spite of the selective system. The sentiment expressed on the sign attempts to challenge the grounds for the inferior status of secondary modern schools. Further attempts at this are evident as John Krish's narration begins to draw the film to an end. He comments that some secondary modern schools: 'can try and keep up with the neighbours, especially if the neighbour is a grammar school'.

There is an absence of any overt criticism of the selective system; instead *Our School* highlights the ways in which this secondary modern school has striven to offer more opportunities to pupils, and there is an implied claim to achieve a parity of esteem with grammar schools (Banks, 1998). Krish's narration implores teachers, parents and employers to help children become 'dissatisfied with second best'. This is a clear rejection of the inferior status and a celebration of the secondary modern school. In the context of growing dissatisfaction with the secondary school, both at a grassroots level as well as a national political level, the film is a bold attempt to reclaim the soul of the secondary modern school (Crook, 2010).

Conclusion

This chapter has examined two short documentary films made to promote a positive vision of the secondary modern school. Secondary modern schools were introduced as part of a post-war reform of secondary education, though they were not a new idea. In the decades preceding World War II, government committees had enquired into developing schooling beyond the elementary stages, eventually leading to the 1944 Act. This represented a shift in educational provision in England and Wales, offering free secondary education beyond the age of 11 with a school-leaving age of 15. The selective system, though not prescribed, became a characteristic of the post-war secondary school landscape. Selection and segregation at age 11 was not universally accepted, and the secondary modern schools attracted a status of being inferior in comparison with the grammar schools. This is an oversimplification, and there is evidence of secondary modern schools as sites of experimental approaches as well as offering external examinations and offering a broad curriculum.

The two films, *The Three A's* and *Our School*, were made at different points in the life of the secondary modern school, but both present visions of schooling that can provide children and young people with a broad and relevant curriculum to prepare them for a life beyond school. Made at the birth of the secondary modern school, *The Three A's* presents a vision of a school in an experimental stage, but one that offers a better education than previous generations could experience. *Our School*, made in the death throes of the secondary modern school, is a bold statement about the quality of education experienced in such a school.

The films are valuable to historians of education not because they are definitive accounts of life in a secondary modern school, but because they constitute a resource of a contemporary vision about secondary modern schools.

Summary points

- The chapter provides a history of the development of secondary education.
- The 1944 Education Act introduced secondary education for all pupils with a selective tripartite system.

- The three types of school included grammar and technical schools which were selective by the 11+ examination, and secondary modern schools for those who 'failed' the examination.
- The tripartite system was intended to ensure that all pupils received an education suited to their 'ability', with parity of esteem between the schools. However, the secondary modern school endured low status against the grammar school and was seen to privilege middle-class pupils and families.
- The technical schools, intended to provide proved high-level education in industry-related subjects proved unpopular, and few were established by local education authorities.
- Because of the perceived social inequality of the tripartite system, in most LEAs it was abolished in favour of comprehensive schools in the late 1960s. The system is still retained in some LEAs.
- Two documentary films about secondary modern schools are analysed showing their attempts to present the benefits of secondary modern schools.

Recommended reading

Brooks, V. (2008) The Role of External Examinations in the Making of Secondary Modern Schools in England 1945–65. *History of Education*, **37**(3), pp. 447–467.

Carter, L. (2016) 'Experimental' Secondary Modern Education in Britain, 1948–1958. *Cultural and Social History*, **13**(1), pp. 23–41.

McCulloch, G. (2002) Local Education Authorities and the Organisation of Secondary Education. *Oxford Review of Education*, **28**(3), pp. 235–246.

McCulloch, G. and Sobell, L. (1994) Towards a Social History of the Secondary Modern Schools. *History of Education*, **23**(3), pp. 275–286.

References

Aufderheide, P. (2007) *Documentary Film: A Very Short Introduction*. Oxford: Oxford University Press.

Baldi, G. (2022) *Ideas, Institutions, and the Politics of Schools in Postwar Britain and Germany*. Basingstoke: Palgrave Macmillan.

Banks, O. (1998) *Parity and Prestige in English Secondary Education*. Abingdon: Routledge.

BBC (2016) *The Grammar School: A Secret History*. 23:00 20/09/2016, BBC4, 60 mins. Online. Available at https://learningonscreen.ac.uk/ondemand/index.php/prog/0234E83D?bcast=122535956 (Accessed 5 June 2022).

Board of Education Consultative Committee (William Spens) (1938) *Report of the Consultative Committee on Secondary Education with Special Reference to Grammar Schools and Technical High Schools*. London: HMSO.

Brooks, V. (2008) The Role of External Examinations in the Making of Secondary Modern Schools in England 1945–65. *History of Education*, **37**(3), pp. 447–467.

Carter, L. (2016) 'Experimental' Secondary Modern Education in Britain, 1948–1958. *Cultural and Social History*, **13**(1), pp. 23–41.

Central Office of Information (1947) *The Three A's: A County Modern School*, 1947. Online. Available at https://www.imdb.com/title/tt2878446/?ref_=ttco_co_tt (Accessed 23 November 2022).

Chapman, J. (2015) *A New History of British Documentary*. Basigstoke and London: Palgrave Macmillan.

Cohen, S. (1996) Postmodernism. The New Cultural History, Film: Resisting Images of Education. *Paedagogica Historica International Journal of the History of Education*, **32**(2), pp. 395–420.

Crook, D. (1993) Edward Boyle: Conservative Champion of Comprehensives? *History of Education*, **22**(1)), pp. 49–62.

Crook, D. (2002) "Local Authorities and Comprehensivisation in England and Wales, 1944–1974," *Oxford Review of Education* **28**(2–3), pp. 247–260. Available at https://doi.org/10.1080/03054980220143405 (Accessed May 13, 2023).

Crook, D. (2010) Local Authorities and Comprehensivisation in England and Wales, 1944–1974. *Oxford Review of Education*, **28**(2–3), pp. 247–260.

Crook, D. (2013) "Politics, Politicians and English Comprehensive Schools," *History of Education* **42**(3), pp. 365–380. Available at https://doi.org/10.1080/0046760X.2013.796777 (Accessed May 13, 2023).

Dean, D.W. (1970) H. A. L. Fisher, Reconstruction and the Development of the 1918 Education Act. *British Journal of Educational Studies*, **18**(3), pp. 259–276.

Dent, H.C. (1971) To Cover the Country with Good Schools: A Century's Effort. *British Journal of Educational Studies*, **19**(2), pp. 125–138.

Elwyn Jones, G. (2002) Policy and Power: One Hundred Years of Local Education Authorities in Wales. *Oxford Review of Education*, **28**(2), pp. 343–358.

Hadow, W.H. (1926) *Report of the Consulative Committee on the Education of the Adolescent*. London: HMSO.

Halsey, A.H., Heath, A.F. and Ridge, J.M. (1980) *Origins and Destinations: Family, Class, and education in Modern Britain*. Oxford: Clarendon Press.

Hargreaves, D. (1967) *Social Relations in a Secondary School*. London: Routledge and Kegan Paul.

Jones, K. (2016) *Education in Britain: 1944 to the Present* (2nd edition). Cambridge: Polity Press.

Krish, J. (1962) *Our School*. Online. Available at http://www.screenonline.org.uk/film/id/1078626/ (Accessed 23 November 2022).

Loukes, H. (1959) The Pedigree of the Modern School. *British Journal of Educational Studies*, **7**(2), pp. 125–139.

McCulloch, G. (2002) Local Education Authorities and the Organisation of Secondary Education. *Oxford Review of Education*, **28**(3), pp. 235–246.

McCulloch, G. (2007) *Cyril Norwood and the Ideal of Secondary Education*. Basingstoke: Palgrave Macmillan.

McCulloch, G. and Sobell, L. (1994) Towards a Social History of the Secondary Modern Schools. *History of Education*, **23**(3), pp. 275–286.

Morris, R. and Perry, T. (2017) Reframing the English Grammar Schools Debate. *Educational Review*, **69**(1), pp. 1–24.

Munden, M. (1962) *Comprehensive School, 1962*. Online. Available at https://player.bfi.org.uk/free/film/watch-comprehensive-school-1962 (Accessed 23 November 2022).

Peterson, A.D.C. (1965) Secondary Reorganisation in England and Wales. *Comparative Education*, **1**(3), pp. 161–169.

Rao, N. (2002) Labour and Education: Secondary Reorganisation and the Neighbourhood School. *Contemporary British History*, **16**(2), pp. 99–120.

Russell, P. (2011) *Our School in a Day in the Life: Four portraits of post-war Britain by John Krish*. London: British Film Institute.

Simon, B. (1991) *Education and the Social Order, 1940–1990*. London: Lawrence and Wishart.

Southern, A. (2016) *The Ministry of Education Film Experiment: From Post-War Visual Education to 21st Century Literacy*. Basingstoke: Palgrave Macmillan.

Tawney, R.H.H. (1922) *Secondary Education for All: A Policy for Labour*. London: George Allen and Unwin.

Taylor, W. (1963) *The Secondary Modern School*. London: Faber and Faber.

Tomlinson, J.R.G. (1991) Comprehensive Education in England and Wales, 1944–1991. *European Journal of Education*, **26**(2), pp. 103–117.

Warmington, P., Van Gorp, A. and Grosvenor, I. (2011) Education in Motion: Uses of Documentary Film in Educational Research. *Paedagogica Historica*, **47**(4), pp. 457–472.

10 Independent schools

Richard Riddell

Introduction

The place of independent schools within the English educational ecosystem has long been controversial. Paradoxically, independent schools are accused both of perpetuating elite privilege and of
failing to provide an adequate education for their learners:

> Probably the battle of Waterloo *was* won on the playing fields of Eton, but the opening battles
> of all subsequent wars have been lost there. One of the dominant facts in English life during the
> past three quarters of a century has been the decay of ability in the ruling class.
>
> (Orwell, 1941: 21)

This quotation, after the Duke of Wellington, was written by George Orwell, who was attempting to
characterise the nature of English life during the middle of the Second World War. Yet it provides a
useful statement of an often-made connection between Eton, one of the best known of English
independent schools, and the privileged nature of the young people that then, and now, attend Eton,
and, for want of a better term, those who rule and govern the United Kingdom.

Robert Verkaik documents some of these links in his pugnacious 2018 account, where he points
out that there had been 20 prime ministers, including the then incumbent, since the post was
established in the eighteenth century (out of 55). A further 18 were old boys (no women) of other
independent schools, with Westminster and Harrow schools being particularly predominant. And at
the time of writing (2022), the current prime minister had attended another well-known independent
school, and the oldest, Winchester College.

To return to Eton College, to give its full and proper title, with current annual fees (2022–2023)
at up to £46,296, its connection with those who rule us and have access to power – and who are
also generally wealthy – seems obvious. But Eton's place in the wider provision of schooling can
only be understood if its history, and those of all independent schools, is considered as a whole.
This is attempted here, but the chapter also argues that the history of independent schools has also
to be further considered, particularly since the mid-nineteenth century, alongside the development
of schooling for all young people. But first, some definitions.

Definitions of independent schools

'Independent', as a description of the schools being considered in this chapter, has become understood more recently to describe schools that are not dependent on, or responsible to, the 'state' at

DOI: 10.4324/9781003039532-11

national (London) or local levels (such as your local council). Nor do they have to implement such requirements as a national curriculum. The word 'independent' is clearly intended to do some persuasive work for those coming to these matters for the first time, because being 'independent' is obviously such a good thing, so their staff can decide what to do in the best interests of their students without outside 'interference' (another persuasive term). This is not quite an accurate description, however, of what they are able to do.

More confusing, or persuasive, is the term 'public school'. This came to prominence quite recently in the schools' history following the publication of the Clarendon Commission in 1861 (more on this in the section "Nineteenth-century developments"). The term denotes just a small number of independent schools that became known as the Clarendon schools because of the Commission's prime focus on them. They are the nine 'top' schools – Eton, Winchester, Westminster, Harrow, Charterhouse, Rugby, Shrewsbury, St Paul's and Merchant Taylors'.

To be more precise, all these independent schools are in fact *private schools*: businesses in the education sector that derive their income from charging fees to (usually) the parents of the young people attending them, and not from the taxpayer, although this too is not quite accurate, as we shall see. Most countries worldwide have a mix of schools to serve children, families and communities. *State schools*, or more properly, *public schools* (as they are termed accurately in the United States because they are in the public sector), are those funded by the taxpayer and overseen in some form by local or national governments.

Generally, the expectation is that these state schools are free to their children and their parents and, in line with international expectations, represent an attempt to make education universally available, especially literacy and numeracy, as a human right. In many countries, including the United Kingdom, however, parents may be expected to make some financial contribution, from buying uniforms to paying small fees. More confusingly still in some countries, the responsibility of the state to provide schooling up to a certain level is provided by private sector schools or organisations (sometimes not for profit) such as Kunskapsskolan in Sweden and UK-based organisations such as GEMS and the Varkey Foundation, often, but by no means solely, in developing countries.

Questions for discussion

Rehearse to yourself what you understand by the term 'independent schools'. What does the term mean?

What are some examples that you know of independent schools and state schools?

The development of independent schools until the nineteenth century

Independent schools are among the oldest institutions in the country, with some reflecting the wealth of their privileged benefactors, having among the most historical and beautiful buildings as well. But obviously, education in the broadest sense – and particularly after human beings discovered a need to keep records and communicate over distance – has been taking place for millennia. We know that wealthier Roman families, for example, ensured their children were educated (mostly their sons) by having a private tutor (Verkaik, 2019), usually a slave, and often in the Romans' case, a Greek.

The most important institution to survive the fall of the Roman Empire, with Christianity established for over 100 years as the de facto state religion, was the organised Christian church. Besides the church's own need for literate monks (in Latin), and choirs to sing the services of the day, there was also a need for the nobility (given a title by the Crown) and wealthier families to have educated boys (again) for their own record keeping, legal documents, estates bookkeeping, accounting and correspondence. The development of schools attached to churches and cathedrals began early, therefore, possibly with the King's School in Canterbury (Verkaik, 2019) in the seventh century CE, but by the Middle Ages there were also local grammar schools in market towns, often charging modest fees (Turner, 2015).

But the first recognisable, we would say, independent or public school, Winchester College, was founded in 1382 by William Wykham, Bishop of Winchester, who also, in the fashion of the time, held high offices of state. Over the next few hundred years, the precursors of what we understand now as these schools, were successively founded either by churchmen (like Wykham), nobles, the king (e.g. Henry VI's Eton in 1440), and gradually other such interested groups including livery companies (guilds of merchants) such as the Merchant Taylors' (1561). Because these schools were founded, or endowed (that is with a sum of money), many of them still bear the name of their benefactors (such as Winchester or Merchant Taylors'). But it must also be understood that these foundations all included a sum of money for the education of 'poor scholars', that is without parents with the means to pay. Scholars received 'scholarships' and, although scholarship boys remained at the heart of these foundations, many of these schools began, not long after their foundation, to take in other boys paid for by their parents. This reflected developing economic need, richer parents with ambitions for their families, and noble families who were seeking a broader education than private tutors could provide in the home, though these continued to be employed into the twentieth century (Turner, 2015).

The much wider networks of grammar schools, later often termed 'endowed schools' – for example, such as that attended by William Shakespeare in Stratford on Avon – continued to serve the needs of merchant families but very often without foundations, requiring the small fees mentioned earlier – such as 5 shillings and a quarter (about £100 in 2023 money) in the sixteenth century and, for children from poor families, far less. These schools have been considered separate from the public schools, but it is not always as simple as that. What is now known as the independent Manchester Grammar School, for example, was founded by the Bishop of Exeter in 1515 as Manchester School, with a foundation for poor scholars.

The important issue for what we now know as 'public schools', however, was how the non-scholarship boys began to increase in importance and number (Verkaik, 2019) and diminish the significance of their scholarship peers. By many accounts, including those previously addressed, they became looked down on snobbishly, as the identification of nobility and wealth with these 'top' schools proceeded apace, and the emergence of Verkaik's 'posh boys' as representatives of a separate class.

At this point, it is also worth mentioning the curriculum and teaching methods of the schools at the time. The most common pattern of schooling was to have one large schoolroom only – a pattern across both 'public' and grammar schools – with a number of 'masters' teaching (termed 'beaks' at Eton), sometimes with assistants, later 'pupils' or apprentice teachers. This is why many surviving old school buildings do have this sort of schoolroom at their heart. This was properly 'instruction' rather than what we describe as 'teaching' today, with memorisation, sometimes by rote, at their heart, and the copying of Latin texts, often without discussion. Corporal punishment, often cruel and excessive by any humanitarian standard, sometimes causing injury, was a major daily part of school life. It should be remembered, however, that corporal punishment was only made illegal at UK state schools in 1986, with independent schools in England and Wales not following until 1998, and in Scotland much later. These formal methods (and the basic 'classics' curriculum) survived for many years and, for many richer families, was complemented by the private tutors they continued to employ.

Questions for discussion

Are there any schools where you come from with an ancient foundation? What do you know about them?

How would you describe the lessons for their future lives that young people (boys to begin with) would take away from being educated in the ways described?

Nineteenth-century developments

The nineteenth century is often considered an important transitional turning point from the older, agriculture-based society, originally rooted in feudalism, to a modern industrialised one. The needs of industry for a mass workforce, allied to great changes in the production of food (the industrial was preceded by the agrarian revolution), led to vast migration from the country to cities and towns and their new factories. As society changed (there are many accounts of this, but try G.M. Young's (1969) book on the Victorians, originally published in 1936, or Harris, 1994), this had several implications that were also to require changes in education.

One was the need for greater levels of literacy and numeracy, for the whole population, because of the developing needs of the economy and employment. Another was the increasing importance of science and technology to industrial development and investment. Another – it was argued by many concerned Members of Parliament in discussion of the 1870 Education Bill – was the need for greater and earlier learning of respect and discipline in urbanised areas where the old ties of church and family were much weaker. And yet another was the need for (literally) an army of officials and others to help run and police the growing British Empire, which provided both a source of raw materials for the factories and a ready market for its exports. The introduction of competitive entry to both the armed forces and the civil service – no longer would it be possible, for example, to become a senior army officer by buying a commission – began to highlight the need for better and relevant career preparation in the curriculum provided in the independent schools.

These social and economic changes required new provision for all the population, and the 1870 Education Act led to compulsory education for all children up to the age of 13 from 1880. But for a 'ruling class', as Orwell termed it, including those overseeing or investing in the new industries, a new understanding of mathematics and science was required, neither of which was available in the traditional 'independent' or public schools with their curriculum based still largely on the classics of Latin and Greek. Although, as Turner says, the older noble families continued to employ tutors to complement the 'education' received at public schools, the increasing requirements of society demanded more than this, animated by increasing concern about other competitor industrialising nations such as France and Germany and whether they were doing things better over there. At the same time, the nineteenth century had seen the foundation of new day schools in the developing urban areas, such as Liverpool, Edinburgh and Leeds, many of whose children were members of the expanding professions such as law and medicine that urbanisation required, as well as service officers' children and those of the officials, industrialists and merchants. All these families saw the old mantra of 'First – Character, Second – Physique, Third – Intelligence' of the older public schools as insufficient preparation. As a result, and despite the increasing importance of the so-called 'modern side' in the grammar schools, a term still in use in some independent schools and denoting a greater emphasis on the sciences (not necessarily mathematics), a number of commissions were set up, and change became endemic.

The most famous of these was the Public Schools Commission, called the 'Clarendon Commission' because its chair was the Earl of Clarendon. It was originally set up to examine financial probity, but it spent most of its report commenting on the curriculum. The Commission's conclusions, sometimes fuelled by comments from the universities that received the graduates of the public schools, embraced standards in English, Mathematics and the knowledge of History and Geography. The Commission, as has been said, confined its attention to the nine top public schools. However, the later Taunton Commission, properly termed 'the Schools Inquiry Commission', went much further in 1868 in commenting on all the public and independent schools and took in the education of girls for the first time. It castigated a system where the need for 'accomplished' young women limited the scope of their education.

This was not seen as a problem by the middle and upper classes, of course, where women did not generally have any economic role, and in whose households it was considered anathema and embarrassing sometimes to have wives more educated than their husbands. But the scope of the curriculum for girls came more and more into the public attention from the 1870s onwards, some of it driven by pioneers of girls' education such as Dorothea Beale, the founder of Cheltenham Ladies' College. The Girls' Public Day (= non-boarding) School Trust was set up in 1872, promoting a curriculum of 'English grammar and literature, French, German, and elementary Science, with Classics and elementary Economics for the older pupils' (Turner, 2015: 151). This trust, now termed the Girls' Day School Trust (from 1906), is still going strong with 23 independent schools and two sponsored academies (see the next section).

Key twentieth-century developments: Relations between independence and the state

Overall, though, despite the original foundations for educating poor scholars, precious few children from working-class backgrounds were attending any of the independent schools. The 1902 Education Act, however, required local education authorities (LEAs, which the Councils became, replacing the direct School Boards of the 1870 Act) to provide secondary education for the children of families living in their areas. This was done in a number of ways, but the flowering of new council grammar schools from the early 1900s, many of whose buildings remain in use, was one result. At the same time, LEAs could purchase places at existing independent schools – a practice that continued until the 1980s in some places – without the need to build new schools. It is important to remember that many of the new Council grammar schools, as well as the providers of these places at independent schools, continued to be able to charge small fees, until the 1944 Education Act (see later in this section).

It is not possible to omit mention of the First World War (1914–1918) even in this very brief history of independent schools. Their old boys suffered the worst casualties: in contrast with just over 10 per cent of the general population who died, some independent schools such as Harrow (Turner, *ibid*) lost nearly a quarter of their boys, with the day schools commonly losing between 10 and 20 per cent. This was partly due to the predominance of independent and grammar school boys in the commissioned ranks (i.e. the officers), based on the strength of their schools' own Officer Training Corps, but officers also wore distinctive uniforms with boots and baggy trousers, making them prominent targets. At Ypres in 1916 and 1917, a furious series of battles, Eton College alone lost over 300 ex-boys.

Arguably, the greater levelling in societal expectations that began in the trenches had two effects. First, the 'separateness' of those from the independent schools, especially the ancient foundations, and the deeper class divisions that it signified (the 'poshness') became even more obvious from close quarters, especially as economic circumstances worsened from the 1920s onwards and in the Great Depression that followed, only really alleviated when the Second World War began with the shift to armaments manufacture and an economy on a war footing. Second, the desire for change developed across all aspects of society, particularly brought into relief during the 1930s, and which deepened during the course of the war. It resulted in the national coalition government-appointed Beveridge inquiry. The publication of its Report in 1944, identifying the five 'evils' affecting society, one of which was 'ignorance', led to the 1944 Education Act and the provision of universal free secondary education for all young people.

The effect was to change the landscape of selective schools and to increase the competitive pressure on the independent schools. This was further intensified by the 1944 Act, allowing nearly 200 independent schools, at which LEAs had been able since 1902 to purchase some places, to offer a quarter of their places to young people from local state schools to be funded from a 'direct grant' from the central government, in addition to the further quarter to LEAs, if they paid the fees, which many did. For some independent schools, such as the North London Collegiate School, this new access to public money provided a budgetary lifesaver in the increasing competition. But at the same time, others, such as those of the Girls' Day School Trust, found the competition from new council-founded grammar schools challenging, said so publicly and did not want to change.

For ambitious parents, the prospect of a selective and academic education became available at any of a combination of the new grammar schools, direct grant schools or the traditional independent and public schools that did not wish to take the state's money. The expansion of more academic secondary education in turn increased the competition for university entrance, putting pressure on the older independent schools, both the boarders and the day schools, to change. Although school certification was not new (the old 'School Cert' at 'lower' and 'higher' levels), this became even more focused with the 1951 introduction of the General Certificate of Education (GCE), at Ordinary Level for age 16 ('O' Level), and Advanced ('A') Level at 18. The latter is still with us, began to feature much more strongly for competitive university admissions and is what a later prime minister, Tony Blair, referred to as the (untouchable) 'gold standard' when reform was mooted in 2005.

The net effect of these pressures, the increased significance of 'credentialism' and the greater ambitions of middle-class parents as the relative proportion of middle-class jobs in the economy was increasing, began a process whereby the independent schools developed a much greater emphasis on examinations and academic outcomes. At that time, it began with looking forward to university entrance. Arguably, this process was intensified with the opening of 'plate glass' universities from the 1960s such as York and Sussex. But the comprehensivisation of secondary schools driven by Labour Governments after 1964, closing grammar schools and moving away from selection at 11 years old, provided a new market opportunity.

The access of middle-class families to schools of their choice in an increasingly competitive and aggressive school-places market has become one of the defining and structuring issues of school history to understand since the 1970s (Ball, 2003, among many others). It should be understood as such, even when masked by discussions that emerged about allowing the 'brightest and the best', disadvantaged or impecunious children access to the 'best schools' as their numbers were allegedly being diminished. This has become the tenor of much public discussion in recent years about independent schools, which are (they assume) the best schools. Reading any independent school website will affirm this statement.

Although there is much public nostalgia for the era of the LEA grammar schools, through which many young people from disadvantaged backgrounds attained professional status, this was due primarily to structural changes in the economy occurring at the time rather than anything these many fine schools did (Goldthorpe, 2016), including the direct grant and other independent schools. It needs also to be remembered that the school-leaving age remained at 15 until 1974, so that many young people actually left school, even grammar school, at that age without qualifications. Beyond that, we know that grammar and other selective schools were attended predominantly by mid-dle-class children from early on, however impecunious their families (Jackson and Marsden, 1962).

This is the context in which to understand the debates and controversies of education reform for the subsequent 50 years. The Direct Grant system was abolished in 1976 by the then Labour Government. The huge public controversy that followed *was* about 'bright boys and girls' having access to these schools, much to the dismay of those leading comprehensive ones. Many direct grant schools decided now to go fully independent in the sense described at the beginning of the chapter. However, the incoming Conservative Government of 1979 led by Margaret Thatcher had promised, as part of introducing 'parental choice' in 1980, to introduce a *replacement* for the direct grant scheme. It was to be called the Assisted Places Scheme, resulted from discussions between the Conservative Party while in opposition and public and former direct grant schools, and sup-ported the first intake of children, who had to satisfy the selective entry requirements of the schools, in September 1981. Throughout its life, the scheme was presented publicly by both Government and the schools concerned, as somehow a twentieth-century version of the provision for 'poor scholars'. Poor some of the students may have been, but we know that the scheme, in turn abol-ished by the incoming Labour Government of 1997, served predominantly the children from mid-dle-class families (Edwards et al., 1989), just as had the grammar schools.

One final piece of the jigsaw has been the attempts by governments of all political persuasions to encourage joint working of some sort between independent schools and state schools, driven partly by the fact that many of the older foundations of the schools we have been discussing had charitable status. In practice, this has been focused on the need to establish what this charitable work was, because in return these schools paid no business rates (a local taxation) and did not need to charge value-added tax on their fees for parents. The 'partnership' work has ranged from sharing facilities such as playing fields and swimming pools, 'lending' teachers in shortage subjects (espe-cially post-16) and, more recently, 'sponsoring' academies (helping improve them), which have become the predominant form of governance in secondary schools since 2010. At the time of writing, 936 schools were involved in 'independent state school partnerships' (ISC, 2022).

Thus, the framework for understanding the role and place of independent schools in contemporary society today, and the nature of the public discussion about them, has in reality been set by the hugely competitive nature of the contemporary school-places market, the 'pecking orders' it has exacerbated and the desire to tap into successful 'independent school DNA', set against the rapidly changing nature (again) of the UK economy. Much of the educational argument has been about the access of 'bright,' more disadvantaged students to the 'best' schools. All this continues to be underpinned by a variety of unspoken and largely inaccurate assumptions about which schools are the best, who should have access to them and how.

Questions for discussion

What are the best schools, do you think, and who should have access to them?
Can some state schools be better than independent schools? How?

Independent schools today

Currently, there are about 2,600 private schools in the United Kingdom, educating about 7 per cent of children and young people, but about 18 per cent post-16. About 80 per cent of the young people attending independent schools in the UK attend schools that are members of the Independent Schools Council (ISC, 2022). This is an advocacy body dating from 1974, set up originally to campaign against the abolition of the Direct Grant system (see the previous section). Outside this group, however, other independent schools provide intense education, sometimes residential, for children with more severe special educational needs or disabilities (SEND). Places at these schools – sometimes costing more than £100,000 a year – are purchased by local authorities, which have the statutory responsibility to meet these children's needs. We do not have the space in this chapter to discuss these schools nor the place of some of the older charities in their development, such as the Royal National Institute for the Blind, the National Autistic Society and the National Deaf Children's Society.

Despite these SEND schools' importance, public discussion in the UK is often concerned with the elite nature (and social purpose) of the independent or private schools, for the reasons discussed. The notion of 'elite' was highlighted earlier and derives – to recap – from their history, their identification with the 'ruling class', notions of 'posh boys' (and now girls, presumably), highly selective entry requirements (though in fewer than 50 per cent according to the ISC) while they have disappeared elsewhere, their fees and, therefore, who is included and, more significantly, excluded by them.

ISC-affiliated schools, including the 'top' ones, say that some £480 million was spent in 2022 on means-tested benefits, which helped the parents of 180,524 young people to pay fees, or about 34 per cent of the total. Other young people receive help for other reasons, but only about 6,000 young people receive 100 per cent help with fees, or just over 1 per cent of all attending, a small minority of a minority. Care must be taken in drawing conclusions from these figures, but fees are clearly possible only for families with higher levels of income, even with assistance. This in itself is important, as academic performance in the UK and other developed countries is often also associated with social background, often measured by income: school performance is a *cipher* for background.

In practice, this has led to 93 per cent of young people who leave ISC schools going on to university, with 58 per cent attending 'top 25' institutions (ISC, 2022 – they mean largely Russell Group research-intensive universities, including Oxford and Cambridge). More than 25 per cent of students offered places at the 'top 25' were from ISC schools in 2020, but 37 per cent at Oxford and 32 per cent at Cambridge.

These results carry through to the dominance of professional occupations, with the predominance from these two universities particularly staggering: 71 per cent of senior judges (65 per cent from independent schools overall), 56 per cent (59 per cent from independent schools) of heads of central government departments and 44 per cent (44 per cent from independent schools) of top journalists, to give a few examples. More of this data can be found in *Elitist Britain* (Sutton Trust/ Social Mobility Commission, 2019). In fact, recent research (Reeves et al., 2017) has found that young people attending the 'top' nine (Clarendon) public schools were, in the period from 1897 onwards, 94 times more likely to enter elite positions in society (as measured by occupation and income) than *all other schools put together*. So these are very successful institutions.

We also now know something about the highly effective mechanisms whereby they achieve these outcomes with young people, often from the early years of secondary schooling. They include a relentless focus from an early age on examination outcomes (and a restricted choice of subjects better regarded by targeted 'top' universities), coaching for self-presentation including writing university applications, and regular access to people from similar backgrounds who have been successful in their careers (Riddell, 2010). We know that some state schools apply these mechanisms too, but in more limited numbers, as only a minority of their students (and their parents) might require them.

In a sense, if access to these top professional positions depends on good academic qualifications, preparation and self-presentation, then these high-performing independent schools *will* be over-represented in these 'top' universities and 'top' professions. These are the people best suited, the schools argue, to go on to the best universities and to run our society (Riddell, 2010). And this is also, very often, what the students from these schools tell themselves too, as Verkaik (2019) and Green and Kynaston (2019) argue, together with many others. But you may be surprised to know that winners of Oscars, BAFTAs and BRIT awards are also disproportionately from independent schools (Kirby, 2016). And 32 per cent of Team GB's medallists at the Rio Olympics in 2016 were from an independent school, though this was down from 36 per cent at the London games.

More recently, we have also come to understand some of the mechanisms whereby, *after* independent school, and *after* university, all the wider group of professions make assumptions about the 'best fit' for vacancies they need to fill. Most of their criteria, apparently, after academic performance, indeed include how candidates present and describe themselves to prospective employers, and this too seems to be a cipher for the 'products' of independent schools and the top universities (Friedman and Laurison, 2019).

Unsurprisingly, therefore, in the context of discussion in developed countries about limited and slowing social mobility and apparently restricted social access to the professions, this elite-reproductive role of independent schools – often the children of elites go to the most elite schools and then often the elite universities – is often commented on academically, politically and in print, broadcast and social media. This is why the existence of a well-funded private sector of independent schools remains politically controversial in some quarters, leading more recently to calls for the revoking of their charitable status and tax advantages.

To conclude, and to return to the George Orwell quotation with which this chapter began, the concern Orwell had was, in addition to where the 'ruling class' came from, and how, is whether they are any good or not at what they do. If the process of their selection has been 'fair' and based on 'merit' – and this continues to be doubted by Friedman and Laurison, among many others – it may not matter *if* the government, industry, commerce and public services appear to be led efficiently and well. But, besides the wider political discussion that is beyond the scope of this book, this also has been questioned by academics such as Davis (2018) as well as Reeves et al. (2017). Davis in particular found some destructive tendencies in current national leaders and leaderships. Discussion about what sort of country the UK will be after emerging from the Coronavirus epidemic – and who leads it and where they come from and how they are chosen – will continue long after the publication of this book.

Questions for discussion

How have independent schools become so effective over the years?
Do they produce the 'best people' for the 'best jobs'? Isn't that what we need?
Should they receive privileged tax status?

Summary

- The ancient origins of many independent schools today reflect a steadily growing desire and need over the years to educate ever-wider groups of the population.
- What are often termed 'public schools' in the UK are actually an elite group of fee-paying independent institutions, many boarding.
- The best way to understand the history of what we now term 'independent schools' is alongside the provision made by the state of free schooling for the whole population. Very often, this has involved discussion about whom to select for which schools and on what basis.
- About 7 per cent of children in the UK are educated in the independent sector currently, with more at post-16. They are 'over-represented' in higher education (in other words, they attend in greater numbers and proportions than their size might warrant) and at the top of key professions.
- The fact that only about 1 per cent of young people attending independent schools receive 100 percent of relief on their fees suggests that they are not socially representative of the wider population.

Recommended reading

You will have gathered from this chapter that much of contemporary writing about independent schools is partisan, so you must read carefully and try to remain objective. In this sense, you might find dipping into James and Lunnon (2019) helpful, as it sets out voices from within the sector about the future challenges facing these schools – remember this is what they are.

Some of the early history is well-covered by Turner in particular, but you will find partisan treatments in a number of the books below; Green and Kynaston in particular received extensive coverage when it was published.

One of the problems – as you will also perceive from the titles in the References – is that gaining research access to independent schools has proved difficult for many academics in recent years, because a partisan treatment is exactly what is feared! You may find Chapters 2–4 in the author's own 2010 book helpful, however, as they present first-hand interview data from two independent schools in different parts of the country.

References

Ball, S. (2003) *Class Strategies and the Education Market: The middle classes and social advantage*. London: Routledge/Falmer.

Davis, A. (2018) *Reckless Opportunists. Elites at the end of the establishment*. Manchester: Manchester University Press.

Edwards, T., Fitz, J. and Whitty, G. (1989) *The State and Private Education. An evaluation of the assisted place scheme*. Basingstoke: The Falmer Press.

Friedman, S. and Laurison, D. (2019) *The Class Ceiling: Why it pays to be privileged*. Bristol: Policy Press.

Goldthorpe, J. (2016) Social Class Mobility in Modern Britain: Changing Structure, Constant Process. *Journal of the British Academy*, **4**, pp. 89–111.

Green, F. and Kynaston, D. (2019) *Engines of Privilege: Britain's Private School Problem*. London: Bloomsbury.

Harris, J. (1994) *Private Lives, Public Spirit: Britain 1870–1914*. London: Penguin Books.

Independent Schools Council (2022) *ISC Census and Annual Report 2020*. Online. Available at isc_census_2022_final-v2.pdf (Accessed 27 October 2022).

Jackson, B. and Marsden, D. (1962) *Education and the Working Class*. Harmondsworth: Penguin Books.

James, D. and Lunnon, J. (Eds) (2019) *The State of Independence: Key Challenges Facing Private Schools Today*. Abingdon: Routledge.

Kirby, P. (2016) *Leading People 2016: The Educational Backgrounds of the UK Professional Elite*. Online. Available at Leading-People_Feb16-1.pdf (suttontrust.com) (Accessed 27 October 2022).

Orwell, G. (1941) *The Lion and the Unicorn. Socialism and the English Genius*. London: Penguin Books.

Reeves, A., Friedman, S., Rahal, C. and Flemmen, M. (2017) The Decline and Persistence of the Old Boy: Private Schools and Elite Recruitment 1897 to 2016. *American Sociological Review*, **82**(6), pp. 1139–1166.

Riddell, R. (2010) *Aspiration, Identity and Self-Belief. Snapshots of social structure at work*. Stoke-on-Trent: Trentham Books.

Sutton Trust/Social Mobility Commission (2019) *Elitist Britain 2019: The Educational Backgrounds of Britain's Leading People*. London: The Sutton Trust/Social Mobility Commission.

Turner, D. (2015) *The Old Boys. The Decline and Rise of the Public School*. New Haven: Yale University Press.

Verkaik, R. (2019) *Posh Boys – How English Public Schools Ruin Britain*. London: Oneworld Publishing.

Young, G.M. (1969) *Victorian England, Portrait of an Age*. Oxford: Oxford University Press.

11 The history of Special Education in England

Divisions, divergences and coalitions

Deborah Robinson and Nicholas Joseph

Introduction

This chapter focusses on the history of Special Education in England through exploring its relationship with Ordinary Education. It critiques dualist notions of *Special Education* and *Ordinary Education*, in part to reveal that distinctions between these are far from simple in our contemporary situation. Policy and legislation developed between 1880 and 1969 to divide Special and Ordinary Education at the same time as dividing children as 'educable' or 'ineducable'. Policy iterations between 1970 and 2014 illustrate the way in which Special and Ordinary Education have come to diverge and then coalesce. This has been in a context where parents, and children and young people (CYP), were to have more choice over school placement (at least in principle) and where there has been more interest in the right of disabled people to be included in mainstream society.

With a particular focus on learning disabilities, the purpose of this chapter is to tell the story of Special and Ordinary Education as their relationship progresses through the periods of division (1880 to 1969), divergence (1970 to 1993) and growing coalition (1994 to 2014).

The current context for SEND and Special Education in England

Between the nineteenth and early twenty-first centuries, the status and position of Special Education has shifted as the status and position of persons with disabilities has shifted in a context of societal change. Much of this has been catalysed by activism in the disability rights arena. Change has taken the form of resistance to labelling, segregation and marginalisation by disabled people and their advocates. Such activism has led to legislative reform. For example, the 1970 Education (Handicapped Children) Act enshrined the right to education for all, to include those with severe and profound learning disabilities, a group previously considered *uneducable* and assumed to have no need for schooling. England's most recent educational legislation, the 2014 Children and Families Act, mandated that local authorities (LAs) give CYP and their families more control over decisions about the provisions made to support their education and care, with this mandate being a direct result of lobbying and campaigning by disabled people and their advocates. LAs were asked to pay particular attention to the 'views, wishes and feelings of children and their parents', ensuring their participation 'as fully as possible' in decision-making, with support helping CYP with SEND to achieve 'the best possible educational and other outcomes' (Children and Families Act, Section 19 [3]), including a transition into the 'least restrictive' adulthood possible (DfE and DoH, 2015). The concept 'least restrictive' refers to maximal opportunities for independent living, community participation,

DOI: 10.4324/9781003039532-12

employment, education and good health; it means being in mainstream society and education as far as is possible. Hence, the purpose of legislation has been to facilitate the participation, self-determination, freedom and choice of disabled people in society.

An enquiry into SEND by the parliamentary committee for education concluded that, 'We have a system of unmet need and strain' (House of Commons Education Committee, 2019: 89). A key recommendation was that government should give more attention to ensuring quality of provision for SEND in Ordinary Schools (known as 'mainstream' schools in England). In part, this was to build parental confidence in mainstream schools such that they did not see Special Education as their only option. It was also to reduce the proportion of children requiring more expensive, specialist support. The notion was that if mainstream education was more effective, fewer children would have difficulty learning. At the same time, improvements in the fit of education delivered in the mainstream to the needs of CYP with SENDs, would make it a more viable choice (Lamb, 2019).

In what follows, the current structure of educational placement for children with disabilities is explored to reveal its complexity and to illustrate how divisions between Special and Ordinary Education are less clear than may be assumed.

Defining special and ordinary education: complexities, fluidity and cross-fertilisation

There is a common assumption that Special Education happens only in special schools. But this assumption needs to be challenged. Currently in England, a special school is usually for pupils aged between 3 and 19 who have special educational needs and/or disabilities (DfE, 2021). Placements in special schools are usually reserved for CYP with more complex and exceptional levels of need, such as those with profound and multiple learning difficulties (PMLD), severe learning difficulties (SLD), communication and interaction needs or social and emotional needs (DfE and DoH, 2015). The identification of exceptional and/or complex need is confirmed when, following a request for assessment, the CYP is provided with an Education, Health and Care plan. This is a legally binding document that outlines needs, outcomes and provisions within a consultative framework. About 3.7 per cent of all children at school in England have an EHCP, a rise from 2.8 per cent in 2016 (DfE, 2021). Though it is recognised that individual CYP with SEND are likely to have interacting types of need, special schools can also specialise further to support, for example, pupils with physical needs, sensory needs (visual impairment, hearing impairment, multi-sensory impairment) and autism spectrum disorder (ASD). Alternatively, children with EHCPs are educated in Ordinary schools. In fact, legislation has held the presumption of mainstream since the 1981 Education Act. This means that it is assumed that the CYP with SENDs will be educated in a mainstream rather than a special school. This presumption is sustained in the 2014 Children and Families Act, except in cases where: (a) the family or CYP do not want it, or (b) a placement in Ordinary school is likely to interfere *unavoidably* with the efficient education of other CYPs in the school. If refusing a CYP with SENDs on this basis, an LA must be able to show that there are no reasonable steps that can be taken to remove this incompatibility. About 50 per cent of CYP with EHC plans are in Ordinary schools (DfE, 2021).

Table 11.1 summarises some shifts in the proportion of children in special schools since 2003, and there are clear indications that, although the number of special schools in England has been falling, the number of children attending those schools has been rising (Black, 2019).

Table 11.1 Percentage of pupils in special schools out of all pupils

Year	2003	2005	2007	2009	2011	2013	2015	2018
Proportion of pupils in special schools out of all pupils (per cent)	1.16	1.12	1.13	1.15	1.17	1.21	1.26	1.38

Source: Derived from Black (2019).

Table 11.1 illustrates that, although the percentage of pupils attending special schools has fluctuated over the 15 years between 2003 and 2018, special schools have been retained despite a context where UK policy and international declarations have moved toward support for their diminution (Slee, 2019). However, it is recognised that, in reality, provision for CYP with SEND is in a hybrid form rather than a dualist one, as demonstrated in Figure 11.1.

Figure 11.1 illustrates how Special Education and Ordinary Education for SEND sits on a continuum ranging from full inclusion in an ordinary class to long-term hospital or custodial placements. Where the term 'forensic' is used, it refers to secure placements for CYP with SEND who have been convicted of criminal offences and whose offences have warranted detention. In England, there has been a 40-year commitment to a continuum model of schooling for CYP with SEND, as expressed in the 1981 Education Act onward and in non-statutory guidance (DfE and DoH, 2015). It is fair to say that the presence of Special Education and special schools in the system has been vociferously debated, with some antagonism. For example, in the UK, the Centre for Studies on Inclusive Education (CSIE) and the Alliance for Inclusive Education (ALFIE) have campaigned against all forms of segregation. We return to this later in our historical review.

Special Education and special pedagogy

Practice is usually defined as Special Education when specialist pedagogies are applied to support the development of CYP with SEND. Such pedagogies are usually impairment specific. This means they are developed for groups of learners who share common characteristics, needs and propensities in the form of 'types' of learning difficulty or disability (such as ASD or Down syndrome).

A useful model for conceptualising special pedagogy is offered by Lewis and Norwich (2005), who argue for a more fluid idea of pedagogy for SEND. Rather than presenting special pedagogy and 'ordinary' pedagogy as an either-or, Lewis and Norwich argue for a continuum of specialisation. At the 'less intense and specialised' end of the continuum, teaching and learning is enacted in larger steps with longer-term goals and less intensive teacher intervention. At the 'more intense and specialised' end of the continuum, there are smaller steps, detailed and frequent assessment and monitoring, overlearning, repetition, frequent teacher intervention, high levels of individuation and multi-modal approaches to mastering the same content or skill (e.g. multisensory approaches). Figure 11.2 provides an illustration. Lewis and Norwich (2005) argue that the full continuum can be delivered in special or ordinary schools.

The continuum illustrated by Figure 11.2 is useful because it prevents the unhelpful and inaccurate splitting of teaching for SEND from teaching for all pupils. Care must be taken when defining Special or Ordinary Education since one is enriched by the effective practices of the other. As

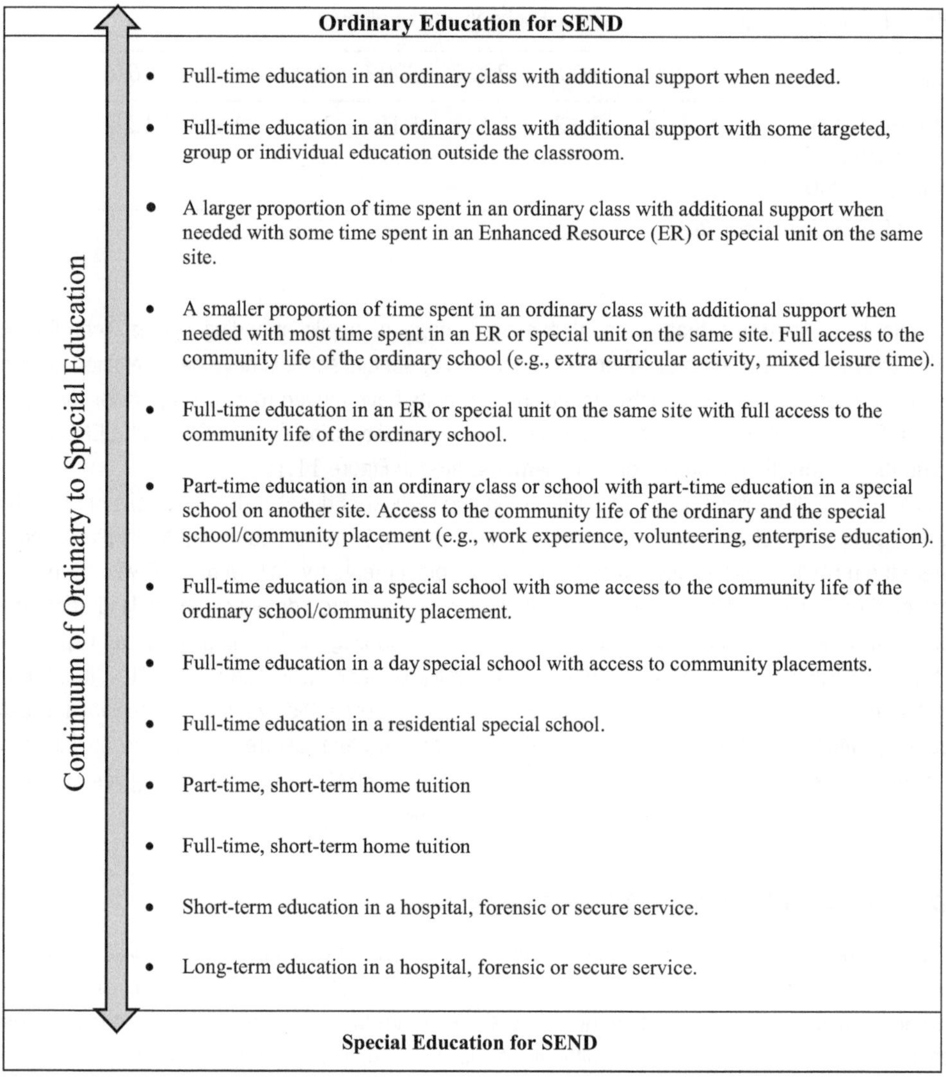

Continuum of Ordinary to Special Education

Ordinary Education for SEND

- Full-time education in an ordinary class with additional support when needed.

- Full-time education in an ordinary class with additional support with some targeted, group or individual education outside the classroom.

- A larger proportion of time spent in an ordinary class with additional support when needed with some time spent in an Enhanced Resource (ER) or special unit on the same site.

- A smaller proportion of time spent in an ordinary class with additional support when needed with most time spent in an ER or special unit on the same site. Full access to the community life of the ordinary school (e.g., extra curricular activity, mixed leisure time).

- Full-time education in an ER or special unit on the same site with full access to the community life of the ordinary school.

- Part-time education in an ordinary class or school with part-time education in a special school on another site. Access to the community life of the ordinary and the special school/community placement (e.g., work experience, volunteering, enterprise education).

- Full-time education in a special school with some access to the community life of the ordinary school/community placement.

- Full-time education in a day special school with access to community placements.

- Full-time education in a residential special school.

- Part-time, short-term home tuition

- Full-time, short-term home tuition

- Short-term education in a hospital, forensic or secure service.

- Long-term education in a hospital, forensic or secure service.

Special Education for SEND

Figure 11.1 A continuum of Ordinary to Special Education and provision

explored later, this coalescence stance on Special and Ordinary Education became stronger in policy from 1994 onwards.

Defining 'Special Education'

To summarise the analysis of Special Education as placement and pedagogy, it is useful to note that Special Education is understood as an educational placement in a school or specialist unit where all children have SENDs, most have an EHC plan, and specialised pedagogies are used. However, it is recognised that, whilst there are clear divergences, there are crossovers and fluidities between Special and Ordinary Education that the following historical analysis will illustrate and explain.

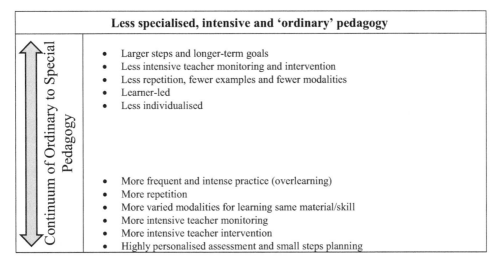

Less specialised, intensive and 'ordinary' pedagogy
• Larger steps and longer-term goals • Less intensive teacher monitoring and intervention • Less repetition, fewer examples and fewer modalities • Learner-led • Less individualised
• More frequent and intense practice (overlearning) • More repetition • More varied modalities for learning same material/skill • More intensive teacher monitoring • More intensive teacher intervention • Highly personalised assessment and small steps planning

Figure 11.2 Continuum of 'ordinary' to 'special' pedagogy

Source: Derived from Lewis and Norwich (2005).

The era of division: 1880–1969

In Britain, the beginning of compulsory, state-funded education for the majority of children emerged in the period 1840 to 1900 with compulsory education for children between the ages of 5 and 12 mandated in the 1870 Elementary Education Act (also known as the Forster Act). At this time, there was very little interest in the education of disabled children. Special Education existed only as private, denominational and/or philanthropic schooling. Usually, this was available only to wealthier families. An example was the Worcester College for the Blind Sons of Gentlemen (founded in 1866) which was available to 'blind children of opulent parents' and offered 'education suitable to their station in life' (Thomas, 1957: 32).

Segregation, institutionalisation and isolation for the uneducable

In 1846, the first private school in England for children with learning disabilities (who at that time were termed 'mental defectives') opened in Bath, and similar establishments proliferated to serve a constituency of 'idiots' and 'imbeciles', so termed in the parlance of the day. The following extract from a newspaper advertisement for a private school, the Heigham Retreat in Norwich, manifests prevailing attitudes about the social position and education of CYP with learning disabilities:

> The Proprietors of Heigham Retreat have determined to make an addition to their Establishment for the purpose of EDUCATING and TRAINING a limited number of IDIOTIC and IMBECILE CHILDREN … When it is considered that there is a very large proportion of imbecile children in every country, and no opportunity of giving them a fitting education, the proprietors think that the means now offered to the upper and middle classes will be eagerly seized. No parents having the misfortune to possess such children can fail to perceive how injurious it is to them to mix with boys of stronger powers, who can make no allowances for deficiencies they cannot

discern: consequently, the weak are annoyed and oppressed by the stronger in all schools, private and public. Nor is the mode of education common in schools suitable for the imbecile, who require a system of training adapted to the animal frame, as well as to the mental capacity of each individual case, pursued with patience, perseverance, and kindness.

(Advertisement for the Heigham Retreat, *Manchester Guardian*, 11 January 1851)

The advertisement represents a cultural stance that positions CYP with learning disabilities as unfortunates whose tragic status in life was deserving of charity and whose needs were best met through segregating them from more able people.

A common argument was that segregation was protective not only to those with 'mental deficiencies', but also to society, which would be more likely to thrive if its gene pool were not contaminated by the presence of those with undesirable traits (Inge, 1907). Deficiencies of mind (rather than body) were considered to be particularly undesirable because of the cultural prizing of the intellect and rationality. The following extract is from a popular newspaper of the time and illustrates, what was, a mainstream view.

Idiots or feeble-minded people are either born so or become so in the course of their development. In any case, the existence of some evil taint in the parents will generally be found … One important thing is that the idiot child should not be allowed to play about or mix with other children who are healthy. He cannot share their games, he cannot enjoy their companionship, and he can only feel a sense of his own inferiority. If he is too idiotic to feel that then he should be kept from others because his company would be very unwholesome for the healthy minded ones. Confinement to an asylum is the most humane and kind treatment for idiots beyond a doubt.

(*News of the World*, 23 August 1900)

This editorial argues for the confinement of people with learning disabilities in asylums, carrying this argument with an assumed righteousness given its presumption that such practices are both *practical* and *moral*. The extract also represents a concern to protect schools from the contagion of those considered less human and inferior to those who are 'healthy minded'. In the nineteenth and early twentieth centuries, attention to the educational needs of CYP with learning disabilities reflected a rather bizarre contradiction. One was about *saving* these people through philanthropic clemency, and the other was about *condemning* them to isolation through removal from their families and communities. Whatever the purpose, the outcome was often the marginalisation of disabled people from ordinary, public life.

Questions for discussion

The motives of those making decisions for CYP with SENDs were mixed and contradictory.
Are you aware of any similarly mixed motives in decision-making around the education of CYP today?
Can mixed motives ever be avoided when balancing the rights and needs of varied individuals?

The origins of un-educability

In the late nineteenth and twentieth centuries in England, in a context where successive legislation had made state-funded elementary education almost universal, one of the biggest challenges to be managed by local education authorities (LEAs) was what to do with those children who were not able to cope with the school curriculum because of their disabilities. The Committee for Defective and Epileptic Children (part of the Government's Education Department) considered how this could be managed. In an 1898 report from the Egerton Commission, the identification and management of children with severe learning disabilities was considered:

> From the normal child down to the lowest idiot, there are all degrees of deficiency of mental power; and it is only a difference of degree which distinguishes the feeble-minded children, referred to in our inquiry, on the one side from the backward children who are found in every ordinary school, and, on the other side, from the children who are too deficient to receive proper benefit from any teaching which the School Authorities can give.
>
> (The Egerton Commission, Committee on Defective and Epileptic Children, 1898, Part 2: 13)

This extract illustrates the established belief that some children with learning disabilities had capacities that were so low that schooling was irrelevant. It signalled the emergence of an 'uneducable' group in policy. For others, with mental deficiencies that were not so low grade, the challenge was to find an educational or care placement that matched their needs. In this way, assessment became paramount, with a key question being how to divide those who were educable from those who were not, and how to classify children in ways that helped with the match to the right placement. This became a preoccupation among policy makers and in many ways continues to pre-occupy today. The Egerton Commission (1889) and its next iteration, the Sharpe Committee (1898) were influential in the formation of the Elementary Education (Defective and Epileptic Children) Act, 1899. The 1899 Act divided children with learning disabilities ('mentally defective') into two groups: the educable (defined by the term 'feeble-minded') and the uneducable (defined by the terms 'imbecile' and 'idiot'). With further reinforcement in the Education Act of 1902, LEAs were empowered to identify children who were 'feebleminded' and place them in Special Education in segregated schools. Though they were given the power to do this, such provisions were not mandated. Patchy provision for Special Education emerged with the result that many children with learning and other disabilities were not in school. Those considered ineducable (defined as 'imbecile' and 'idiot') did not have the right to education, and provision was in the form of institutionalised care.

Eugenics and the reification of the ineducable

Eugenics is the philosophy of genetic purification. In the late nineteenth and early twentieth centuries, children and adults with learning disabilities were assessed and certified by medical officers serving LEAs. The certification would inform decisions about whether an individual's mental deficiency was so severe that it warranted the identification of ineducability and/or incarceration. This was mandated in the 1913 Mental Deficiency Act which gave legislative credence to the grading of human intelligence. It established systemic medical measurement of intelligence as a basis for ascertaining educability, defining grades of intelligence with legally sanctioned terms. Categories included the

least severe, *'feeble-mindedness'* for children 'that appeared incapable by reasons of such defectiveness of receiving proper benefit from instruction in ordinary school', to *'imbeciles'* for children whose
deficiency was so pronounced that they were incapable of being taught to manage themselves or
their affairs, to the most severe level of *'idiot'*. The term 'idiot' was applied to 'persons in whose case
there exists mental defectiveness of such a degree that they are unable to guard themselves against
common physical dangers' (2013 Mental Deficiency Act, Part 1: 1). Such assessments were used to
select the most appropriate placement which might include education in existing primary schools,
education in special schools or institutionalisation (for education and/or care).

Lobbying of and by politicians at the time that the 1913 Mental Deficiency Act became law,
demonstrates how the Eugenicist philosophy of genetic purification was part of mainstream political
thought. As an illustration, in 1910, Winston Churchill, MP Home Secretary, argued for compulsory
sterilisation for people with learning disabilities, noting, in a letter to the prime minister, that:

> The unnatural and increasingly rapid growth of the feebleminded classes, coupled with a steady
> restriction among all the thrifty, energetic, and superior stocks constitutes a race danger. I feel
> the source from which the stream of madness is fed should be cut off and sealed up before
> another year has passed.
>
> (Oxford, Asquith 12)

Though forced sterilisation was debated in Parliament, it was not made law, in part because it was
seen as an unconscionable betrayal of human rights. However, practices of institutionalisation and
incarceration for those deemed mentally deficient also served as a eugenicist practice, and such
practices continued over several decades (Cavaliere, 2018). This illustrates a eugenic motivation
for educational policy. Segregation enabled the 'improvement of the human race' (Inge, 1907: 26)
through measurement and restricted breeding such that:

> Between the present time and the end of the period when the earth will remain habitable, there
> shall be the largest possible number of men and women who to the largest extent realise the
> ideal of what a human ought to be.
>
> (Inge, 1907: 26–27)

Following the passing of the Mental Deficiency Act, 1913, systems of intelligence measurement and
classification as elements of educational policy were given state assent. For the educable, the
Defective Children Act, 1914, made educational provision for so-called 'feeble-minded' children a
duty for local education authorities. Emerging from the legislation between 1899 and 1914 was a
clear LEA duty to 'ascertain defect', 'determine educability', ensure provision of Special Education
and 'notify custodial cases' (i.e. cases of ineducability) to local mental deficiency authorities such
that those with severe mental deficiencies could be placed in institutions for their care and rehabil-
itation (Board of Education, 1917). This marks the increasing presence of dividing practices in the
form of categorisation. The educable were the responsibility of local educational authorities, and
the uneducable were the responsibility of mental deficiency, custodial boards.

Despite attempts to refine, and make more fitting, the diagnostic criteria for 'educable' and
'uneducable', the continuing vagueness of definition meant that decisions were in the hands of
school medical officers and dependent on their personal interpretation of the criteria (Jackson,
2017). Some diagnostic manuals included lists of 'stigmata' indicative of 'sub-human powers' to

include assessments of the size and setting of ears and the extent to which the lower jaw protruded from the head (Royal Commission on the Care and Control of the Feeble-Minded, 1908: 865). This may represent the way in which pseudoscience was used to escape subjectivity and to create the illusion of objective judgement. In essence, though there was unequivocal belief in the rectitude of division and the existence of measurable grades of human defectiveness, the processes of division were based on shaky and unreliable criteria (Goodey, 2011).

Questions for discussion

Do you think society today is more willing to compromise individual human rights in return for public health benefits?

Should we be worried about that?

A century ago, eugenics was 'the Science.' Consider the role of the teacher:

Should teachers promote modern scientific consensus above old-fashioned social values, or vice versa?

Does the previous question actually miss the point about what teachers *should* be doing? If so, how?

The growth of special education for the educable

The 1918 Education Act was formulated as a landmark change of direction for Special Education and for education generally in a period of peacetime reconstruction following the First World War (Doherty, 1966). This represented a new moral consciousness since government wanted to compensate the public for the hardships they had suffered as the consequences of war. From 1918 Local Authorities were more clearly mandated to provide grant aid to charitable schools providing Special Education. Invariably, these were in the form of special schools (day schools or residential) and heralded a journey toward universal state funding for Special Education. However, the right to education for children with physical and sensory disabilities took some time to reach all children. During this hiatus, those categorised as 'physically defective', for example, were left without an education where there were no special schools. They were also assumed unsuitable for Ordinary Education in mainstream schools. Accounts by disabled people (Humphries and Gordon, 1992: 45), relate the impact of the policies of categorisation prevalent at the time. An example is from Gerald Turner, a person with cerebral palsy:

> I wasn't allowed to go to the school with the rest because they said it wouldn't be fair, that the other children might look at me. But I couldn't understand because I knew them all anyway. I saw them all and played with them in the village. I used to get so frustrated and scream a lot, I wanted to know what they were learning at school.

Assumptions about 'fit' then, were generically applied according to *category* rather than actual, individual propensity. In the context of policy implementation, the concept 'uneducable' evolved beyond its original statutory construction as applicable to children who were deemed mentally deficient to a severe degree. In actuality, it came to apply to *any* child who was thought unable to access ordinary education because the infrastructure was not in place to support them (Marsh, 2019).

Though clear definitions of, and criteria for, educability and ineducability were lacking in legislation and the wider system, the purpose of special schools for children with 'mental deficiencies' was clear. Largely based on a German model, the special school (and hence Special Education) was:

> Intended solely for children of inferior brain power who yet possess sufficient intelligence to be amenable to the discipline of their own homes, and who are capable of benefiting by instruction sufficiently to enable them to pass out of school at the limit of school age with a probability of earning their own living.
>
> (Eicholz, 1901: 595)

The purpose of Special Education, then, was to prepare those children who were capable of it for an independent life. This signals the way in which Special Education was considered relevant only for those CYP who were capable of self-sufficiency after school (Mills Daniel, 1997). Where self-sufficiency was in question, education was not considered to be an investment worth making, nor was it considered sensible when longer-term incarceration was more likely to fulfil the needs of the individual and the needs of society (Mills Daniel, 1997).

The 1944 education act and the identification of the 'cusp' cohort

The 1944 Act began to propose that some children with disabilities could be educated in ordinary schools with some special adaptions (e.g., aids and equipment), although there were fewer concessions for those described as 'educationally subnormal.' In the case of the educable cohort of ESN pupils, Special Education could be delivered in ordinary schools, either within a division of the class, or in a separate special class for 'special instruction in the subjects they are especially backward' (Ministry of Education, 1945: 30).The children for whom ordinary school was considered appropriate were a 'cusp' cohort because, although they had disabilities, the best fit of educational placement was considered to converge at the Special/Ordinary divide. In a context where it was conceded that, where possible, it was best to educate disabled children in ordinary schools, the Handicapped Pupils and Medical Services Regulations of 1945 allowed for special equipment, furniture and aids to be provided, along with tuition for lip reading if pupils were partially deaf. It was at this point that the Ministry of Education (1945, para 106: 29) identified a cohort who could be supported by Special Education delivered in ordinary schools more clearly:

> Besides aiming at the ordinary goals of education, the teacher giving special educational treatment must also have in mind the rehabilitation of a child suffering from a handicap, either temporary, or possibly lifelong, which to some extent marks him out from his fellows. It must, therefore, be the design of any system for providing special educational treatment to enable the teacher as fully as possible to perform this additional task, which will involve appreciating peculiarities in the child's outlook. To this end it is better to remove some children entirely from the environment of an ordinary school in which they are too conspicuous, and to educate them in a special school; but others, the majority, are better retained in the group of children in which they are found and educated to form members of that group. Hence the new Act recognises that special educational treatment may be given in ordinary schools where the child would benefit more from this than from education in a special school.

This extract also expounds the concept of benefit: that the school placement chosen should be the most beneficial. This is the beginning of the idea of *least restrictive* influential during the later part of the twentieth century and explained in the earlier part of this chapter. However, categorisation still served a dividing function for those considered very different. It was argued that the conspicuousness of their difference would expose them to suffering and, at the same time, require too much of teachers in ordinary schools.

Continuing medical classification of children worked against the policy of mainstreaming, and the number of children with disabilities receiving Special Education rose from 38,499 in 1945 to 106,367 in 1972. There were 11 such categories described in the 1944 Act to include blind, partially sighted, deaf, delicate, diabetic, epileptic, maladjusted, physically handicapped and speech defected. In the case of learning disabilities, the two categories were 'educationally subnormal' (ESN) and 'severely educationally subnormal', with the latter replacing the terms 'imbecile' and 'idiot' as an indicator of ineducability.

Hence, the 1944 Act continued the era of division in terms of categorisation, educability and school placement (Haines and Ruebain, 2011). The so-called 'uneducable' remained divided from the population of children with disabilities now being served by education.

The era of divergence: 1970 to 1993

In the 1960s and 1970s, the civil rights movement in the United States inspired disabled people to take direct action against inequality, segregation and institutionalisation. One of the first disability activist groups was the Union of the Physically Impaired Against Segregation (UPIAS), which was established when Paul Hunt (a disability rights campaigner) wrote to *The Guardian* newspaper in September 1972 to argue that people with severe physical disabilities were living in 'isolated and unsuitable institutions where their views are ignored, and they are subject to authoritarian and often cruel regimes' (Hunt, 1972). Paul Hunt's letter (and people's response to his invitation to join in a campaigning group), catalysed activism for societal change. Further influential activists proposed a social model of disability to emphasise the way in which society constructs barriers to participation (e.g., inaccessible transport, inaccessible curricula, segregated schooling) and, in doing so, intensifies the disabling impact of impairment. Mike Oliver, a leading activist in the field, argued against the medicalisation of disability to purport that it was 'a social state and not a medical condition' (Oliver, 1990: 2). In this way, the social model was offered as an alternative to medical or deficit models, and activist groups concerned with learning disability also used it to argue against segregation in education and in society (Tomlinson, 1982).

Lobbying prior to the formation of UPIAS in 1972 had contributed to the 1970 Education (Handicapped Children) Act which signalled a major change in the educational rights of children with learning disabilities. It discontinued the classification of some children as uneducable and instated a universal right to state-funded schooling for all. The term 'mentally handicapped' replaced the term 'educationally sub-normal', and it was no longer legal to classify 'children suffering from a disability of mind' as children unsuitable for education at school (1944 Education Act, 1970, c.2: para 1(1) a). The 1970 Education Act also determined that *all* children (including those who were severely mentally handicapped) would be under the care of the Local Education Authority, rather than the NHS as hitherto. However, medicalised, deficit language still dominated, with the term 'special educational treatment' being used to describe schooling for disabled children in a manner that constructed special pedagogy as *distinctly* clinical and rehabilitative. In this way, teaching and learning for CYP in Special Education developed in ways that diverged from developments in Ordinary Education (Tomlinson, 1982) because of the presence (and influence) of educational psychologists and health-care workers in the formation of special schools and their practices. For example, the TEACCH curriculum for children with autism applies highly individualised, behaviourist principles to pedagogy.

The 1970 Education Act led to further growth in the number of Special Schools in England since there was a new cohort of pupils to be served, that is, those previously defined as uneducable. This group had previously been supported in non-educational establishments and institutions providing care rather than education. Table 11.2 is drawn from the School Census data for 1975 and 1980 (DES, 1975, 1980) to show changes in the numbers of children with learning disabilities being educated in state funded Special Schools during this period.

Census data for Special Schools prior to 1975 was not collected, but nonetheless the data in Table 11.2 is useful as an illustration of how many CYP who would have been categorised as uneducable were now being educated in Special Schools. Table 11.2 shows that about 1,600 Special Schools were in existence between 1975 and 1980. Of these, 480 schools had children on roll who had severe or profound learning disabilities. By 1980, a total of 48,325 children with severe ESN were receiving education in a special school.

During the period of expansion in Special Education from 1944 onwards, the structure and practice of schooling began to diverge as special schools for those categorised as educable and 'Educationally Sub Normal' (ESN) developed specialised practices. Special schools were tending to pursue more clinical and specialised approaches such as applied behaviour analysis, an intervention that uses systematic reinforcement and reward to develop more prosocial behaviour. Such approaches crystalised Special Education as distinctive, specialised and separate (Hick et al., 2008).

Hence, the divergence between Ordinary Education and Special Education was not just about practice, it was also about philosophy, making cross-fertilisation challenging (Dyson and Howes,

Table 11.2 School census data on Special Schools educating children categorised as 'Educationally Sub-Normal' (ESN)

	1980	*ESN Pupils*	*Severe*	*1975*	*ESN Pupils*
Total Special Schools	1,598	82,228	48,325	1,604	42,087
Hospital Schools for Severe ESN	59			69	
Special Schools for Moderate and Severe ESN	40			13	
Special Schools for Severe ESN	381			382	
Special Schools for Moderate ESN	514			562	

Note: The 1975 School census data did not identify how many pupils categorised as ESN were assessed as 'severe'.
Source: DES (1975, 1980).

2008). Special education had tended to adopt a more clinical and rehabilitative approach to peda-gogy (and was positivist), whereas ordinary education was influenced by social and sociological formulations for education (and was more relativist). This was a concern in a context where policy makers were giving increasing attention to the 'cusp' cohort of children with disabilities whose most fitting placement was considered to be in ordinary schools but with some Special Education provision.

The Warnock report and the 1981 education act

By the early 1970s, most children with learning disabilities were in Special Education, but many mainstream schools (about 40 per cent) contained special classes for children with learning disabil-ities or behavioural disorders, as had been encouraged by the 1944 Education Act and subsequent regulations (Cole, 1989). There was a growing interest in making greater provision for disabled children in mainstream schools for the cusp cohort. In 1974, the Department of Education and Science formed the Warnock Committee to review provision in England, Wales and Scotland. When the Warnock Report (DES, 1978) was published, it created the concept of 'Special Educational Needs' (SEN), in part to replace the 1944 Education Act's medicalised concept of schooling as treatment with more holistic, educational ones. It also abolished the 11 categories established in 1944 and replaced the term ESN with, 'learning difficulties'. The aim was to perpetuate more per-sonalised, descriptive assessments of difficulty/educational need so that a child would be seen not in terms of a 'category' (like ESN or epileptic), but 'in relation to everything about him, his abilities as well as his disabilities – indeed, all of the factors have a bearing on his education progress' (DES, 1978: 37). In this way, the report was anti-labelling and sought to soften the divisions (categorisa-tion, educability) established by educational legislation during previous decades.

The report demonstrated a continuing interest in the cusp cohort and established a more fluid conception of special educational need to accommodate those with more severe, complex and exceptional needs and those whose educational difficulties were more moderate and usual. To break down the divide between Special and Ordinary Education, the Warnock Committee proposed a flexible model and proposed that up to 20 per cent of the whole school population may require some form of special provision, and that *the majority of those* would be identified and supported within mainstream schools. This continued the assumptions of the 1944 Act. Assessment would now be staged and, rather than being in the hands of LEA-appointed medical officers alone, would involve increasing involvement from professionals (e.g. educational psychologists) where the com-plexity of need demanded this. Parents were to be actively involved in this process, for the first time. Where children's disabilities were exceptional or complex, they would receive a 'statement of SEN', a legally binding plan for their provision. Children with statements could be educated in main-stream schools where practical but would be the group served by special schools.

Further deconstructing the divide between Special Education and Ordinary Education, and the schools where such practices take place, Warnock proposed three ways of 'integrating' children with special educational needs into mainstream schools (DES, 1978: 100–101), as shown in Figure 11.3.

Figure 11.3 is reminiscent of Figure 11.1 since it represents an overlapping concept of Special and Ordinary Education. In essence, the Warnock Report (DES, 1978) was recommending a more flexible placement model for children in the cusp cohort. It introduced the idea of a 'continuum of

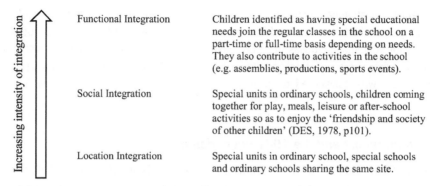

Increasing intensity of integration

Functional Integration — Children identified as having special educational needs join the regular classes in the school on a part-time or full-time basis depending on needs. They also contribute to activities in the school (e.g. assemblies, productions, sports events).

Social Integration — Special units in ordinary schools, children coming together for play, meals, leisure or after-school activities so as to enjoy the 'friendship and society of other children' (DES, 1978, p101).

Location Integration — Special units in ordinary school, special schools and ordinary schools sharing the same site.

Figure 11.3   Warnock's continuum of integration

needs' (DES, 1978: 102), which was intended to span full-time integration into ordinary classes to long-term, segregated education in hospitals or other establishments.

As explained in the earlier part of this chapter, the continuum model is still in place today, and we can identify the Warnock Report as one of the clearest attempts to soften the division and divergence of Special and Ordinary Education. The subsequent 1981 Education Act contained many of the Warnock Committee's recommendations including parental involvement, a continuum of need/placement (rather than categorisation) and better linkage between professional services from different sectors. It also strengthened the idea of state-funded resourcing for special educational provision in mainstream schools (seen in Ministry of Education publications in 1945), providing flexible definitions of this as 'educational provision that is additional to or different from, the educa-tion provision made generally for children of his age in schools maintained by the local education authority' (1981 Education Act, C.60, Preliminary, 1: 3). The message was that special educational provision could be made in both special or ordinary schools, and that where it was practicable: 'the child engages in the activities of the school together with the children who do not have special educational needs' (1981 Education Act, C.60, Preliminary, 2:7). This also perpetuates the idea that provision should be in its *least restrictive* form to maximise opportunities for integration with main-stream peers.

Though the Warnock Report and the 1981 Education Act continued with the assumption that the *majority of children with disabilities* would be educated in mainstream schools (sometimes with additional support), it did not promote inclusion in ordinary schools (or mainstreaming) for *all*. In 2005, Warnock and Norwich (2010) revisited the question of placement to note that children with statements of Special Educational Needs (currently in the form of EHC plans) should be included flexibly 'within a common educational project', which did not mean that they should all, 'be included under one roof'. Rather than being a call for the full integration (inclusion) of children with state-ments of SEN in mainstream schools, the Warnock Report (DES, 1978) established the idea of a continuum. The focus should be on finding the school placement/combination of placements that was *least restrictive*, rather than on the belief that fewer children with disabilities should be edu-cated in special schools (Booth, 1981). However, in concrete and influential ways, the Warnock Report and the 1981 Act did work against the simplified division of children according to category, instigated more positive language to describe children with learning disabilities and encouraged a less divergent view of the relationship between Special and Ordinary Education that continues to influence the structure of schooling for SEND today.

The era of coalescence: 1994 to 2014

The framework for SEN emerging from Warnock and the 1981 Education Act held ground during the 1990s. During this period, there was growing commitment to the integration of children with disabilities, including those with learning disabilities, into mainstream schools. In 1997, the newly elected Labour government endorsed the Salamanca Statement (UNESCO, 1994) which called on governments to adopt the principle of inclusive education (DfEE, 1997: 5), with the expectation that 'ordinary schools must recognise the diverse needs of their students, whilst also having a contin-uum of support and services to match these needs'. The Salamanca Statement (UNESCO, 1994: 7) also used the caveat phrase: 'all children should learn together, *where possible*' (emphasis added) and in its principles reflected an idea established in 1945; for education policy to assume that the ordinary school is the right choice for disabled children where it is deemed both practicable and beneficial. This idea was strengthened in the 1981 Education Act, where special educational provision was considered to be possible in both special and mainstream schools.

However, the Salamanca Statement (UNESCO, 1994: 6) introduced the concept of the 'inclusive school', one that was neither special nor ordinary but was committed to 'developing a child-centred pedagogy capable of successfully educating all children, including those who have serious disad-vantages and disabilities'. Special Education was recognised as a pedagogically successful (though divisive) movement at Salamanca, and there was a call for Special Education to support the devel-opment of the inclusive school, a call that left special educators feeling as if their status and profes-sion was at risk (Conner, 2016).

Many of the principles of the Salamanca Statement reflected those argued for by the Warnock Committee, including the rally against 'one-size-fits-all' approaches in favour of flexible, personalised ones, capable of transformation around the needs of the child and in the context of a continuum. Despite (a) vociferous campaigning against segregated schooling for CYP with disabilities in the 1980s and 1990s by disabled people and their advocates (e.g. CSIE, ALFIE), and (b) the intensifi-cation of educational rights for people with disabilities as compounded in the 2001 Special Educational Needs and Disability Act (SENDA), policy in England never reached the point where Special Schools and Special Education were to be removed or minimised. Rather, policy encour-aged and expected the inclusion of children with Special Educational Needs (with statements) in mainstream schools, but only in cases where the adjustments required were 'reasonable', and where inclusion was 'not incompatible with the efficient education of other children' (DfES, 2001: 14). Hence, England has maintained a dual system spanning a structural continuum of placements (Figure 11.1), and one in which the 'inclusive school' has come into existence as a third space. This third space was being developed to include children with exceptional needs as well as a cusp cohort, with a concern for the right of parents and CYPs to choose where they wanted to be edu-cated (though of course, there were caveats). In a context where there were wide variations across all LEAs, the national percentage of 5- to 15-year-olds in special schools across England's 149 authorities fell from 1.39 per cent in 1997 to 1.32 per cent in 2001. This continued a trend that had lasted 20 years and continued to 2011 (1.15 per cent), when it began to rise (see Table 11.1).

In 2011, at the start of a SEN reform process, a new coalition government led by David Cameron pledged, 'we will remove the bias towards inclusion and propose to strengthen parental choice by improving the range and diversity of schools from which parents can choose' (DfE, 2011: 3). However, much public debate and parent/carer concern had centred on the lack of inclusive provi-sion in mainstream schools as much as it had centred on concerns about the lack of capacity in special schools (Slee, 2019). In essence, though, the removal of bias to inclusion was not really much of a departure from policy since 1981, and parental choice was still to be mediated by caveats already in place in the 1981 Education Act; these supported parental choice unless (a) the parents' preferred placement would not meet the needs of the child, (b) the preference was too expensive and (c) the placement was 'incompatible with the efficient education of other children' (DfE, 2011: 6). However, many saw the pledge of removing bias to inclusion as an expression of validation for Special Education, in a context where Inclusive Education had been promoted over it, sometimes to the detriment of children's education (Imray, 2017).

Hence the policy period between 1994 and 2014 continued with a concern to blur the boundaries between Special and Ordinary Education, but to validate both (and their cross over spaces) as relevant sites for the effective education of CYP with SENDs. More recently, the establishment of some special schools as 'teaching schools' (schools which have a remit to deliver CPD, initial teacher training and school to school support) means that special schools are supporting mainstream schools in the development of inclusive practice in terms of 'Quality First Teaching' (effective practice for all) and special educational provision. In this way, Special and Ordinary Education are expected to coalesce, with one supporting the other in a constructive relationship. However, policies have tended to assume that the direction of the support should flow from Special to Ordinary Education rather than the other way around. Though there has been a growing interaction between the two, the practice of reciprocity has some way yet to go.

Questions for discussion

Special education and inclusion became politically contentious in the 2000s.

Is it helpful or unhelpful for these issues to debated adversarially in a democratic political system?

Consider the language and terminology in use at different times in the field of SEND and Special education. Examples might be: idiot, handicapped, Special and Ordinary, segregation, defective.

What does the language used suggest about underlying attitudes and beliefs?

How might the language used influence or perpetuate attitudes and beliefs?

Are you immune to that kind of influence?

Conclusion

This historical analysis of Special and Ordinary Education has sought to illustrate the shifting position of Special and Ordinary Education in policies related to SEND in England. It has demonstrated how the relationship between Special and Ordinary Education was one of division and divergence up until the 1980s. This was in terms of the division of disabled children into categories, the division of disabled children into educable/uneducable cohorts, and the related division of services. However, from 1945, an interest in a cusp cohort began to come to the fore. This cusp cohort included children with disabilities who could be educated in mainstream schools, with additional support. This concern to integrate children with disabilities into ordinary education continued to develop along with commitment to a structural continuum of schooling for children with disabilities to span full inclusion in ordinary classes to segregated, secure education in hospitals or forensic services. Since 1945, there has been a sustained interest in choosing the *least restrictive* environment. In the 1990s, a third type of school, the 'inclusive school', came to be conceptualised with the event of global and national commitments to including children with disabilities in mainstream schools. This was to be achieved through improvements to mainstream practice such that practices were effective for all but also included special educational provision for those who needed it. However, though grassroots activism has tended to persuade policy makers to support this emphasis on inclusive practice, and policy makers continue to expect mainstream schools to work inclusively, policy and legislation has continued to support a dual system of Special and Ordinary Education, albeit across a continuum of placements. Vociferous debate about the place of Special Education and segregated special schools continues among people with disabilities and their activists, but at this juncture, both look likely to prevail in a context where there is a re-energised focus on how mainstream schools can work more effectively to serve the needs of a cusp cohort (those currently identified with the term SEND Support), and in so doing, reduce the reliance on and incidences of EHC plans in ways that make the system both sustainable (financially) and offer parents and CYP real choice about the placement of their education. Whatever the future, skirmishes, and debates around the question of where CYPs with SENDs should be educated, and how to manage the dehumanising impact of division/categorisation are likely to continue. Such dilemmas have, thus far, not been resolved by educational policy in England.

Summary points

- Special Education and Ordinary Education are not as separate or distinctive as they are often assumed to be. This is because children and young people with Special Educational needs and disabilities may receive their education in special schools, ordinary (mainstream) schools or dual placements. When in mainstream schools, CYP may be included in a mainstream classroom full time with support with some time spent in specialist classrooms. It is also true that Special Pedagogy has much in common with Ordinary Pedagogy, and each can be applied (in combination) in ordinary and special schools.
- The history of educational policy for CYP with learning disabilities can be described with reference to three key eras as follows.

    The era of division, 1880–1969, characterised by categorisation and segregation. CYP with severe and profound learning disabilities were not entitled to education because they were considered to be ineducable.

    The era of divergence, 1970–1993. During this period all children (including those with severe and profound learning disabilities) saw the removal of the term ineducable from UK legislation. All children were now entitled to education. This led to the proliferation of Special Schools and diverging practices in Special Schools and Ordinary Schools

    The era of coalescence, 1994–2014. During this period policy promoted more collaboration between Special Education and Ordinary Education such that the former could enrich the latter and improve inclusive practice in mainstream classrooms.

    The dehumanising impacts of categorisation and segregation for CYP with learning disabilities has been illustrated. Debate about the interaction of segregated education and dehumanisation continues.

Recommended reading

Chitty, C. (2009) *Eugenics, Race, and Intelligence in Education*. London: David Fulton.
Imray, P. (2017) *Inclusion Is Dead: Long Live Inclusion*. London: Routledge.
Robinson, D. and Goodey, C. (2017) Agency in the Darkness: 'Fear of the Unknown', Learning Disability and Teacher Education for Inclusion. *International Journal of Inclusive Education*, **26**(2), pp. 15–28.
Warnock, M. and Norwich, B. (2010) *Special Educational Needs: A New Look*. London: Continuum.

References

Black, A. (2019) A Picture of Special Educational Needs in England – An Overview. *Frontiers in Education*, **4**, p. 79. Available at https://doi.org/10.3389/feduc.2019.00079 (Accessed May 13, 2023).
Board of Education (1917) *Annual Report of the Chief Medical Officer for 1917* (BPP 1918, IX).
Booth, T. (1981) Demystifying Integration. In W. Swann (Ed.) *The Practice of Special Education*. Oxford: Blackwell.
Cavaliere, G. (2018) Looking into the Shadow: The Eugenics Argument in Debates on Reproductive Technologies and Practices. *Monash Bioethics Review*, **36**, pp. 1–22.
Cole, T. (1989) *Apart or a Part? Integration and the Growth of British Special Education*. Milton Keynes: Open University Press.
Committee on Defective and Epileptic Children (1898) *Report of the Departmental Committee on Defective and Epileptic Children. Vol I*. (HP C.-8746). London: HMSO.
Conner, L. (2016) Reflections on Inclusion: How Far Have We Come Since Warnock and Salamanca? *Research in Teacher Education*, **6**(1), pp. 18–23.
DES (1975) *Statistics of Education: 1975 Schools: Volume 1*. London: HMSO.
DES (1978) *Report of the Committee of Enquiry into the Education of Handicapped Children and Young People*. London: HMSO.
DES (1980) *Statistics of Education: 1980 Schools. Volume II*. London: HMSO.
DfE (2011) *Support and Aspiration: A New Approach to Special Educational Needs and Disabilities*. Online. Available at: https://www.gov.uk/government/publications/support-and-aspiration-a-new-approach-to-special-educational-needs-and-disability-consultation (Accessed 19 July 2021).
DfE (2021) *Special Educational Needs in England: Academic Year 2020–21*. Online. Available at: https://explore-education-statistics.service.gov.uk/find-statistics/special-educational-needs-in-england (Accessed 17 July 2021).
DfE and DoH (2015) *The Code of Practice for SEND: 0-25*. London: DfE and DoH.
DfEE (1997) *Excellence for All Children: Meeting Special Educational Needs*. Online. Available at: http://www.educationengland.org.uk/documents/pdfs/1997-green-paper.pdf (Accessed 1 August 2020).
DfES (2001) *Special Educational Needs Code of Practice*. London: HMSO.
Doherty, B. (1966). Compulsory Day Continuation Education: An Examination of the 1918 Experiment. *Vocational Aspect of Secondary and Further Education*, **18**(39), pp. 41–56.
Dyson, A. and Howes, A. (2008) Towards an Interdisciplinary Research Agenda. In P. Hick, R. Kershner and P.T. Farrell (Eds) *Psychology for Inclusive Education: New Directions in Theory and Practice*. Abingdon: Routledge.
Eicholz, A. (1901) Report of the Congress on the Education of Feeble-Minded Children, held at Augsburg, April 10–12, 1901. *Special Reports on Educational Subjects*, v. 9. Education in Germany.
Goodey, C.F. (2011) *A History of Intelligence and 'Intellectual Disability': The Shaping of Psychology in Early Modern Europe*. Farnham: Ashgate.
Haines, S. and Ruebain, D. (Eds) (2011) *Disability, Education and Social Policy*. London: Policy Press.
Hick, P., Kershner, R. and Farrell, P.T. (Eds.) (2008) *Psychology for Inclusive Education: New Directions in Theory and Practice*. Abingdon: Routledge.
House of Commons Education Committee (2019) *Special Educational Needs and Disabilities (HC 20)*. London: Parliament UK.
Humphries, S. and Gordon, P (1992) *Out of Sight: The Experience of Disability, 1900–1950*. Plymouth: Northcote House.
Hunt, P. (1972) *Letter to The Guardian*. 20 September 1972.
Inge, W.R. (1907) Some moral aspects of eugenics. *Eugenics Review*, **1**(1), pp. 26–36.
Imray, P. (2017) *Inclusion Is Dead: Long Live Inclusion*. London: Routledge.
Jackson, R. (2017) Politics and intellectual disability in England: An historical perspective. *International Journal of Developmental Disabilities*, **63**(1), pp. 52–58.

Lamb, B. (2019) Statutory Assessment for Special Educational Needs and the Warnock Report: The First 40 Years. *Frontiers in Education*, **4**(1), pp. 51–62.

Lewis, A. and Norwich, B. (2005) *Special Teaching for Special Children*. Maidenhead: Open University Press.

Marsh, A.J. (2019) Special Education Trends and Variations from the United States and United Kingdom (England), 1984 to 2014. *International Journal of School & Educational Psychology*, **7**(4), pp. 229–239.

Mills Daniel, D. (1997) The Ineducable Children of Leeds: The Operation of the Defective Children and Mental Deficiency Legislation in Leeds, 1900–29. *Journal of Educational Administration and History*, **29** (2), pp. 121–141.

Ministry of Education (1945) *The Nation's Schools, Their Plan and Purpose*. London: His Majesty's Stationery Office.

Oliver, M. (1990) The Individual and Social Models of Disability. *Joint Workshop of the Living Options Group and the Research unit of the Royal College of Physicians*, 23rd July 1990. Available at: https://disability-studies.leeds.ac.uk/wp-content/uploads/sites/40/library/Oliver-in-soc-dis.pdf (Accessed 12 June 2015).

Oxford (n.d.) Bodeleian Libraries, MS. *Asquith 12*.

Royal Commission on the Care and Control of the Feeble-Minded (1908) *Vol I, Minutes of Evidence* (BPP 1908, XXXV).

Slee, R. (2019) *Inclusion Isn't Dead, It Just Smells Funny*. Abingdon: Routledge.

Thomas, M. (1957) *Royal National Institute for the Blind, 1858-1956*. London: RNIB.

Tomlinson, S. (1982) *A Sociology of Special Education*. London: Routledge.

UNESCO (1994) The Salamanca Statement and Framework for Action on Special Needs Education. Adopted by the *World Conference on Special Needs Education: Access and Quality*. Salamanca, Spain, 7–10 June 1994.

Warnock, M. and Norwich, B. (2010) *Special Educational Needs: A new look*. London: Continuum.

12 Adult to adult *in loco parentis*

The changing roles of the university from 1968 to 2018

Gavin Rhoades and Peter Harwood

Introduction

This chapter explores the changing nature of the relationships and duties between universities, students and their parents over the last half-century, and considers the impact of these changes on the nature of universities themselves. The principle of '*in loco parentis*' and how it has evolved over this period is discussed and perspectives from both the United Kingdom and the United States are compared. The reduction in the age of majority to 18 in the UK in 1970 arguably reduced the university's duties towards their students. Subsequent developments in education policy sought to open up higher education to a much wider proportion of the population than ever before. There have been calls for universities to re-embrace some of these former duties and to actually take on broader responsibilities for students' health and well-being. There has also emerged a new focus on the importance of avoiding 'harm' that has been extended to coping with challenging academic ideas. This has given rise to allegations of 'infantilisation' within universities. The chapter concludes with a summary and some recommended reading.

The principle of in loco parentis

Any exploration of the role and nature of universities from 1968 must first consider the traditions of participation in the English university system in the immediately preceding period. In the nineteenth and early twentieth centuries there was a sense in which English universities were shaped in line with an ideal 'based unequivocally on a modern version of the elitist Oxbridge ideal' (Barnes, 1996: 305). Prior to the Second World War university education remained largely restricted to a small minority, and as such it had the function of reproducing a socio-professional elite. Universities were, to a large extent, attended and staffed by people drawn from the upper middle class and they remained 'exclusive, high cost per capita institutions' (Sutherland, 2008: 48). The state's willingness to fund them was based in part on an assumption that only the elite, a small percentage of the population, would ever qualify to attend (Sutherland, 2008). This situation endured for decades, and change in the university system was slow. However, in the post-war years fundamental social upheaval was about to happen, and the university, its relationship with students, its purpose and function would be subject to an unprecedented period of challenge and evolution.

> [The father] may also delegate part of his parental authority, during his life, to the tutor or schoolmaster of his child; who is then *in loco parentis*, and has such a portion of the power of

DOI: 10.4324/9781003039532-13

the parent committed to his charge, viz. that of restraint and correction, as may be necessary to answer the purposes for which he is employed.

William Blackstone, *Commentaries on the Laws of England 441* (1769)

The idea that someone can stand in for a parent and be *in loco parentis* has its origins in common law and was outlined by Blackstone in the mid-eighteenth century. For higher education (HE), particularly in the United States, *in loco parentis* has been considered to be 'an insulating' doctrine (Lake, 1999) that offered protection to universities in terms of their duties towards their students, rather than protecting the students themselves. *Loco parentis* placed duties on universities and shaped the way university culture had developed. From 1960 the notion of *in loco parentis* in the United States had already begun to break down, but a particular moment is often highlighted as the most significant point of change.

An incident occurred in which students at the all-black Alabama State College staged anti-segregation lunch counter sit-ins (Weigel, 2004). The students were expelled, and the case highlighted the issues of *loco parentis* in that 'the university actually asserted the right to arbitrarily give some students [due] process and deny it to others' (Weigel, 2004: 1). The US Court of Appeals for the 5th Circuit rejected the school's claim of omnipotence, and effectively college enrolment was newly defined as a contract between the student and the college. This had major implications, as a contract-based agreement was subject to all the scrutiny of any other legal agreement and consequently the nature of the relationship between the university and the student was fundamentally changed.

In the United Kingdom, unlike the United States, the term *in loco parentis* was not set down in statute; instead, it was developed by common law. As such it lacked a clearly stated set of descriptors which meant that the precise responsibilities of the university with regard to the 'children' in its care were *implied* rather than unequivocally stated. Changes to the relationship between students and universities in respect of *in loco parentis* were more gradual in the UK system and harder to pin down to a particular incident. However, the shift away from the long-held certainties of the university as a paternalistic authority for the 'children' in its care echoed to some extent the changes in the United States.

Prior to the 1960s the relationship between the university and the student was considered to be an indirect relationship between the university and the parent. The parent sent the 'child' to university and in so doing entered into an informal agreement with the institution, delegating parental authority to it. In the United Kingdom the shift away and subsequently, as will be explored later, back towards the principle of *in loco parentis*, has been much less overtly legally driven. It has centred instead on a shifting understanding of the purposes of education and the nature of the role that higher educational institutions play in supporting, caring for and educating young people. In both the United States and the United Kingdom, the debate has been largely about rights, duties and responsibilities.

Question for discussion

What is the role of a university? Is it simply to offer an adult environment in which learning takes place, or does it have a duty to its students that extends beyond that primary educational purpose?

The struggle for student rights: 1968–1988

Post-war higher education in Britain

'World War Two highlighted the importance of civil rights' (Hutcheson et al., 2011), and in the post-war period, equality of opportunity became a core, galvanising concept for the nation. Ensuring that a wider pool of both young and more mature people had access to higher education became something of a touchstone issue for a newly aspirational generation emerging from the austerity and horror of world war. The meaning of 'higher education' was up for debate. In truth it had always been contested, but until the mid-twentieth century in the UK it was unequivocally equated with 'University' (Silver, 1982). A wider definition, to take account of professional and advanced technical education and teacher training, began to emerge in response to concerns about disparities in participation (Silver, 1982). This was highlighted by the Anderson Report (Ministry of Education/Scottish Education Department, 1960) that focused on funding and specifically on grants. There was an increasing awareness that barriers to participation had more to do with economics and choice rather than privilege or entitlement. In order to ensure greater equity of opportunity, these financial barriers needed to be addressed. Largely implemented in 1962, Anderson recommended mandatory grants for living costs and tuition fees for full-time, first-time UK undergraduate students. The impact of this was significant and had a fairly immediate effect in attracting a much wider group of potential students to the opportunities of funded higher education. The notion that university was a closed shop for a minority elite was being overtly challenged and the ground was prepared for a massive period of expansion in the HE sector.

The Robbins report and the expansion of higher education

The Robbins Report (Committee on Higher Education, 1963) argued for a huge increase in HE provision. Following its publication there was a period of rapid expansion of provision and participation. Higher education, which now included the polytechnic sector (formed by the merger of local authority colleges) was beginning to be seen 'as a form of human capital investment' (Sutherland, 2008: 48), and therefore something of value to the country as a whole. Higher education numbers had already expanded in the post-war period; the number of students had doubled between 1945 and the end of the 1950s, and had doubled again to 217,000 by 1962 (Gillard, 2018).

The Representation of the People Act (1969) lowered the voting age to 18 and in doing so recognised the need, expressed by the Latey Committee, to acknowledge the 'capacity' of young adults (Latey, 1967). The way in which young people were viewed was changing in many ways and across many aspects of society. There was increasing recognition of the potential of this younger generation to be marshalled and developed through a higher education system that was more widely available and open to a broader cross-section of society. Consequently, as the 1960s drew to a close, universities faced a profound, double-edged challenge. They had to find ways to accommodate significantly increased numbers of students from wider sections of society. Additionally, they had to consider, in many ways for the first time, the implications of an adult-to-adult relationship. This required fundamental reform of the role of universities in the education and care of students and significantly challenged the prevailing notion of *in loco parentis*. Until the Family Law Reform and Age of Majority (Scotland) Acts (1969) passed into law, the age at which young people gained the legal status of an adult (the age of majority), in the UK, was 21. Anyone under that age, as traditionally, a significant number of undergraduates were, was legally regarded as a child. Consequently, for many decades prior to the 1970s universities had been responsible for the education and care of young adults who had the status of children in law.

Perhaps for this reason, prior to changes to the age of majority, universities had to consider a range of issues in relation to their duty to students who lacked adult status. Where students lived and the nature of student accommodation are useful indicators of how attitudes changed significantly in response to the change in legal status of many university students. During the period immediately after the Second World War, faced with significant growth, all UK universities had a major concern with the accommodation of their students, and this concern was, 'expressed literally in bricks and mortar, with university or college-owned rooms available for the majority of undergraduates on or near to the campus' (Tight, 2011: 109).

The responsibility that universities had, *in loco parentis*, informed policy positions that meant they sought to monitor and control the living conditions of their students and wherever possible, just as parents would do, keep them close to 'home'. If, as was often the case, a young student had to move away from the family home but could not secure a room in a university hall of residence, many universities would require them to live in 'approved lodgings' that were licensed by the institution. Of course, as minors, students would not have been able to easily enter into tenancy agreements, and this may have been a part of the motivation, but it also resulted in a degree of informal supervision of young people considered by law to be in the care of the university.

Given the lack of a clearly defined set of responsibilities, set out in a contract or governed by law, the concept of *in loco parentis* was mostly evident through the universities' attitude towards students. In standing in for parents, universities took on oversight of aspects of students' lives that, it could be argued, any parent would be interested in. This included not only where they lived, but who they associated with and how they behaved. Some of this included pastoral concerns typical of any educational institution, but for decades prior to the post-war period, in exercising their duties as stand-in parents, university authorities implemented regulations governing student behaviour that would seem excessive and oppressive to most students nowadays. In addition to the expectations that current students would recognise in terms of the academic requirements and even attendance patterns, students could be required to follow dress codes, attend acts of worship, live within a certain distance of the university, consent to keep particular hours and, centrally, agree to live somewhere approved of by the university. Furthermore, for the students in halls of residence, there were often quite strict and demanding regulations including curfews and prohibitions on overnight guests.

Question for discussion

The experience of higher education could be considered to be as much about learning to be an independent adult as it is about the subject of study. What challenges are universities faced with in seeking to balance these two aspects of university life?

Student protests

To some extent the expectations of behaviour reflected wider social norms, and it might be argued that universities, in fulfilling their duties *in loco parentis*, were simply reflecting more conservative attitudes typical of the post-war era. However, by the 1960s expectations had shifted, and this was a time of significant social change across the world with social norms being challenged in many domains. The student-initiated protests of 1968 in Paris, were just one example from a year of seismic change that saw protesters not only demonstrating against particular causes of concern but 'beginning to explore the potential for a very different way of organising work, study and society' (Hewlett, 2018: 115).

In the United States, widespread student protests forced courts to recognise fundamental changes in educational philosophy and campus life that made *in loco parentis* an outdated concept. Many courts acknowledged the new nature of the student-university relationship and struggled for ways to characterise these changes (Jackson, 1991). With the shift in expectations and norms of behaviour, it was increasingly difficult for universities to continue to impose what would, by today's standards, be seen as excessive regulations governing student life. In parallel the numbers of people going to university were increasing significantly, making it much more difficult for universities to continue to provide the level of support and supervision that had included high ratios of personal tutors, warden-led halls of residence and supervised lodgings.

Students became much more resistant to rules and regulations. Overturning paternalism was a key demand of the student-led revolts of the late 1960s and early 1970s. With these significant and widespread changes in social attitudes, and a new sense of freedom and possibility, university rules seemed outdated. Universities continued to look back to a previous epoch for many of their expectations (Malcolm, 2018), but family life had changed, and young people's experience was very different to that of the previous generation.

The Latey Report had been welcomed by both the National Union of Students and the Committee of Vice-Chancellors and Principals (CVCP, the predecessor of Universities UK, the organisation which collectively represents the UK's universities) in a joint statement that acknowledged the shift in attitudes towards recognising 18-year-olds as adults. However, neither the Latey Report nor the legislation reducing the age of majority required universities to immediately drop the regulations, and the paternalistic attitudes that had characterised university relationships with their students continued into the 1970s.

With the removal of the legal basis for *in loco parentis*, as well as the relative decline of traditional halls in favour of self-contained flats and the private rented sector by the end of the 1970s, most of the rules around accommodation and behaviour had all but disappeared. The demise of *in loco parentis* was arguably the consequence of radical protest for greater freedom and individual rights. However, it was not long before the tensions in the HE sector created by the continuation of expansion and an increased focus on the rights of the individual resulted in further recasting of roles and responsibilities in the nature of the student-university relationship.

The struggle between identity and academic values: 1988–2018

It is impossible to separate politics from education in modern western societies. Education policy is formed by the particular government of the day, and it reflects their values and priorities. From at least the 1970s onwards, many of these governmental policies have been shaped by neoliberalism. This period of increasing globalisation has seen the marketisation of education, and alongside it widespread changes to the nature of students and their characteristics, behaviours and expectations of their relationship with their university. The principle of *in loco parentis* has experienced something of a renaissance, but in stark contrast to its previous existence where universities placed requirements on students, it is now driven by student expectations that their university owes them a broad range of responsibilities in order to protect their interests.

Neoliberalism

Neoliberalism can trace its origins to economic theories from as far back as the 1930s. After being credited for some economic successes, principally in West Germany after the Second World War, by the 1980s neoliberalism had developed into a series of policy initiatives characterised by deregulation of markets, a drive for privatisation, and the dismantling of the welfare state. Throughout the 1990s the concept expanded widely into political, social and cultural areas of public life in countries all around the world. In doing so it moved beyond its economic beginnings towards a focus on power and class rule, and became a fully fledged ideology (Venugopal, 2015: 3–4). Neoliberalism is particularly insidious because 'It has pervasive effects on ways of thought to the point where it has become incorporated into the common-sense way many of us interpret, live in, and understand the world' (Harvey, 2007: 72). When this happens, it becomes very difficult to even think about challenging the paternalistic *status quo*.

The influence of neoliberalism is not limited to the national stage. In our increasingly globalised world, intense 'peer' pressure drives countries to embrace neoliberal practices in an attempt to secure the same competitive advantages perceived to be held by competitor countries further along the road of neoliberalism. The 'Washington Consensus' was a phrase coined in 1989 by the British economist John Williamson that described a set of ten policies that collectively came to be seen as a standard 'solution' to be deployed whenever developing countries were in crisis, and later became a synonym for neoliberalism itself (Williamson, 2009). Neoliberalism came to be seen as a panacea to global economic crises, and a way to structure and organise government and associated functions such as education.

Neoliberalism argues that in order to maximise social good, governments need to create the conditions that are most conducive to free trade and free markets and then leave the markets alone to operate. Where markets do not already exist, they should be created, and no area of human activity is immune, for 'it seeks to bring all human action into the domain of the market' (Harvey, 2007: 72). In the UK markets for education did not exist, and therefore, from a neoliberal perspective, they had to be created.

Questions for discussion

If universities are increasingly in competition with each other to attract students, what impact might this situation have on academic standards?

Do you know anybody who received an unconditional offer of a place at a university, providing they firmly accepted it?

The marketisation of higher education

In the UK a series of governments that embraced neoliberal ideas created an education system that operates as a quasi-market. Part of the justification for this development is to deal with increased competition from other countries in an increasingly globalised world. In order to be competitive, countries need well-educated workforces. The election of Margaret Thatcher in May 1979 heralded an unprecedented era of marketisation in education within the UK, beginning with secondary education following the passage of the Education Reform Act (1988). The same conditions that created the market at the secondary school level can now be seen emerging within higher education.

Although certain universities had always competed against others for prestige and research funding, in competing for students in higher education there was no real market until the government created a quasi-market through the introduction of student fees payable by the students themselves, and later on the removal of the cap on student numbers. The introduction of fees did not work as intended. When fees were trebled to £9,000 per annum in 2012–2013, the government wanted an outcome whereby the 'best' universities would charge the highest fees and those seen to be less prestigious would charge smaller fees. In reality, all universities quickly moved to charging the maximum fee. Graham Henderson, vice chancellor of Teesside University clearly identified the key reason for this when he said, 'Our students have been checking we are not charging the bottom of the spectrum because they don't want it to be seen as second rate'. (Paige, 2011: 12).

The removal of the cap on student numbers in 2015–2016 by the coalition government meant that UK universities were for the first time free to recruit as many students as they wished. The government estimated there would be an additional 60,000 entrants per year to universities, which would be a 20 per cent increase in full-time undergraduate numbers, but this seems to have been an overestimate (Bekhradnia and Beech, 2018). A direct consequence of the removal of the cap has been a marked increase in the number of early so-called 'conditional-unconditional offers' made to potential students, particularly by 'red brick' universities and those in the Russell Group. These offers guarantee a student a place irrespective of their A-level results, but only if they firmly select the institution as their first choice. The Office for Students (OfS) has reported that the dropout rate for students who have accepted these offers is 10 per cent higher than those students who accepted traditional conditional offers (Office for Students, 2019). This raises the question of whether these offers are good for students or not. Universities could be seen as acting against the best interests of their students for whom government and society increasingly expect them to act *in loco parentis*. The government has accused the universities of pressure sales tactics (Weale, 2019), which can be seen as somewhat ironic given the lengths they went to in order to create a market in the first place.

Students as customers?

With the commodification of higher education, a key question is the extent to which students should be considered to be customers, especially in the light of increased individual responsibility for tuition fees. The UK does not have a higher education inspectorate to assess the quality of teaching through direct observations (which approach is in itself potentially problematic and of varying reliability). Therefore, the metrics chosen as a proxy to measure universities' performance in order that potential students can make an informed decision are those around 'student satisfaction', as measured via the National Student Survey (NSS) and included in the Teaching Excellence and Student Outcomes Framework (TEF).

Lawson, Leach and Burrows (2012: 8) argue that universities exist 'not to satisfy students, but to educate them and provide an environment in which they may learn and develop'. Finney and Finney (2010: 276) found in their US study that students who viewed themselves as customers were more likely to 'hold attitudes and to engage in behaviors that are not conducive to success'. Students may dislike engaging with challenging activities and assessments that are designed to help them develop, and therefore their satisfaction level may be adversely affected. Customers usually have the right to request what they want, and there may be an inherent tension between their wants and what faculty may perceive they need, as expressed through course design and assessment processes.

Whilst academics in the UK might struggle to adapt to this paradigm shift, the reality is that there is now legislation such as the Consumer Rights Act (2015) and the Higher Education Research Bill (2016) which means that students have consumer rights, and if an institution fails to deliver as promised, then remedies will be available, such as repeat performance and damages (Neary, 2016). Students themselves are increasingly self-identifying as customers. A ComRes survey in 2017 found that 47 per cent of students saw themselves as customers (Universities UK, 2017), and they are developing expectations in line with that perception, such as having any significant changes to courses communicated at least a year in advance.

It is difficult to understate the impact that this has had on the relationship between the university and the student. Along with contractual obligations, there are now consumer protections, and greatly enhanced expectations from students and their families. In assessing satisfaction, the converse level of student dissatisfaction is automatically measured, and where this becomes a focus, there is potential for a 'culture of complaint' to arise where the student becomes the 'personification of market pressures on an otherwise archaic and unresponsive university' (Molesworth et al., 2010: 3). Given that a marketisation viewpoint believes the customer is always right, it follows that the university should listen to the students. This may lead to a more defensive form of university education where a key driver of change is the avoidance of potential disputes that can turn into complaints which can give rise to litigation. In this kind of climate academics are not as free to express their professional opinions, and courses that score low in the NSS may be adjusted to be more customer-friendly. It is not just students who see themselves as customers; certain universities take the same position. The 1994 Group of Universities states, 'Students know how they want to be taught and have ideas about how techniques can be improved' (Molesworth et al., 2010: 3). Depending on one's point of view, this sort of development is either an overdue 'breath of fresh air' that will improve the university experience or a potential 'death knell for academic rigour' that reduces academics to the role of service technicians.

In 1999 Prime Minister Tony Blair set a target to have 50 per cent of young people entering higher education in the next century. This target was reached almost 20 years later when figures from the Department for Education showed that 50.2 per cent of young people went into higher education in 2017–2018. In comparison, in 1990 only 25 per cent of young people stayed in any form of education or training beyond the age of 18 (Coughlan, 2019). This dramatic increase in the number of students entering higher education over a 20-year period inevitably means that the composition of the student population has changed considerably. It still includes privately educated students from wealthy middle-class backgrounds whose families have a tradition of attending university, but increasingly entrants are being drawn from a broader cross-section of society. This includes those who are from lower socio-economic status backgrounds and are often the first in their families to attend university. Unlike their wealthier peers, these students often do not arrive at university with the social or cultural capital that would enable them to independently flourish in higher education. They may have part-time or even full-time jobs alongside their studies, and may also have parental or caring responsibilities, and thus their studies can come second or even third in their list of day-to-day priorities. Unsurprisingly, these students find completing university to be a considerable challenge, quite aside from the academic aspects of being a student.

Questions for discussion

To what extent did you perceive yourself to be a customer during your higher education?

Thinking back on your experiences now, do you think such a perception influenced your behaviour or expectations as a student?

Greater accountability and responsibility to students

Universities have slowly begun to realise that they must do more to address the disadvantage that these students face if they are to be enabled to succeed. It is no longer politically acceptable to receive fees for students who then go on to drop out of courses in large numbers. The new reality of very diverse university student cohorts is not likely to change anytime soon. This diversity should be celebrated, representing as it does both the make-up of modern multicultural society and a fundamental break with the elite university populations of the early twentieth century.

Launched in early 2018, the Office for Students (OfS) has a clear role in holding universities accountable. One of the key metrics in the TEF is that of 'continuation', which is double-weighted and therefore seen as very important in terms of the overall grade the university receives. If a university does not perform well in this area, it cannot hope to achieve the highest 'Gold' TEF rating, which is now seen as crucial in the higher education marketplace. In this way the university is incentivised to deploy strategies to support their disadvantaged students and ensure that they complete their studies rather than dropping out. Universities are also required to produce an Access and Participation Plan that sets out how they will work to increase equality of opportunity within their provision. The OfS must approve their plan in order for the university to charge the highest level of student fees, and it is monitored on an ongoing basis.

In February 2018, Sam Gyimah MP, the universities minister, delivered a speech at the launch of the OfS that caused consternation amongst university leaders. He said,

> universities need to act *in loco parentis*, that is to be there for students offering all the support they need to get the most from their time on campus. One area where I particularly think work needs to be done is in mental health.
>
> (Gyimah, 2018)

This was unexpected and challenging to universities for at least three reasons. Firstly, as described earlier in the chapter, since late in the last century the relationship between students and the university had been one of a contract with an adult, and the purpose of the contract was the provision of education and, possibly, accommodation. The idea of universities acting *in loco parentis* had fallen out of use, and the sudden expectation that it should be re-introduced came as a shock. The second reason university leaders were concerned was this suggestion that universities should effectively take on aspects of the role of healthcare provider, being responsible for supporting students' mental health. Universities do not have the resources to fulfil this role, and allowing their unqualified staff to do this would open the universities up to litigation. Thirdly, in the form that it was stated, the MP's interpretation of *in loco parentis* was erroneous, broadening the principle considerably from covering some aspects of a parental role to 'offering all the support they need'.

Universities do have a duty of care to their students, but it is legally limited to taking 'reasonable steps to prevent harm occurring, where that harm is caused by their own careless actions or omissions' (Swanton, 2018) The harm must also be reasonably foreseeable, and within the reasonable control of the university. Universities do not and cannot have a parent-child relationship with their students, especially with large numbers of modern students who are commuter students and tend to spend little time on campus outside of taught sessions.

Identity and protest in the twenty-first-century university

The concept of protecting students from harm lies at the heart of a key debate raging in higher education around the world. The media have widely and enthusiastically reported on the apparently growing trend for students to request 'trigger warnings' and 'safe spaces' at university. The concept of trigger warnings first emerged in the United States but has spread to the UK and other European countries. Trigger warnings are a highly contested device originally deployed to protect survivors of sexual violence (Byron, 2017: 118), and take the form of a written or verbal statement warning students about the nature of some upcoming academic content. Proponents argue that trigger warnings offer a chance for the student to consider their mental state and level of resilience before they encounter materials that might cause them to relive their trauma. Critics argue that they are a form of censorship by classifying certain experiences as not suitable for public debate. Others go further and argue that 'the medicalisation of reading serves as a model for regarding other experiences – lectures, seminars, meetings – as a risk to the mental health of students' (Furedi, 2017: 15), suggesting that embracing these ideas supports the government's paternalistic approach to higher education which infantilises students rather than helping them discover their independence. The ongoing debate is around the fact that their usage appears to be broadening to cover ideas and concepts that students might find offensive or even just disagreeable, and many see this as an assault on academic freedoms (Byron, 2017: 119). Distinguishing genuine fear and trauma from discomfort or offence is a subtlety that is often lost in the media reporting, and misunderstood by some students, yet it is key to avoiding the conflation of safety with mere comfort. Another key distinction is between the growth in entrants to higher education, which as discussed earlier necessarily drew on a broader cross-section of society, and these different groups of students.

Safe spaces also have their roots in feminist activities, originally being a space where women could meet without men to discuss issues that they could not freely discuss when men were present (Byron, 2017). Safe spaces do not have to be actual physical spaces but can take the form of a set of rules to govern behaviour at events, and it is easy to see how this concept can be seen as an attack on academic free speech, depending on how those rules are formulated, and whether they permit or deny genuine debate. A criticism of safe spaces is that often the call for them can be seen as 'a cultural and political claim for an entitlement to be validated and recognised' (Furedi, 2017: 12). This can be seen as a form of therapeutic censorship that in the United States is contributing to calls from students for the reinstatement of the concept of *in loco parentis*. This pressure for new rules to govern behaviour and language to prevent harm feeds into the paternalistic style of governance in higher education. The growing trend for students to argue that they are offended rather than that they simply disagree demonstrates the growing habit of viewing emotions as more important and valid than reason (Furedi, 2017: 18), which, within universities at least, contradicts centuries of scholarly tradition.

The impact of the Covid-19 pandemic

If universities had hoped for a period of consolidation in the second decade of the twenty-first century after the unprecedented changes in their relationship with students, they were to be sadly disappointed, and once again forced into a process of intense self-reflection as the result of the global Covid-19 pandemic that started during 2019.

The pandemic began to take hold in the UK in February 2020, with the first national lockdown called by the government on 23 March 2020. Just before lockdown, the National Union of Students (NUS) carried out research in January and February 2020 involving 3,097 college and university students. This research found that almost half of students claimed coping with course workload had a negative impact on their mental health (Douglas Oloyede *et al.*, 2020). This was before the extent and longevity of the pandemic was to be fully realised, and even as this chapter was written in the middle of 2021, it is too soon to be able to properly evaluate the full extent of the mental health crisis in higher education that the pandemic will have caused. It is, however, the case that once again the relationship between universities and their students was the subject of intense debate, with the pandemic highlighting and exacerbating a range of issues from the value and justice of course-fee structures to the nature and cost of accommodation and to the duty of care owed by a university to its students in times of challenge and threat.

Students were at times the subject of institutional and media anxiety about their perceived role in potentially spreading the virus, and by August 2020, the University and College Union (UCU) was insisting that universities must scrap plans to reopen campuses in September 2020 in order to prevent a major public health crisis (UCU, 2020). Students were seen as potential 'super spreaders' with fears that the migration of over a million students across the UK would risk doing untold damage to people's health, and that it would exacerbate what the UCU called the worst health crisis of our lifetimes.

After a summer of gradual relaxation, the country entered another cycle of infection in the autumn and winter of 2020 and the majority of student learning was delivered online, with all but a very few universities switching to blended and online learning and assessment. Students, parents and their sponsors began to question both the learning and teaching experiences and the wisdom of keeping students on campus whilst effectively learning online. By January 2021 BBC News was reporting that growing numbers of students in England had pledged to withhold rent on university accommodation they were unable to use during the national lockdown (Burns, 2021). This was seen to be developing into a major protest, with an estimate at the time of 15,000 students at dozens of universities having signed up. Students were demanding a rebate on rent as they were being kept off campus. However, because of the changes in the ways in which students' accommodation is provided, the universities themselves were accountable for only around 20 per cent of student accommodation. Universities UK (2020) stated at this time that 'in most cases decisions on refunds will be made by private landlords and other providers'.

By the spring of 2021 it was becoming clear that the student experience had changed dramatically and that some of this change could in turn have a profound impact on the relationship between universities and students in the post-pandemic recovery period and beyond. As students remained isolated either at home or in their privately rented accommodation near to their university, the long-term challenges facing higher education were becoming much clearer. Concern about the burden on students' mental health, the focus on value for money during the pandemic in the face of steep tuition fees, and the general level of unemployment and economic hardship for young adults stimulated renewed questioning of the fairness of the prevailing 'business model' for universities. This questioning was not restricted to the UK. As reported by the *Financial Times* (FT), in February 2021, more than 50 colleges in the United States, including George Washington University and New York University, faced lawsuits from students who were seeking compensation for amenities that had remained closed during the pandemic (Allnutt, 2021). In the same article, it was further reported that in January 2021 there was a series of demonstrations in Paris drawing attention to poverty and declining mental health at universities. Rent strikes and protests proliferated with, for example, students in Glasgow protesting against their circumstances and perceived injustice by erecting a fence around their vice-principal's lodgings.

In February 2021, the Sutton Trust published a report which found that, whilst almost 60 per cent of students reported taking part in student societies, volunteering or sport in autumn 2019, only 36 per cent did so by the autumn of 2020, and just under a third by the spring (Montacute and Holt-White, 2021). The wider student experience had been significantly diminished, with students less likely to have taken part in work experience or to be studying abroad. The number of students who did not take part in these types of activities had increased by more than half. There are clear indications highlighted by the Sutton Trust report that the participation gap has widened significantly. Participation has fallen more significantly for poorer students, with 44 per cent of middle-class students during the autumn 2020 term taking part in student societies, sport or volunteering, compared to just 33 per cent of students from a working-class background.

The move to online learning has seen the majority of students learning from home, and this is another significant factor in deterring students from taking part in wider university life. It is the case that those from less well-off homes are more likely to live at home, with almost two-thirds of those from low-income backgrounds saying they were living at home in the spring term of 2021. Student satisfaction surveys clearly indicate that for all the efficiency of online platforms and the swift introduction of blended models of learning, students continue to want a university campus experience and the social interaction that goes with it. The Sutton Trust report reported that in the autumn 2020 term just under a third of students said they were not taking part in activities beyond their academic course because they were put off by a lack of social interaction during online activities, and a further quarter cited 'Zoom-fatigue' as a barrier (Montacute and Holt-White, 2021).

Many universities have instituted a range of interventions and regulation changes to try to support their students. Laptop and wireless broadband loan schemes were established to attempt to address the yawning digital divide that was laid bare by the consequences of the pandemic and the move to online-only learning. Universities amended regulations and assessment practices to try to avoid disadvantaging students who were struggling with grief for deceased friends and family, working from home, home schooling their children and trying to manage their own mental health issues, all whilst trying to complete a degree course online. During the pandemic, the mental health and well-being services of universities saw a massive increase in demand for their support with much less resistance to the idea that this sort of *in loco parentis* service is something that universities should be providing. Nicola Dandridge, chief executive of the Office for Students, actually stated in September 2020 the clear expectation on universities that 'It is more important than ever that students can access good mental health support to help them settle in, particularly where they are being asked to self-isolate' (Office for Students, 2020).

Conclusion

The last 50-plus years have seen unprecedented change and growth in higher education in the UK, the United States and many other countries around the world. Driven partly by changes in society and partly by student protests, higher education has evolved, although many would argue it needs to evolve faster. As with many aspects of society, the Covid-19 pandemic has forced universities to respond and adapt provision, and this has happened with varying levels of success both across and within countries, with many students, particularly those from lower socio-economic backgrounds, suffering or being disadvantaged as a result. *In loco parentis* has come full circle during this time. From restricting and protecting students in a very paternalistic manner, it gradually fell out of favour until it became unsustainable. Then, as the relationships between universities and students and between universities and society has changed, seemingly out of nowhere there are many calls for the principles at least of *in loco parentis* not necessarily to be formally reinstated, but to act as a guiding light to offer protection demanded by adult students themselves. Students are unwittingly fitting into a neoliberal paternalistic government agenda that argues that the public need protection and the government are best placed to offer it.

Summary points

- Changing social norms, the decrease in the age of majority to 18 and student protests led to the removal of *in loco parentis* and the recognition of students being adults rather than children.
- The marketisation of higher education inevitably led to the introduction of performativity measures such as the Teaching Excellence Framework, because they perform the necessary market function of enabling effective choice by the customer.
- Seeing students as customers and concentrating on addressing levels of student satisfaction seem inevitably to lead to the erosion of academic rigour and values. Together with the rise of identity as the prime issue of importance to students, it can be argued that this is leading to the suppression of anything that can 'harm' students.
- The situation appears to have gone full circle, from a position of an imposed *in loco parentis* in the middle of the last century, to one of a demanded *in loco parentis* by some students in this century.

Recommended reading

Furedi, F. (2017) *What's Happened to the University? A Sociological Exploration of Its Infantilization*. Abingdon: Routledge.
Molesworth, M., Scullion, R. and Nixon, E. (2010) *The Marketization of Higher Education*. London: Routledge.

References

Allnutt, C. (2021) *High Fees and Lockdown Blues: Why Students Are in Revolt.* Online. Available at: https://www.ft.com/content/3ab48f92-f779-4f77-b39a-8fae7ff9f452 (Accessed 10 May 2021).

Barnes, S. (1996) England's Civic Universities and the Triumph of the Oxbridge Ideal. *History of Education Quarterly,* **36**(3), pp. 271–305.

Burns, J. (2021) *Students Pledge Rent Strike over Unused Uni Rooms.* Online. Available at: https://www.bbc.com/news/education-55576471 (Accessed 10 May 2021).

Byron, K. (2017) From Infantilizing to World Making: Safe Spaces and Trigger Warnings on Campus. *Family Relations,* **66**, pp. 116–125.

Bekhradnia, B. and Beech, D. (2018) *Demand for Higher Education to 2030.* London: HEPI. Online. Available at: https://www.hepi.ac.uk/2018/03/15/demand-higher-education-2030/ (Accessed 8 November 2019).

Committee on Higher Education (Robbins Committee) (1963) *Higher Education.* London: HMSO.

Coughlan, S. (2019) *The Symbolic Target of 50% at University Reached.* Online. Available at: https://www.bbc.co.uk/news/education-49841620 (Accessed 8 November 2019).

Douglas Oloyede, F., Bridger, K. and Lawson, B. (2020) *Improving Mental Health and Wellbeing Support for Scotland's Students.* Online. Available at: https://www.nusconnect.org.uk/resources/executive-summary-improving-mental-health-and-well-being-support-for-scotland (Accessed 10 May 2021).

Finney, T. and Finney, R. (2010) Are Students Customers of Their Universities? An Exploratory Study. *Education and Training,* **52**, pp. 276–291.

Gillard, D. (2018) *Education in England: A History.* Online. Available at: http://www.educationengland.org.uk/history (Accessed 8 November 2019).

Gyimah, S. (2018) *A Revolution in Accountability.* London: DfE. Online. Available at: https://www.gov.uk/government/speeches/a-revolution-in-accountability (Accessed 8 November 2019).

Harvey, D. (2007) *A Brief History of Neoliberalism.* Oxford: Oxford University Press.

Hewlett, N. (2018) Disorder, *les forces de l'ordre* and the Re-ordering of Capitalism in May–June 1968. *Modern & Contemporary France,* **26**(2), pp. 115–128.

Hutcheson, P., Gasman, M. and Sanders-McMurtry, K. (2011) Race and Equality in the Academy: Rethinking Higher Education Actors and the Struggle for Equality in the Post-World War II Period. *Journal of Higher Education,* **82**(2), pp. 121–153.

Jackson, B. (1991) The Lingering Legacy of *in loco parentis*: An Historical Survey and Proposal for Reform. *Vanderbilt Law Review,* **44**, pp. 1135–1164.

Lake, P. (1999) The Rise of Duty and the Fall of *in loco parentis* and Other Protective Tort Doctrines in Higher Education Law. *Missouri Law Review,* **64**, pp. 1–28.

Latey, J. (1967) *Report of the Committee on the Age of Majority.* London: HMSO.

Lawson, A., Leach, M. and Burrows, S. (2012) The Implications for Learners, Teachers and Institutions of Using Student Satisfaction as a Measure of Success: A Review of the Literature. *Education Journal,* **138**(21), pp. 7–11.

Malcolm, D. (2018) *As Much Freedom as Is Good for Them: Looking Back at in loco parentis,* WONKHE. Online. Available at: https://wonkhe.com/blogs/much-freedom-good-looking-back-loco-parentis/ (Accessed 8 November 2019).

Ministry of Education and the Scottish Education Department [Anderson Committee] (1960) *Grants to Students.* London: HMSO.

Montacute, R. and Holt-White, E. (2021) *Covid-19 and the University Experience.* Online. Available at: https://www.suttontrust.com/our-research/covid-19-and-the-university-experience-student-life-pandemic (Accessed 10 May 2021).

Neary, M. (2016) Teaching Excellence Framework: A Critical Response and An Alternative Future. *Journal of Contemporary European Research,* **12**(3), pp. 690–695.

Office for Students (2019) *Update to Analysis of Unconditional Offers.* Online. Available at: https://www.officeforstudents.org.uk/media/306770e1-0c36-4754-a952-8a8ea697e61c/unconditional-offers-data-analysis-update.pdf (Accessed 8 November 2019).

Office for Students (2020) *Universities Must Provide Clarity for Students, Says Regulator.* Online. Available at: https://www.officeforstudents.org.uk/news-blog-and-events/press-and-media/universities-must-provide-clarity-for-students-says-regulator/ (Accessed 10 May 2021).

Paige, J. (2011) *University Fees Table – Why Charge Less than the Max?* Online. Available at: https://www.theguardian.com/higher-education-network/2011/may/16/university-fees-why-charge (Accessed 8 November 2019).

Silver, H. (1982) Institutional Differences: Expectations and Perceptions. *Studies in Higher Education*, **7**(1), pp. 1–11.

Sutherland, J. (2008) Higher Education, the Graduate and the Labour Market: From Robbins to Dearing. *Education & Training*, **50**(1), pp. 47–51.

Swanton, G. (2018) *University Life: In loco parentis?* Online. Available at: https://universitybusiness.co.uk/Blog/university-life-in-loco-parentis/ (Accessed 8 November 2019).

Tight, M. (2011) Student Accommodation in Higher Education in the United Kingdom: Changing Post-War Attitudes. *Oxford Review of Education*, **37**(1), pp. 109–122.

Universities UK (2017) *Education, Consumer Rights and Maintaining Trust: What students want from their university*. Online. Available at: https://www.universitiesuk.ac.uk/policy-and-analysis/reports/Pages/what-students-want-from-their-university.aspx (Accessed 8 November 2019).

Universities UK (2020) *COVID-19: FAQ: Student accommodation and testing*. Online. Available at: https://www.universitiesuk.ac.uk/covid19/faqs-links-relevant-bodies/Pages/student-accommodation.aspx (Accessed 10 May 2021).

University and College Union (UCU) (2020) *Universities Must Not Become the Care Homes of a Covid Second Wave*. Online. Available at: https://www.ucu.org.uk/article/10964/Universities-must-not-become-the-care-homes-of-a-Covid-second-wave (Accessed 10 May 2021).

Venugopal, R. (2015) Neoliberalism as Concept. *Economy and Society*, **44**(2), pp. 165–187.

Weale, S. (2019) *Students Who Have Unconditional Offers More Likely to Quit*. Online. Available at: https://www.theguardian.com/education/2019/oct/30/students-who-had-unconditional-offer-more-likely-to-quit-university (Accessed 8 November 2019).

Weigel, D. (2004) Welcome to the Fun-Free University. *Reason*, **36**(5), pp. 41–47.

Williamson, J. (2009) A Short History of the Washington Consensus. *Law and Business Review of the Americas*, **15**(1), pp. 7–23.

Index